SOFTENG 2017

The Third International Conference on Advances and Trends in Software Engineering

April 23 - 27, 2017

Venice, Italy

SOFTENG 2017 Editors

Mira Kajko-Mattsson, Stockholm University & Royal Institute of Technology, Sweden
Pål Ellingsen, Bergen University College, Norway
Paolo Maresca, Verisign, Inc., USA

Printed from e-media with permission by:

Curran Associates, Inc.
57 Morehouse Lane
Red Hook, NY 12571

Some format issues inherent in the e-media version may also appear in this print version.

Printed by Curran Associates, Inc. (2017)

International Academy, Research, and Industry Association (IARIA)
412 Derby Way
Wilmington, DE 19810

Phone: (408) 893-6407
Fax: (408) 527-6351

petre@iaria.org

Additional copies of this publication are available from:

Curran Associates, Inc.
57 Morehouse Lane
Red Hook, NY 12571 USA
Phone: 845-758-0400
Fax: 845-758-2633
Email: curran@proceedings.com
Web: www.proceedings.com

TABLE OF CONTENTS

SOFTENG 1: SOFTWARE TESTING AND VALIDATION I

SOFTENG 2: SOFTWARE TESTING AND VALIDATION II

SOFTENG 3: SOFTWARE DESIGNING AND PRODUCTION I

SOFTENG 4: SOFTWARE REUSE

SOFTENG 5: SOFTWARE RELIABILITY, ROBUSTNESS, SAFETY

SOFTENG 6: SOFTWARE DESIGNING AND PRODUCTION II

SOFTENG 2017

Forward

The Third International Conference on Advances and Trends in Software Engineering (SOFTENG 2017), held between April 23-27, 2017 in Venice, Italy, continued a series of events focusing on challenging aspects in the field of software engineering.

Software engineering exhibits challenging dimensions in the light of new applications, devices and services. Mobility, user-centric development, smart-devices, e-services, ambient environments, e-health and wearable/implantable devices pose specific challenges for specifying software requirements and developing reliable and safe software. Specific software interfaces, agile organization and software dependability require particular approaches for software security, maintainability, and sustainability.

The conference had the following tracks:

- Software designing and production
- Software testing and validation
- Software reuse
- Software reliability, robustness, safety

We take here the opportunity to warmly thank all the members of the SOFTENG 2017 technical program committee, as well as all the reviewers. The creation of such a high quality conference program would not have been possible without their involvement. We also kindly thank all the authors that dedicated much of their time and effort to contribute to SOFTENG 2017. We truly believe that, thanks to all these efforts, the final conference program consisted of top quality contributions.

We also gratefully thank the members of the SOFTENG 2017 organizing committee for their help in handling the logistics and for their work that made this professional meeting a success.

We hope that SOFTENG 2017 was a successful international forum for the exchange of ideas and results between academia and industry and to promote further progress in the field of software engineering. We also hope that Venice, Italy provided a pleasant environment during the conference and everyone saved some time to enjoy the unique charm of the city.

SOFTENG 2017 Committee

SOFTENG Steering Committee

Mira Kajko-Mattsson, Stockholm University & Royal Institute of Technology, Sweden
Miroslaw Staron, University of Gothenburg, Sweden
Yoshihisa Udagawa, Tokyo Polytechnic University, Japan
Ulrike Hammerschall, Hochschule München, Germany

SOFTENG Industry/Research Advisory Committee

Philipp Helle, Airbus Group Innovations - Hamburg, Germany
Sigrid Eldh, Ericsson AB, Sweden
Tomas Schweigert, SQS Software Quality Systems AG, Germany
Michael Perscheid, Innovation Center Network, SAP, Germany
Janne Järvinen, F-Secure Corporation, Finland
Paolo Maresca, VERISIGN, Switzerland
Doo-Hwan Bae, Software Process Improvement Center - KAIST, South Korea

SOFTENG 2017
Committee

SOFTENG Steering Committee

Mira Kajko-Mattsson, Stockholm University & Royal Institute of Technology, Sweden
Miroslaw Staron, University of Gothenburg, Sweden
Yoshihisa Udagawa, Tokyo Polytechnic University, Japan
Ulrike Hammerschall, Hochschule München, Germany

SOFTENG Industry/Research Advisory Committee

Philipp Helle, Airbus Group Innovations - Hamburg, Germany
Sigrid Eldh, Ericsson AB, Sweden
Tomas Schweigert, SQS Software Quality Systems AG, Germany
Michael Perscheid, Innovation Center Network, SAP, Germany
Janne Järvinen, F-Secure Corporation, Finland
Paolo Maresca, VERISIGN, Switzerland
Doo-Hwan Bae, Software Process Improvement Center - KAIST, South Korea

SOFTENG 2017 Technical Program Committee

Ibrahim Akman, Atilim University, Turkey
Issam Al-Azzoni, King Saud University, Saudi Arabia
Jocelyn Aubert, Luxembourg Institute of Science and Technology (LIST), Luxembourg
Doo-Hwan Bae, School of Computing - KAIST, South Korea
Alessandra Bagnato, SOFTEAM R&D Department, France
Anna Bobkowska, Gdansk University of Technology, Poland
Luigi Buglione, Engineering SpA, Italy
Azahara Camacho, Universidad Complutense de Madrid, Spain
Pablo C. Cañizares, Universidad Complutense de Madrid, Spain
Byoungju Choi, Ewha Womans University, South Korea
Morshed U. Chowdhury, Deakin University, Australia
Cesario Di Sarno, University of Naples "Parthenope", Italy
Sigrid Eldh, Ericsson AB, Sweden
Faten Fakhfakh, University of Sfax, Tunisia
Fausto Fasano, University of Molise, Italy
Rita Francese, Università di Salerno, Italy
Barbara Gallina, Mälardalen University, Sweden
Matthias Galster, University of Canterbury, Christchurch, New Zealand
Alessia Garofalo, COSIRE Group, Aversa, Italy
Pascal Giessler, Karlsruher Institut für Technologie (KIT), Germany

Ulrike Hammerschall, Hochschule München, Germany
Noriko Hanakawa, Hannan University, Japan
Rachel Harrison, Oxford Brookes University, UK
Qiang He, Swinburne University of Technology, Australia
Philipp Helle, Airbus Group Innovations, Hamburg, Germany
Jang-Eui Hong, Chungbuk National University, South Korea
Fu-Hau Hsu, National Central University, Taiwan
Shinji Inoue, Tottori University, Japan
Janne Järvinen, F-Secure Corporation, Finland
Hermann Kaindl, TU Wien, Austria
Atsushi Kanai, Hosei University, Japan
Imran Khaliq, Media Design School, Auckland, New Zealand
Abdelmajid Khelil, Bosch Software Innovations, Germany
Herbert Kuchen, Westfälische Wilhelms-Universität Münster, Germany
Vinay Kulkarni, Tata Consultancy Services Research, India
Dieter Landes, University of Applied Sciences Coburg, Germany
Karl Leung, Hong Kong Institute of Vocational Education (Chai Wan), Hong Kong
Chu-Ti Lin, National Chiayi University, Taiwan
Panos Linos, Butler University, USA
Francesca Lonetti, CNR-ISTI, Pisa, Italy
Ivano Malavolta, Vrije Universiteit Amsterdam, Netherlands
Paolo Maresca, VERISIGN, Switzerland
Alessandro Margara, Politecnico di Milano, Italy
Sanjay Misra, Covenant University, Nigeria
Masahide Nakamura, Kobe (National) University, Japan
Risto Nevalainen, Finnish Software Measurement Association (FiSMA), Finland
Flavio Oquendo, IRISA - University of South Brittany, France
Fabio Palomba, University of Salerno, Italy
Fabrizio Pastore, University of Milano – Bicocca, Italy
Antonio Pecchia, Federico II University of Naples, Italy
Andréa Pereira Mendonça, Amazonas Federal Institute (IFAM), Brazil
Michael Perscheid, Innovation Center Network, SAP, Germany
Heidar Pirzadeh, SAP SE, Canada
Pasqualina Potena, SICS Swedish ICT Västerås AB, Sweden
Oliviero Riganelli, University of Milano Bicocca, Italy
Michele Risi, University of Salerno, Italy
Alvaro Rubio-Largo, Universidade NOVA de Lisboa, Portugal
Gunter Saake, Otto-von-Guericke-University of Magdeburg, Germany
Kazi Muheymin Sakib, University of Dhaka, Bangladesh
Rodrigo Salvador Monteiro, Universidade Federal Fluminense, Brazil
Akbar Siami Namin, Texas Tech University, USA
iroyuki Sato, University of Tokyo, Japan
Tomas Schweigert, SQS Software Quality Systems AG, Germany
Paulino Silva, ISCAP - IPP, Porto, Portugal

Maria Spichkova, RMIT University, Australia
Praveen Ranjan Srivastava, Indian Institute of Management (IIM), Rohtak, India
Miroslaw Staron, University of Gothenburg, Sweden
Tugkan Tuglular, Izmir Institute of Technology, Turkey
Yoshihisa Udagawa, Tokyo Polytechnic University, Japan
Sylvain Vauttier, Ecole des Mines d'Alès, France
Miroslav Velev, Aries Design Automation, USA
Colin Venters, University of Huddersfield, UK
Laszlo Vidacs, Hungarian Academy of Sciences, Hungary
Hironori Washizaki, Waseda University, Japan
Ralf Wimmer, Albert-Ludwigs-University Freiburg, Germany
Guowei Yang, Texas State University, USA
Cemal Yilmaz, Sabanci University, Turkey
Mansooreh Zahedi, IT University of Copenhagen, Denmark
Peter Zimmerer, Siemens AG, Germany
Alejandro Zunino, ISISTAN-UNICEN-CONICET, Argentina

Copyright Information

Visualizing Execution Models and Testing Results

Bernard Stepien, Liam Peyton
School of Engineering and Computer Science
University of Ottawa
Ottawa, Canada
Email: (Bernard | lpeyton)@uottawa.ca

Mohamed Alhaj
Computer Engineering Department
Al-Ahliyya Amman University
Amman, Jordan
Email: m.alhaj@ammanu.edu.jo

***Abstract*—Software engineering models typically support some form of graphic visualization. Similarly, testing results are shown as execution traces that testing tools, such as TTCN-3 can display as message sequence charts. However, all TTCN-3 tools avoid presenting data directly in the message sequence chart because some of it may be complex structured data. Instead, they simply display the data types used. The real data is made available through detailed message inspection representations when the datatype shown is clicked on. Thus, validation of test results requires a tedious message by message inspection especially for large tests involving sequences of several hundred test events. We propose the capability to specify which data can be displayed in the test results message sequence chart. This provides overview capabilities and improves the navigation of test results. The approach is illustrated with an example of SIP protocol testing and an example of testing an avionics flight management system.**

Keywords-sofware modelling; testing; TTCN-3.

I. MOTIVATION

Modeling and testing of software applications are intricately linked. The first describes the expected behavior while the second describes a trace of real behavior of a system. The first preoccupation of a software engineer is to ensure that both expected and actual behaviors do indeed match. While formal modelling techniques abound (Unified Modeling Language (UML), [1], Specification and Description Language (SDL)[2], Use Case Maps (UCM)[3]), testing is often performed with ad hoc coded tests using frameworks such as JUnit [5]. There is very little code reuse between tests and displaying the results often accounts for 50% of the code written to define tests.

Formal models frequently use Message Sequence Charts (MSCs) [4] (Figure 1) (Pragmadev studio) to enable the software engineer to visualize the behavior of a system even before it has been implemented giving them the possibility to detect design flaws early and thus avoid costly testing iterations [6][7].

The formal test specification language Testing and Test Control Notation (TTCN-3) [8] provides advantages over frameworks like Junit, with strong typing, a powerful matching mechanism, and a separation of concerns between the abstract test specification layer and the concrete layer that handles coding/decoding data which can result in significant code reuse [16].

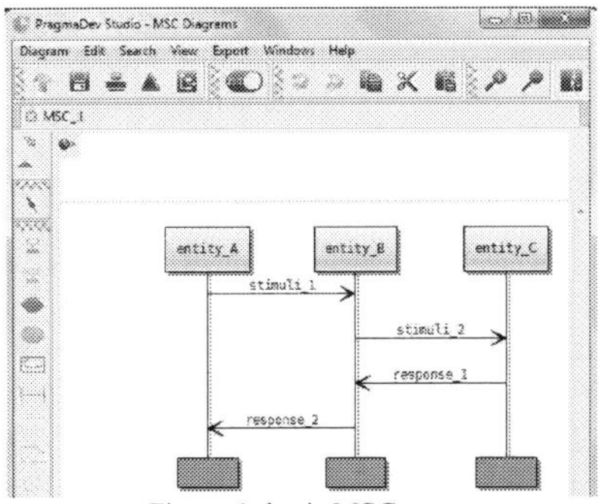

Figure 1. basic MSC

Especially interesting is the support of MSCs to display test results that is provided by commercially available TTCN-3 execution tools like TTworkbench, [9], Testcast [10], PragmaDev Studio [11], Titan [12]. All of these tools use MSCs to display test results which is especially efficient when the system is composed of multiple components that interact with each other as shown in Figure 2.

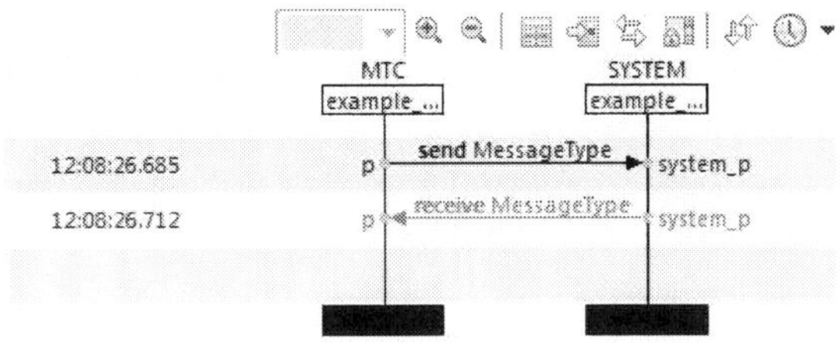

Figure 2. Test results as MSC

However, all of these tools are confronted with the same problem of displaying complex structured data in the limited space provided by MSCs. Thus, they avoid the display problem altogether by showing only the data type of the message (Figure 2 shows TTworkbench) and show the content of the message in a separate table (Figure 3 for TTworkbench) when clicking on one of the arrows of the MSC. This requires a tedious message by message inspection of the MSC. However, this feature is critical in order to allow to spot errors efficiently. The TTworkbench tool is particularly interesting because it is the only one that shows the test oracle, the expected message against the data received from the SUT and flags any mismatches in red.

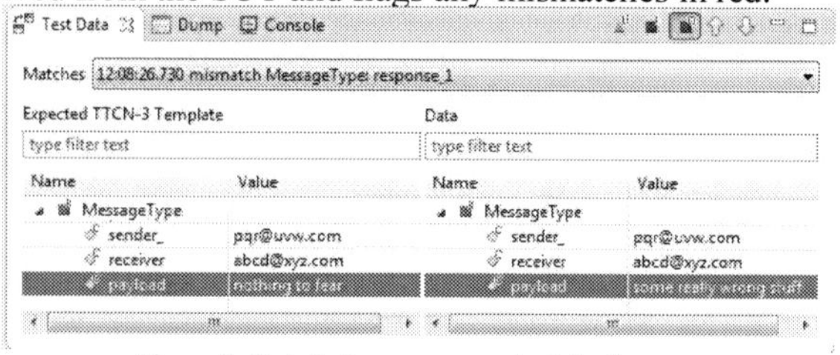

Figure 3. Detailed message content display

II. TTCN-3 CONCEPT OF TEMPLATE

The central concept of TTCN-3 is the template language construct that enables describing both test stimuli and test oracles as structured data in a single template. This in turn is used by the TTCN-3 tools internal matching mechanism that compare the values of a template to the actual values contained in the response message both on message based and procedure based communication. More important is that the template has a precise name and is a building block that can be re-used using its name to specify the value of an individual field or another template that itself can be re-used by specifying a modification to its values. This is a concept of inheritance. For example, one may specify the templates for the sender and the receiver entities separately:

```
template charstring entityA_Template
                        := "abcd@xyz.com";
template charstring entityB_Template
                        := "pqr@uvw.com";
```

A stimuli message can then be specified as:

```
template MessageType stimuli_1 := {
    sender := entityA_Template,
    receiver := entityB_Template,
    payload  :=  "it  was  a  dark  and
stormy night"
}
```

The response template can itself reuse the above entity addresses by merely reversing their roles (sender/receiver):

```
template MessageType response_1 := {
    sender := entityB_Template,
    receiver := entityA_Template,
    payload := "nothing to fear"
}
```

The TTCN-3 template modification language construct can be used to specify more stimuli or responses for the same pairs of communicating entities:

```
template MessageType stimuli_2
              modifies stimuli_1 := {
    payload := "the sun is shining at
last"
}
```

Templates can then be used either in send or receive statements to describe behaviors in the communication with the SUT. Such behavior can be sequential, alternative or even interleaved behavior. The TTCN-3 receive statement does more than just receive data in the sense of traditional general purpose languages (GPL). It compares the data received on a communication port with the content of the template specified. The following abstract specification means that upon sending template *stimuli_1* to the SUT, if we receive and match the response message to the template *response_1* we decide that the test has passed. Instead, if we receive and match *alt_response* we decide that the test has failed.

```
myPort.send(stimuli_1);
alt {
    [] myPort.receive(response_1){
       Setverdict(pass)
    }
    [] myPort.receive(alt_response){
       Setverdict(fail)
    }
}
```

III. SELECTING DATA FIELDS TO DISPLAY

While most of the tools provide test results in form of an XML file precisely for enabling users to use their own proprietary test results display methodology, instead, we decided to modify the tool's source code. The motivation for this approach was to avoid having to re-develop the MSC display software and especially the message selection mechanism that displays the detailed structured data table but also to maintain consistency between the abstract layer and the TTCN-3 tool. Thus, we preferred to modify the display software source code itself to display selected data so that the existing detailed data features when clicking on the arrows of the MSC are preserved and don't need to be re-developed. Our approach is a first in TTCN-3 tools.

The central concept of our approach is to use the standard TTCN-3 extension capabilities that can be specified at the abstract layer using the *with-statement* language construct. TTCN-3 extensions were devised in the TTCN-3 standard to precisely allow tools to handle various non-abstract aspects of a test such as associated codecs and display test results in the most appropriate way the user desires. While the language is standardized, there is no standardization on how a tool operates and, in particular, how it displays test results. Here, we use the template definition itself and its associated *with-statement* in the abstract layer as a way to specify the fields that will be displayed on the MSC during test execution since the template is used by the matching mechanism. In the following example, we are testing some database content for information about cities that is a well multi-layered data structure with fields and sub-fields as follows.

```
template CityResponseType response_1
                                  := {
   location := {
      city := "ottawa",
      district := "ontario",
      country := "canada"
   },
   statistics := {
      population := 900000,
      average_temperature := 10.3,
      hasUniversity := true
   }
} with { extension "{display_fields
    { location {city},
      statistics { population }}}"; }
```

The above TTCN-3 *with-statement* uses the standard TTCN-3 *extension* keyword. It contains a user definition that is represented as a string. The content of this string is not covered by the TTCN-3 syntax but by syntax defined by the user. Thus, it is the responsibility of the user to handle syntax and semantic checking of that string's content. First, we have defined a keyword called *display_fields* to indicate that the specification is about selecting the fields to display. Then, we specify a list of fields and subfields to display. The curly brackets indicate the scope of subfields. For example, we specified that we want to see the *city* subfield of the *location* field and the *population* subfield of the *statistics* field. This hierarchy is necessary because various fields may have subfields with identical names.

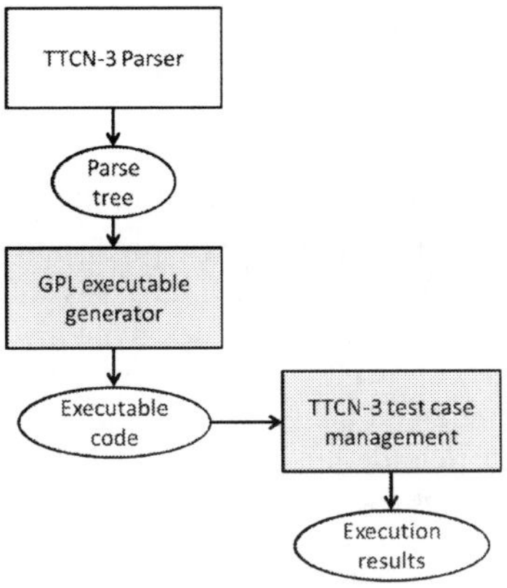

Figure 4. Structure of a TTCN-3 tool

We have implemented this feature on the Titan [12] open-source TTCN-3 execution tool software since this feature requires modifying the source code of the tool. None of the commercial TTCN-3 tool vendors make their source code available. Two areas of the Tool's source code (see Figure 4) were modified:

- the source code for the executable (GPL) code generator that will propagate the selected fields to display.
- the TTCN-3 test case management code that handles the MSC display

This did not require modification of the parser since the content of the *with-statement* is user defined, thus not modifying the grammar of the TTCN-3 language. However, the user definition turns up in the parse tree that is used for test execution code generation. It is during this code generation that we take into account this extension for the display specification. Most TTCN-3 execution software is based on execution code generated in a general purpose language (GPL) like Java for TTworkbench or C++ for Titan and PragmaDev studio and multiple strategies for TestCast. The general principle of these GPL generated code is to transform the abstract TTCN-3 definitions into executable GPL code, for example, in the TITAN tool, the abstract TTCN-3 template definition *response_1* shown previously becomes a series of C++ definitions, one for defining constants and the other to define the template matching mechanism as follows:

```
static const CHARSTRING cs_7(2, "75"),
cs_2(6, "canada"),
cs_8(6, "france"),
cs_4(8, "new york"),
cs_3(13, "new york city"),
cs_1(7, "ontario"),
cs_0(6, "ottawa"),
cs_6(5, "paris"),
...
```

The above definitions are in turn used to generate the C++ source code for the template definition as follows:

```
static void post_init_module()
{
TTCN_Location
current_location("../src/NewLoggingStudy
Struct.ttcn3", 0,
TTCN_Location::LOCATION_UNKNOWN,
"NewLoggingStudyStruct");
current_location.update_lineno(42);
#line 42
"../src/NewLoggingStudyStruct.ttcn3"
template_request__1.city() = cs_0;
template_request__1.district() = cs_1;
template_request__1.country() = cs_2;
current_location.update_lineno(48);
#line 48
"../src/NewLoggingStudyStruct.ttcn3"
{
LocationType_template& tmp_0 =
template_response__1.location();
tmp_0.city() = cs_0;
tmp_0.district() = cs_1;
tmp_0.country() = cs_2;
}
```

Thus, we had to use the same technique of C++ variable definitions to pass on our field display definitions since at run-time, the parse tree is no longer available. The test result MSC is considered as logging activity. Here this is illustrated by calling TITAN function *log_event_str()* that actually writes the template in the source code because this is the test oracle as follows:

```
alt_status
AtlasPortType_BASE::receive(const
CityRequestType_template&
value_template, CityRequestType
*value_ptr, const COMPONENT_template&
sender_template, COMPONENT *sender_ptr)
{
...
TTCN_Logger::log_event_str(": extension
{display_fields { location {city},
statistics { population, temperature}}}
@NewLoggingStudyStruct.CityRequestType :
"),
my_head->message_0->log(),
TTCN_Logger::end_event_log2str()),
msg_head_count+1);
...
```

Using the above source code, during the test execution, the Titan tool writes a log file that contains the matching mechanism results, i.e. the field names and instantiated values of the TTCN-3 template but also after the code modifications, the *display_fields* specifications as follows:

```
09:33:49.443373 Receive operation on
port atlasPort succeeded, message from
SUT(3): extension { display_fields {
location {city}, statistics {
population, temperature}}}
@NewLoggingStudy.CityResponseType : {
city := "ottawa", district := "ontario",
country := "canada", population :=
900000, average_temperature :=
10.300000, hasUniversity := true } id 1
```

The above data is used by the MSC display tool (on Eclipse) and shows two different kinds of information. The first is the content of our *display_fields* definition and the second is the full data that was received and matched. In fact all we had to do was to prepend the field selection logic to the actual log data that remained unchanged. The first will enable the MSC display software to display only the data requested like on Figure 9 while the second one is used for the detailed message content table that is obtained traditionally by clicking on the selected arrow of the MSC like on Figure 3.

While in open source Titan the execution code is written in C++, the actual Eclipse based MSC display is written in Java. Thus we had to modify the Java code that displays the MSC as well. Now, this is the implementation that is valid for Titan tool only. Each tool vendor has different coding approaches and would require different code generation strategies. Unfortunately since they do not make their source code available, all we can do is to strongly encourage these tool vendors to implement our MSC display approach.

IV. THE SIP PROTOCOL TESTING EXAMPLE

The SIP protocol (Session Initiation protocol) [13] is a very complex protocol using complex structured data including a substantial proportion of optional fields. The SIP protocol TTCN-3 test suites are available from ETSI [14] Traditional TTCN-3 tools will display all the fields in the detailed message content table. The user must click on some fields of interest to see the structured content. However, most real application messages make use of only a fraction of all the available fields. Thus, our approach can easily display this fraction of available fields in the MSC.

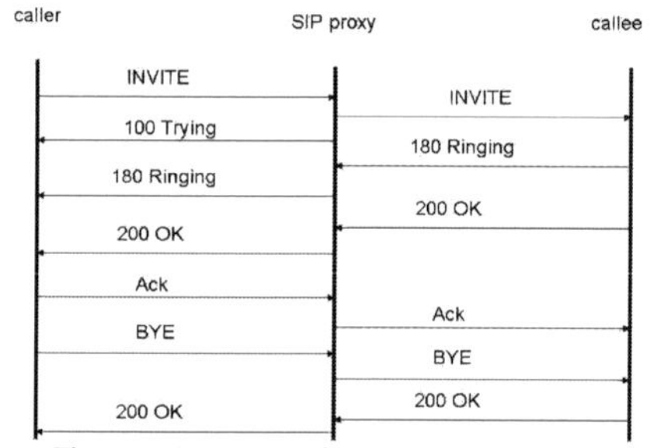

Figure 5. SIP protocol example model MSC

The ETSI definitions for the SIP protocol have used a strategy to try to alleviate the data type display problem in test result MSCs. The approach consists of redefining several times the same structured data type giving different names like in the following excerpt where there is a type for an INVITE method and the BYE request that are absolutely identical from a field definition point of view but they will display differently on the MSC using data types only:

```
type record INVITE_Request {
      RequestLine requestLine,
      MessageHeader msgHeader,
      MessageBody messageBody optional,
      Payload payload optional
}
type record BYE_Request {
      RequestLine requestLine,
      MessageHeader msgHeader,
      MessageBody messageBody optional,
      Payload payload optional
}
```

Where the main field is defined as:

```
type record RequestLine {
      Method method,
      SipUrl requestUri,
      charstring sipVersion
}
```

And the method type is an enumerated type:

```
type enumerated Method {
      ACK_E,
      BYE_E,
      CANCEL_E,
      INVITE_E,
      ...
}
```

All of this can be used to specify a template that has all its fields set to any value except for the method as follows:

```
template INVITE_Request
            INVITE_Request_r_1 := {
   requestLine := {
      method := INVITE_E,
      requestUri := ?,
      sipVersion := SIP_NAME_VERSION },
   msgHeader := {
     callId := {
        fieldName := CALL_ID_E,
        callid := ?
     },
     contact := ?,
     cSeq := {
      fieldName := CSEQ_E,
      seqNumber := ?,
      method := "INVITE" },
      fromField := ?,
      toField := ?,
      ...
}
```

We can select the field for the SIP method to display in the test results MSC by adding the *with-statement* to the above template as follows:

```
with { extension "{display_fields
     { requestLine { msgHeader {cSeq
{method} }} }}"; }
```

This will produce exactly the test results MSC that will be identical to the model MSC shown on Figure 5.

V. AN AVIONICS TESTING EXAMPLE

The whole idea of selecting data to display on a test results MSC originated specifically in an industrial application that we have worked on for testing the Esterline Flight Management System (FMS) [15]. The FMS shown on Figure 6 enables pilots to enter flight plans and display the flight plan on the FMS screen. A flight plan can be modified as a flight progresses. Flight plans and modifications are entered by typing the information using the alphanumeric key pad that consist of letters of the alphabet, numbers and function keys. For test automation purposes, key presses can be simulated by sending messages to a TCP/IP communication port. The content of a screen can be retrieved anytime with a special function invocation that will return a response message on the TCP/IP connection. Thus, we have the behavior of a typical telecommunication system sending and receiving messages with the difference that the response message must be requested explicitly, it is not coming back spontaneously and is subject to response delays that must be handled carefully in case of time outs.

Figure 6. Flight Management System

In this case, stimuli messages are simple characters or names of function keys. These messages are by definition very short and can easily be displayed in full on the test results MSC. For such short messages, we have devised a default display option where if there is no with-statement with a display field specification for a given template, the MSC will display all data of this message. This is particularly optimal for short message content like the FMS key presses. The original test results MSC provided by Titan was displayed using useless message type names as shown on Figure 7 .

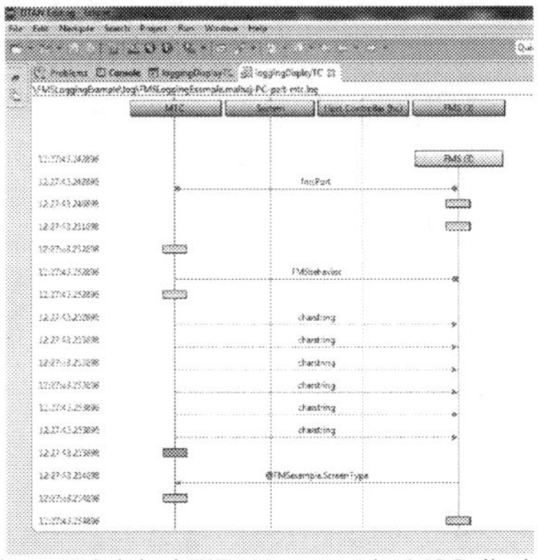
Figure 7 Original TITAN test results MSC display

It is clear from looking at Figure 7 that this MSC is not useful from an overview point of view while our approach on Figure 9 shows the messages values which allows the user to explore rapidly the test results before deciding to go for a fully detailed view of the results when for example the matching of the test oracle with the resulting response shows a failure. This is where the comparison with a model such as UCM is particularly easy to achieve as shown on Figure 8.

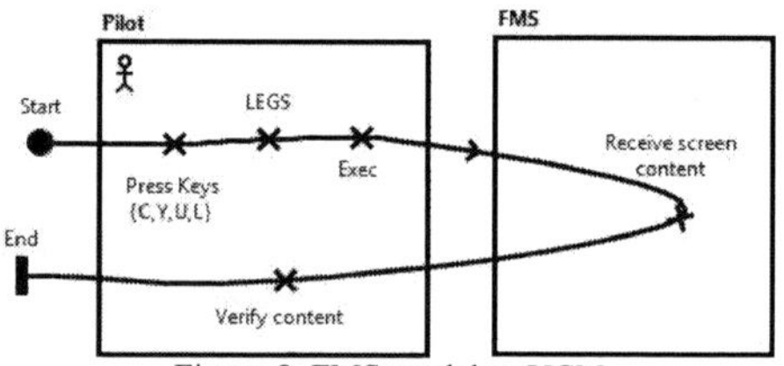

Figure 8. FMS model as UCM

The content of the screen is mapped to a data structure that contains fields for the various lines of the screen and also subfields to describe the left and the right of the screen. The FMS has 26 such fields, a title line, 6 lines structured into 4 subfields and a scratch pad line. Normally a test is designed to verify a given requirement which consists in verifying that a limited number of fields have changed their values. For example, the result of a sequence of stimuli may have changed the field that displays the destination airport on line 2 in the right part of the screen.

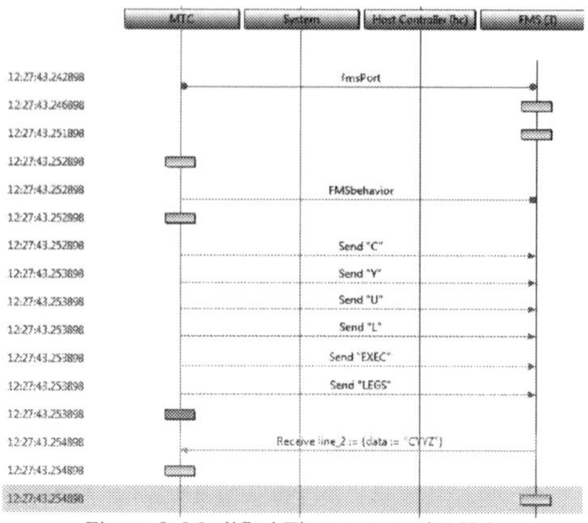

Figure 9. Modified Titan test result MSC

VI. CONCLUSION

In this research, we have shown that when using TTCN-3, it is an advantage to display selected information of complex structured data so as to have an overview on the test results and be able to locate an area of interest quickly and efficiently in test results.

ACKNOWLEDGMENT

We would like to thank CRIAQ, MITACS, ISONEO SOLUTIONS and CMC Esterline for their financial support on this project.

REFERENCES

[1] S. Jagadish, C. Lawrence and R.K. Shyamasunder, cmUML - A UML based Framework for Formal Specification of Concurrent, Reactive Systems, Journal of Object Technology (JOT), Vol. 7, No. 8, Novmeber-December 2008, pp 188-207.

[2] A. Ollsen, O. Færgemand and B. Møller-Pedersen, Systems Engineering using SDL 92, Elsevier Science B.V., Amsterdam, The Netherlands, 1994.

[3] R.J.A. Buhr and R. S. Casselman, Use Case Maps for Object-Oriented Systems, Prentice Hall Inc., Upper Saddle River, New Jersey, USA, 1995. ISBN:0-13-456542-8

[4] R. Alur, and M. Yannakakis, Model checking of message sequence charts, International Conference on Concurrency Theory. Springer Berlin Heidelberg, 1999, pp 114-129

[5] Y. Cheon, and G. T. Leavens, A simple and practical approach to unit testing: The JML and JUnit way. In European Conference on Object-Oriented Programming, June 2002, pp. 231-255. Springer Berlin Heidelberg.

[6] A. Miga, D. Amyot, F. Bordeleau, C. Cameron, and M. Woodside, Deriving Message Sequence Charts from Use Case Maps Scenario Specifications. Tenth SDL Forum (SDL'01), Copenhagen, Denmark, June 2001.. LNCS 2078, 268-287

[7] J. Kealey, and D. Amyot, (2007) Enhanced Use Case Map Traversal Semantics. In: E. Gaudin, E. Najm, and R. Reed (Eds.): *13th SDL Forum (SDL 2007)*, Paris, France, September 2007. LNCS 4745, Springer, 133-149.

[8] ETSI ES 201 873-1 version 4.6.1 (2014-06) The Testing and Test Control Notation version 3 Part 1: TTCN-3 Core Language

[9] TTworkbench,Spirent, https://www.spirent.com/Products/TTworkbench

[10] Testcast, Elvior: http://www.elvior.com/testcast/introduction

[11] PragmaDev Studio, http://www.pragmadev.com/

[12] Titan, https://projects.eclipse.org/proposals/titan

[13] SIP RFC 3261, https://www.ietf.org/rfc/rfc3261.txt

[14] SIP TTCN-3, ETSI http://www.ttcn-3.org/index.php/downloads/publicts/publicts-etsi/27-publicts-sip

[15] FMS, href= http://www.esterline.com/avionicssystems/en-us/productsservices/aviation/navigationfmsgps/flightmanagementsystems.aspx

[16] B. Stepien, L.Peyton, M. Shang and T.Vassiliou-Gioles, "An Integrated TTCN-3 Test Framework Architecture for Interconnected Object-based Internet Applications", International Journal of Electronic Business, Inderscience Publishers, Vol. 11, No. 1, pp. 1-23, 2014. DOI: http://dx.doi.org/10.1504/IJEB.2014.057898

A Comparative Study of GUI Automated Tools for Software Testing

Peter Sabev
Department of Informatics and Information Technologies
"Angel Kanchev" University of Ruse
Ruse, Bulgaria
e-mail: psabev@uni-ruse.bg

Katalina Grigorova
Department of Informatics and Information Technologies
"Angel Kanchev" University of Ruse
Ruse, Bulgaria
e-mail: kgrigorova@uni-ruse.bg

Abstract—**Nowadays, a main resort for delivering software with good enough quality is to design, create, implement and maintain test cases that are executed automatically. This could be done on many different levels. However, graphical user interface (GUI) testing is closest to how the real user interacts with the software under test (SUT). The aim of this paper is to determine the most popular GUI automated tools for software testing among a list of 52 candidates and to compare their features, functional and non-functional characteristics.**

Keywords-GUI; software; quality assurance; QA; automated testing; test automation; testing tools; UI; GUI; tests; Selenium; RFT; UFT; TestComplete; Ranorex; OATS.

I. Introduction

Testing is an essential activity to ensure the quality of software systems. Automating the execution of test cases against a given software or system can greatly improve test productivity, and save time and costs.

However, many organizations refuse to use test automation or have failed to implement it because they do not know how to deal with the implementation of a test automation strategy.

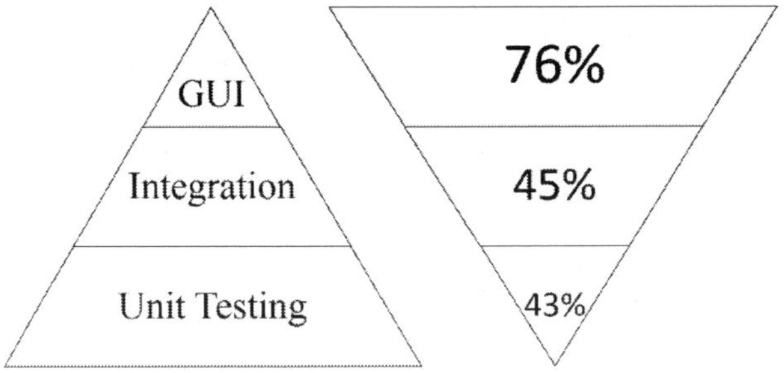

Figure 1. The ideal test automation pyramid on the left and the reversed reality on the right.

In 2009, Mike Cohn proposed the test automation pyramid (Fig. 1) that has become a best practice in the software industry. According to the pyramid, unit testing should form the majority of tests, creating the foundation of the testing strategy, later to be expanded by service-level integration tests and topped by GUI automated tests [1]. Because GUI tests are time-consuming, harder to maintain, they are placed on the top of the pyramid, aiming to do as little user interface tests as possible. However, reality shows a completely reversed situation. In many companies, due to the isolation of the role of quality assurance (QA) engineers and tasking them to write GUI tests only, the ratio of GUI tests to unit tests is inversed. Although it is not possible to collect the ratio for test distribution in each project, reports from 2016 show that unit testing is performed in only 43% of the software companies, while 45% of them perform integration testing, and GUI test automation is performed in 76% of the companies. 60% of quality assurance engineers claim to design, implement and maintain scripted testing, and 39% claim to do user simulations. The report also shows that 94% of software engineers consider functional automation and scripting important, and 67% find automation tools challenging or extremely challenging [2].

All the above indicate that choosing a satisfactory GUI automated testing tool or framework is a very important task, and a challenging problem to solve at the same time. The incorrect choice of proper GUI testing tool may result in a significant loss of time and money, and may even lead to impossibility of automating GUI testing altogether. This paper conducts a comparative analysis of 52 state-of-the-art tools and provides comparison tables that could direct towards the most suitable tool according to specific requirements.

In the next section, a methodology for creating a comprehensive list of tools is described. In Section III, the list of GUI tools is filtered by popularity and maturity. In Section IV, a final assessment is made of the top candidates, scoring them in eight different categories. The outcome of that assessment is shown in Section V, and as the scores are quite close, details for each finalist are given in Section VI. A conclusion based on this paper is made in Section VII.

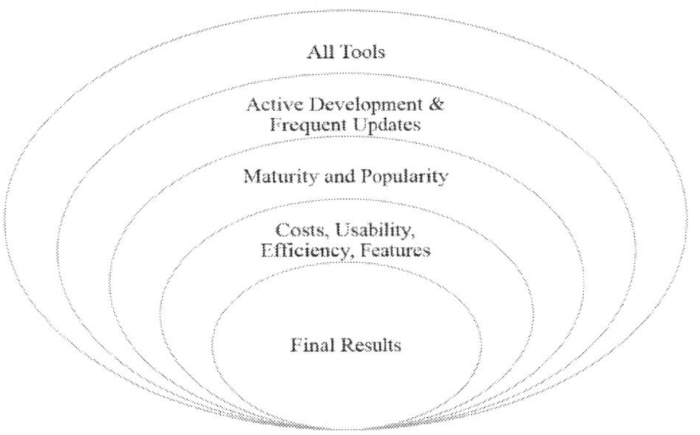

Figure 2. Automation Tools Selection Criteria

II. METHODOLOGY

A comprehensive list of 52 automated testing tools is created (Table I), based on [3]-[5] and the information available in the websites listed in the said table.

The list consists of both free and proprietary tools that are web-based or work at least on one of the following operating systems: Windows, Linux or MacOS. Only proprietary tools with available demo versions are considered. Some tools are then discarded from the list, according to the criteria shown on Fig. 2.

The active development of a testing tool is very important, so tools with no active development after 2015, as well as all deprecated tools are later discarded from the list.

As Table I shows, only 30 tools have active development after 2015, and those tools were listed in Table II. The percentages of active, inactive and discontinued development tools are shown on Fig. 3.

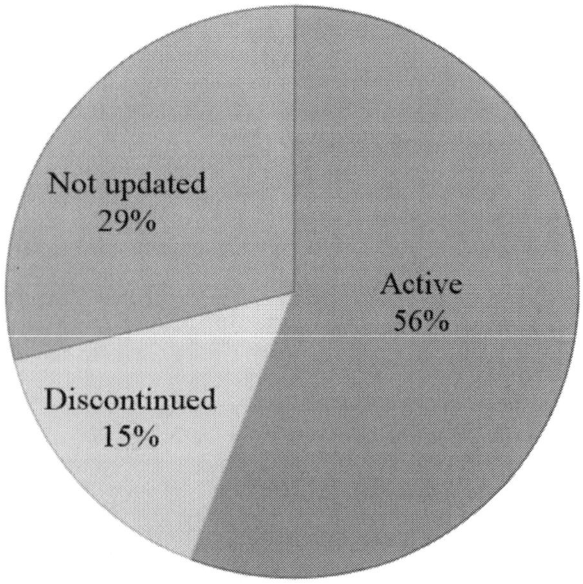

Figure 3. Distribution of active, discontinued and inactive development of automated GUI testing tools.

Only the 10 most popular tools that are mature enough made it to the final stage where a comparison against cost effectiveness, functional and non-functional characteristics is made. This is further explained later in this paper.

III. MATURITY AND POPULARITY

It is very important that automated testing tools are mature enough, i.e. being on the market for at least 3 years, as it takes time until the tools are polished according to the needs of their users. All of the tools remaining are on the market since 2014 or earlier, with SilkTest being the oldest tool with active development in this study (since 1999). It is also very important for a testing tool to be popular in the software engineering industry (so as many professionals as possible know about the product, its features and how to use it). It should be popular also among scientific researchers (so innovations are presented continuously) and the QA community (as people need to help each other, contribute and give suggestions for improvements). That is why the following criteria are chosen to determine tools popularity:

- Google Results (GR Rank) – Google Search [6] is conducted with the name of the tool and the vendor together. When the product is community-driven or there is an ambiguous tool name (e.g., Selenium), the phrase "testing tool" is added to the search. All results are recorded, the list is then sorted by the number of the search results, and finally ranking is assigned and recorded in the GR Rank column. The search results were returned using Google Chrome in incognito mode with Bulgarian IP address. Last, but not least, it is hard, if not impossible to distinguish positive and negative mentions in the search results. Popularity, however, consists of both, i.e., if one knows about a given tool but they do not like it, the tool is still popular;
- To assess the popularity in the scientific community, a search similar to the one above is performed in Google Scholar (GS Rank) [7] and ResearchGate (RG Rank) respectively [8];
- Website popularity is assessed according to Alexa website rank [9]. Although this rank is focused towards the website and respectively the software vendor, popular vendors are expected to be more reliable and software to have longer support lifecycle. The rankings are recorded under A Rank column;
- Wikipedia page views are measured using a Web statistics tool [10] (0 is written for the tools with no dedicated Wikipedia page), and ranking is recorded under W Rank column.

The different criteria may have different importance for the different researches, so the popularity can be calculated in many ways. For the general case of this study, an average of the GR, GS, RG, A and W columns is calculated and recorded under the Popularity Index column and Table II is then sorted according to that criteria. The top 10 tools based on their popularity index are considered for the next stage.

IV. FINAL ASSESSMENT

In the final stage, each of the top 10 candidates is assessed in eight different categories. In each category, maximum 5 points are given, forming a maximum of 40 points per tool. The scores given to some of the categories are not normalized intentionally, to allow adding future tools without changing the scoring system.

A. Popularity (P)

Popularity assessment is performed as described above. 5 points are given to tools with popularity index below 3.0; 4 points when the index is from 3.1 to 6.0; 3 points - 6.1 to 7.5; 2 points - 7.6 to 9.0; 1 point - 9.0 to 15 and no points are given for popularity index that is more than 15. As mentioned, it is a challenging task to determine popularity objectively and with good precision. The main idea is to give similar points according to tools popularity index. That is why border values are chosen in a way to provide equal distribution of points for relatively equal segments of tools with similar popularity indexes.

B. Licensing Costs (LC)

Licensing costs are very important factor in many software companies. Thus, the maximum of 5 points is given to the free tools, 4 points are given to tools that cost under $1000 per single license, 3 points - for tools with single license between $1000 and $2000; 2 points - from $2001 to $5000; 1 point - from $5000 to $10000, and no points are given for license above $10000. For period-based licenses, the period considered is 3 years. Again, border values are chosen with equal distribution of points in mind.

C. Installation, Configuration and Online Documentation Availability (IC)

The first experience that a given user has with an automation testing tool is its installation and configuration. If the tool can be installed, configured and a simple application can be run within 60 minutes, the tool is considered easy to install and configure, so it receives 2 points. Online documentation availability is also considered during that process and an additional point is given for that. The last 2 points are given if the tool supports at least one (1 point for one, 2 points for more than one) system for continuous integration and continuous delivery (CI/CD). The list of CI/CD systems was taken from Wikipedia [11].

D. Usability (U)

According to ISO 9241-11, usability is the extent to which a product can be used by specified users to achieve specified goals with effectiveness, efficiency and satisfaction in a specified context of use [12]. System Usability Scale (SUS) questionnaire [13] was filled by 10 different software QA engineers at different level of expertise. Points are given as follows: 5 points are given for SUS score between 85 and 100; 4 points – for SUS score from 73 to 84; 3 points – from 52 to 72; 2 points – from 39 to 51; 1 point – from 26 to 38. No points are given for SUS score of 25 or less.

E. Programming Skills Needed (PS)

Programming skills and the number of programming languages available are also a very important factor when assessing GUI automation test tool. If the tests can be created and executed without (or minimum) programming skills, this means that much more people would be able to use the tool and the final cost is expected to be less. 5 points were given to tools which require no programming skills; 4 points when simple programming scripts are needed, and the tool gives a choice of programming language; 3 points are given when no choice of programming language is available. For complex scripts, 2 points are given where choice of programming language is available and 1 point if there is no such choice. No points are given where scripts are too complex and even a professional programmer is not able to automate the test cases needed. Of course, it is not necessarily true that the maintenance of tools requiring programming is more expensive compared to record-and-play ones, and this assessment is handled by the next metric.

F. Recording and Playback of Test Scripts (RP)

Once installed, recording and replay of test script becomes a major part of tool usage. Inaccurate recording and replay usually causes more maintenance effort. Data-driven approach separates the logic from the test data, and this makes the maintenance easier. Thus, one point is given to all tools that support data-driven testing. When recording is possible via both scripts and UI, playback is easy and no problems are found, the maximum of 4 additional points is given. One point less is given when there is only one option for recording and replay has no problems. Same is done when both options for recording are available and minor problems are found while replaying. When there is only one option for recording and minor problems are found, 2 points are given. If there are major problems, 1 point is given if there is a workaround, and 0 points – when there is no workaround.

G. Efficiency (E)

Quick test execution is also very important for a test tool, especially when there are many test cases to be automatically executed. A simple set of 4 test cases is recorded on the different tools, testing Windows Calculator and Google Calculator (network delay times are removed), exercising addition, subtraction, multiplication and division. 5 points are given when the whole execution takes less than 5 seconds. From there on, 1 point is subtracted for doubling the execution period, i.e. 4 points are given for execution times from 5 to 10 secs; 3 points – from 11 to 20 secs; 2 points – from 21 to 40 secs; 1 point – 41 to 90 secs. No points are given for test execution that take more than 90 secs.

H. Quality of Reports (QR)

Last but not least, test reporting provides important information on how the test execution went. 5 points are awarded for automatically generated and highly configurable test reports, 4 points – for reports that are automatically generated but not configurable; 3 points – for reports that can be manually created or easily integrated; 2 points – when there is at least possibility to integrate the tool with other reporting tools or systems; 1 point – if such integration is not supported but possible with workarounds. No points are given if such integration is not possible.

TABLE I. FULL LIST OF GUI AUTOMATED TOOLS FOR SOFTWARE TESTING CONSIDERED

Name	Developer or Vendor	Website (URL)	Latest version	OS[1]	Supported Languages	License	Demo	St[2]	Last Update
Abbot Java GUI Test Framework	Timothy Wall	http://abbot.sourceforge.net/	1.3.0	WLM	Java	EPL	N/A	NU	2015
App Test	AppPerfect	http://www.appperfect.com/products/app-test.php	14.5	WLM	Java	$299-$399 per user	15 days	Act	2016
Ascential test	Zeenyx Software, Inc.	http://www.zeenyx.com/AscentialTest.html	6	Web	Java, .NET	Proprietary	On request	Act	2016
AutoIt	AutoIt	https://www.autoitscript.com/site/autoit/	3.3.14.2	W	Own BASIC-like language	Freeware (closed source)	N/A	NU	2015
Coded UI Test	Microsoft	https://docs.microsoft.com/en-us/visualstudio/test/use-ui-automation-to-test-your-code	(part of Visual Studio)	W	.NET	$1200 per user	No	Act	2016
CubicTest	CubicTest	https://github.com/cubictest/	2.21.0	WLM	Java	EPL	N/A	Dis	2012
Dojo Objective Harness	Dojo Foundation	https://dojotoolkit.org/	1.11.3	Web	JavaScript	AFL	N/A	Act	2017
eggPlant Functional	Test Plant Ltd	http://www.testplant.com/	17.0.2	WLM	Java, .NET, C#, Ruby, C++, Python	Proprietary	5 days	Act	2017
eZscript	Universal Test Solutions	http://www.uts-global.com/eZscript.html	0.375	W	XML, keyword driven	Proprietary	On request	NU	2010
Fake	Celestial Teapot	http://fakeapp.com/	1.9.1	M	AppleScript, JavaScript	$30	Freemium	Act	2016
FEST	Google Code / Atlassian	https://code.google.com/archive/p/fest/wikis/Github.wiki	0.30	WLM	Java	Freeware (open source)	N/A	Dis	2013
FitNesse	Community-driven	http://fitnesse.org/	20160618	WLM	Java, Python, C#	Freeware (open source)	N/A	Act	2016
Gauge	Thought Works, Inc.	http://getgauge.io/	0.7.0	WLM	.NET, Java, Ruby	GPLv3	N/A	Act	2017
Google Test	Google Inc.	https://github.com/google/googletest	1.8.0	WLM	C++	Freeware (open source)	N/A	Act	2016
GTT (GUI Test Tool)	Prof. Woei-kae Chen	http://gtt.sourceforge.net/	3.0	WLM	Java	Freeware (open source)	N/A	Dis	2009
IcuTest	NXS-7 Software Inc	http://www.nxs-7.com/icu/	1.0.7	W	.NET	Proprietary	N/A	Dis	2010
iMacros	Ipswitch, Inc.	http://imacros.net/	11.2	WWeb	JavaScript	Proprietary	30 days	Act	2016
IronAHK	Community-driven	https://github.com/polyethene/IronAHK	0.7	W	.NET	Freeware (open source)	N/A	NU	2010
Jameleon	Community-driven	http://jameleon.sourceforge.net/	3.3	WLM	Java, XML	Freeware (open source)	N/A	NU	2013
Jubula	Eclipse & BREDEX GmbH	http://www.eclipse.org/jubula/	8.4.0	WL	Java, Swing, HTML	Freeware (open source)	N/A	Act	2017
Linux Desktop Testing Project	Community-driven	https://ldtp.freedesktop.org/	3.5.0	WLM	Java, .NET, Python, Ruby, Perl, Clojure	GNU LGPL	N/A	NU	2013
Marathon	Jalian Systems	https://marathontesting.com/	5.0.0.0	WLM	Java, Swing, Ruby	$1480 per user	30 days	Act	2016
Maveryx	Maveryx srl	http://www.maveryx.com/	1.5	WLM	Java	2000 EUR per year	Freemium	Act	2016
Oracle Application Testing Suite	Oracle	http://www.oracle.com/technetwork/oem/app-test/index.html	12.5.0.3.0	Web	Own, OpenScript (Java)	Proprietary	Freemium	Act	2016

[1] Supported Operating System (OS): W – Windows, L – Linux, M – MacOS, Web – Web-Based Applications
[2] Update Status: NU – Not updated since 2015, Dis – Officially discontinued, Act - Active

Pounder	Community-driven	http://pounder.sourceforge.net/	0.95	WLM	Java	GNU LGPL	N/A	NU	2002
QA Liber	Community-driven	http://qaliber.org/	1.0	W	.NET	GPLv2	N/A	NU	2011
QF-Test	Quality First Software GmbH	https://www.qfs.de/en.html	4.1.1	WLMWeb	Java, Swing	2000 EUR per user	30 days	Act	2016
Ranorex	Ranorex GmbH	http://www.ranorex.com/	6.2.0	WWeb	.NET	$2590/user	30 days	Act	2016
Rational Functional Tester	IBM	http://www-03.ibm.com/software/products/en/functional	8.6.0.7	WL	Java, VBScript	$6820/user	30 days	Act	2016
RCP Testing Tool	Eclipse	https://eclipse.org/rcptt/	2.2.0	WLM	Eclipse Common Language	Freeware (open source)	N/A	Act	2017
RIATest	Cogitek Inc.	http://www.cogitek.com/riatest.html	6.2.6	WM	Own, RIAScript	Proprietary	30 days	NU	2015
Robot Framework	Community-driven	http://robotframework.org/	3.0	WLM	Java	Apache	N/A	NU	2015
Sahi	Tyto Software	http://sahipro.com/	6.3.2	Web	Java	$695 per user/year	30 days	Act	2016
Selenium	Community-driven	http://www.seleniumhq.org/	3.0.1	Web	Java, .NET, JavaScript, Python, Ruby, PHP, Perl, R, Objective C, Haskell	Apache	N/A	Act	2016
SikuliX	MIT	http://sikulix.com/	2.0.0	WLMWeb	Ruby, Python, Java, Jython	MIT	N/A	NU	2015
SilkTest	Micro Focus Int.	https://www.microfocus.com/products/silk-portfolio/silk-test/	17.5	WL	Java, .NET, own (C++ like)	Individual offer ($5K-9K)	45 days	Act	2016
Squish GUI Tester	froglogic GmbH	https://www.froglogic.com/squish/	6.2	WLM	Keyword-driven	4000 EUR per user	60 days	Act	2016
SWAT	Community-driven	https://sourceforge.net/projects/ulti-swat/	4.1	WWeb	.NET	GPLv2	N/A	Dis	2012
SWTBot	Eclipse	http://www.eclipse.org/swtbot/	2.5.0	WL	Java	Freeware (open source)	N/A	Act	2016
Telerik Test Studio	Progress	http://www.telerik.com/teststudio	2016.4.1208.2	WWeb	HTML, .NET, JavaScript, Ruby, PHP, own (NativeScript)	$2499	30 days	Act	2016
Tellurium	Grant Street Group	http://www.te52.com/	N/A	Web	Java, Perl Python, Ruby	Freeware (closed source)	N/A	Act	2016
Test Complete	SmartBear Software	https://smartbear.com/product/testcomplete/	42804	WWeb	JavaScript, Python, VBScript, JScript, Delphi, C++, C#	3730 EUR	30 days	Act	2016
Testing Anywhere	Automation Anywhere, Inc.	https://www.automationanywhere.com/testing	9.3	W	Keyword-driven	Proprietary	On request	NU	2015
TestPartner	Micro Focus Int.	https://www.microfocus.com/products/silk-portfolio/silk-testpartner/	6.3.2	W	.NET	Proprietary	45 days	Dis	2014
TestStack.White	Community-driven	https://github.com/TestStack/White	0.13	W	.NET	Freeware (open source)	N/A	NU	2014
Tosca Automate UI	Tricentis GmbH	https://www.tricentis.com/resource-assets/tosca-automate-ui/	10.1	W	VBScript	Proprietary	14 days	Act	2017
Twist	Thought Works, Inc.	https://www.thoughtworks.com/products/twist-agile-testing	Unknown	WLM	Java	Proprietary	N/A	Dis	2014
UI Automation Powershell Extensions	Community-driven	https://uiautomation.codeplex.com/	0.8.7	W	PowerShell	Freeware (open source)	N/A	NU	2014

Unified Functional Testing (UFT)	HP Enterprise	https://saas.hpe.com/en-us/resources/uft	12.54	W	Own, keyword driven, VBScript	$3200 per user/year	30 days	Act	2016
VisualCron	NetCart	http://www.visualcron.com/	8.2.3	W	PowerShell, SQL, Batch	$149 per server/year	45 days	Act	2016
Watir	Community-driven	https://watir.com/	6.1	Web	Ruby	MIT	N/A	Act	2017
WinRunner	HP Enterprise	https://softwaresupport.hpe.com/document/-/facetsearch/document/KM01033448	9.2	W	Own, scripting	Proprietary	N/A	Dis	2008
Xnee	Community-driven	https://www.gnu.org/software/xnee/	3.19	L	X11 protocol used	GPLv3	N/A	NU	2014

TABLE II. FILTERED TOOLS SORTED BY POPULARITY INDEX

Tool Name	Since Year	Google Results	GR Rank	Google Scholar Results	GS Rank	Research Gate Results	RG Rank	Alexa Site Rank	A Rank	Wikipedia Views	W Rank	Popularity Index
Selenium	2006	1000000	1	1490	1	580	1	24147	10	21637	1	**2.8**
Rational Functional Tester	2007	425000	3	518	4	8	3	614	4	767	12	**5.2**
Google Test	2008	114000	12	437	5	5	6	61	2	2431	4	**5.8**
Unified Functional Testing	2000	418000	4	100	10	3	8	3629	8	4416	2	**6.4**
TestComplete	1999	553000	2	112	9	3	8	32279	11	1326	5	**7**
FitNesse	2009	328000	5	690	2	17	2	586115	21	1162	6	**7.2**
Coded UI Test	2010	73700	13	50	16	6	4	40	1	1036	7	**8.2**
SilkTest	1994	191000	7	615	3	3	8	61962	13	792	10	**8.2**
Ranorex	2007	125000	10	169	7	2	12	161122	15	901	9	**10.6**
Oracle Application Testing Suite	2008	190000	8	41	18	2	12	348	3	604	13	**10.8**
iMacros	2001	3950	23	201	6	4	7	35068	12	942	8	**11.2**
Watir	2011	125000	11	138	8	6	4	881518	24	789	11	**11.6**
Jubula	2012	4870	22	91	11	3	8	2956	7	23	22	**14**
RCP Testing Tool	2014	143000	9	88	12	0	17	2956	5	0	30	**14.6**
SWTBot	2001	51200	15	70	13	2	12	2956	6	0	29	**15**
Telerik Test Studio	2002	29100	16	22	21	0	17	4655	9	544	15	**15.6**
Dojo Objective Harness	2011	747	29	10	24	0	17	86069	14	3277	3	**17.4**
eggPlant Functional	2013	24200	17	23	20	0	17	522174	18	489	16	**17.6**
QF-Test	2001	8540	20	68	14	2	12	2001348	27	241	18	**18.2**
Gauge	2014	12900	19	65	15	0	17	526578	19	112	21	**18.2**
Maveryx	2010	256000	6	16	23	0	17	7029069	30	258	17	**18.6**
Tricentis Tosca	2011	13000	18	24	19	2	12	281142	17	0	27	**18.6**
Sahi	2010	3210	25	22	22	0	17	534433	20	555	14	**19.6**
VisualCron	2005	69300	14	5	27	0	17	910942	25	175	20	**20.6**
App Test	2003	2050	28	42	17	0	17	877243	23	0	25	**22**
Marathon	2005	5780	21	7	25	0	17	3542542	28	0	23	**22.8**
Tellurium	2010	3320	24	7	26	0	17	630725	22	0	26	**23**
Squish GUI Tester	2003	2820	26	5	28	0	17	202006	16	0	28	**23**
Fake	2010	2440	27	5	29	0	17	1816998	26	0	24	**24.6**
Ascentialtest	2006	524	30	1	30	0	17	4692844	29	197	19	**25**

V. Final Results

After the final assessment in the eight different categories above, Table III containing the final rankings is produced:

TABLE III. FINAL CANDIDATES ASSESSMENT RESULTS

№	Tool Name	P	LC	IC	U	PS	RP	E	QR	TOTAL
1	Selenium	5	5	4	3	4	2	3	2	26
2	UFT	4	1	3	4	4	4	4	5	24
3	CUITs	2	3	4	3	3	4	4	2	23
4	Ranorex	1	2	3	4	4	5	3	4	22
5	Google Test	4	5	3	1	1	2	5	1	21
6	FitNesse	3	5	3	2	2	2	3	1	20
7	TestComplete	3	2	3	3	3	3	2	3	19
8	SilkTest	2	1	3	3	4	2	3	2	18
9	RFT	4	1	2	3	3	1	3	2	17
10	OATS	1	1	3	3	3	3	2	4	16

VI. Final Candidates

The top 10 GUI automation tools that are taken into the final comparison are different in many areas– environment, installation, usage, test script creation and maintenance, etc. That is why this section is dedicated to providing more detailed description of each finalist, so one could pick up the best candidate according to their specific needs.

A. Selenium

Selenium is currently the most popular software testing framework for Web applications. Selenium is portable and provides a record/playback tool for authoring tests without learning a test scripting language (Selenium IDE). It also provides a test domain-specific language (Selenese) to write tests in a number of popular programming languages, including C#, Groovy, Java, Perl, PHP, Python, Ruby and Scala. Selenium WebDriver accepts commands (sent in Selenese, or via a Client API) and sends them to a browser. It does not need a special server to execute tests. Instead, the WebDriver directly starts a browser instance and controls it. However, Selenium Grid can be used with WebDriver to execute tests on remote systems. Selenium allows parallel executions, has multi-platform and multi-browser support (although there are some issues with Safari and Internet Explorer). Selenium supports a variety of CI/CD tools; however some programming may be needed for full setup. A big amount of programming and setup is needed to integrate with report generation tools or database (for data-driven testing). From recording and playback perspective, there is no option to run the test from a point or state of application, so tests need to be started from the very beginning each time. Test execution speed highly depends on the locator used, e.g., Xpath selectors are much slower compared to getting elements by their ID.

B. Rational Functional Tester

IBM Rational Functional Tester (RFT) provides automated testing capabilities for functional, regression, GUI, and data-driven testing. Installation is straight forward. The RFT can generate VBScript and Java statements, requiring some programming experience. Test execution is generally stable, but occasionally it has memory issues, which can be solved easily. During playback, Rational Functional Tester uses the Object Map to find and act against the application interface. However, during development it is often the case that objects change between the time the script was recorded and when a script was executed. For example, testing with multiple values selected using the Shift key pressed does not work. RFT supports data driven commands to generate different test cases, however the expected outputs need to be manually entered. RFT allows one script to call another script, so redundant activities are not repeated. However, scripts quickly become too long and hard to maintain. From a reporting point of view, RFT supports results logs containing a lot of information, making it hard to find the data really needed. It also supports customized reports but integration takes a lot of time. CI/CD integration is supported only for IBM products.

C. Google Test (with Google Mock)

Google Test (also known as Google C++ Testing Framework) is a unit testing library for the C++ programming language, based on the xUnit architecture. Google Test cannot be used for GUI automation tests as a standalone tool. In this study, it is used together with Google Mock, so one can create mock classes trivially using simple macros, supporting a rich set of matchers and actions, and handling unordered, partially ordered, or completely ordered expectations. The framework uses an intuitive syntax for controlling the behavior of a mock, however it has been intended to support unit tests rather than GUI, so most testers find its installation, configuration and coding too complex. Google Test is good to consider for a team of highly skilled developers in test.

D. Unified Functional Testing (UFT)

HPE Unified Functional Testing (UFT) software, formerly known as HP QuickTest Professional (QTP), provides functional and regression test automation for software applications and environments. UFT is targeted at enterprise QA, supporting keyword and scripting interfaces and features a graphical user interface. The keyword view allows a novice tester to easily work with the tool. However, UFT often has problems recognizing customized user interface objects and other complex objects which need to be defined as virtual objects, requiring technical expertise. UFT can be extended with separate add-ins, e.g., support for Web, .NET, Java, and Delphi. UFT runs primarily on Windows, relying on obsolete ActiveX and VBScript which is not an object-oriented language. CI/CD integration is limited, as Test Execution engine is combined with the GUI Test Code development IDE. It is not possible to run the tests independent of HPE Unified Functional Testing. High licensing costs often mean that the tool is not widely used in an organization, but instead is limited to a smaller testing team, encouraging testing to be performed as a separate phase rather than a collaborative approach (as advocated by agile development processes). Test execution is quick, although it causes high hardware load.

E. *TestComplete*

TestComplete is a functional automated framework for Microsoft Windows, Web, and smartphone applications, providing separate modules for each platform. Tests can be recorded, scripted or manually created with keyword-driven operations and used for automated playback and error logging. The tool records only the key actions necessary to replay the test and discards all unneeded actions, supporting data-driven testing. Biggest product drawbacks are crashes, hangs and long waiting times (especially for DOM objects), as well as problems with reading XPath values for some browsers. Regular expressions and descriptive programming are not supported. TestComplete has good integration with CI/CD and reporting tools, although it might require technical expertise.

F. *FitNesse*

FitNesse is an integrated framework consisting of a Web server, a wiki and an automated testing tool for software, focused on GUI acceptance tests. FitNesse was originally designed as a highly usable interface around the Fit framework. As such, its intention is to support an agile style of black-box testing acceptance and regression testing. Installation is simple. Tests are described in wiki as decision tables, with coupled inputs and outputs. The link between those tables and the system under test is made by a piece of Java code called a fixture. FitNesse comes with its own version control but also can be integrated with external one. People with no programming skills are unable to use FitNesse, except adding or maintaining test cases in the wiki. The major drawbacks are that those tests are often limited. Also, recent FitNesse releases have issues with backward compatibility and lack of error messages or feedback on what during test execution went wrong.

G. *Microsoft Coded UI Tests (CUITs)*

Automated tests in Microsoft application that go through its user interface are known as coded UI tests (CUITs). These tests include functional testing of the UI controls. CUITs are available as separate project in Microsoft Visual Studio (VS). Recording and playback actions can be easily done with Microsoft Test Manager or VS, and scripts can be maintained on the fly. Data-driven testing is supported for any data source supported by .NET framework. CUITs seamlessly integrates with Team Foundation Server (TFS), supports Application Lifecycle Management (ALM) and can even execute web-based test on Internet Explorer browser only. CUITs are very easy to use by people who are familiar with VS development but not an option for those who are not.

H. *SilkTest*

SilkTest is focused on automated function and regression testing of enterprise applications and consists of two parts: a host that contains all the source script files and an agent that translates the script commands into GUI commands. Separation of test design and test implementation, together with keyword-driven framework, object-oriented approach and both ability to capture objects from UI or use descriptive programming, makes the tool a great candidate to consider. SilkTest was originally developed by Segue Software, acquired by Borland in 2006, which was also acquired by Micro Focus International in 2009. Those acquisitions, and the fact this is the oldest tool among the finalists (more than 23 years), logically brings some issues, e.g., GUI interface is not modern and looks too complex to non-developers. While installation is smooth, recording mode generates code that is hard to read, and sometimes there is no other way to interact with specific objects other than coordinate-based. Also, online documentation needs improvement.

I. *Ranorex*

Ranorex is a GUI test automation framework for desktop, web-based and mobile applications that also supports unit tests. Installation is straightforward, and there is plenty of online documentation and video tutorials. Element recognition is very reliable (XPath and image-based) and both record/replay tool and descriptive programming in C# and VB.NET are supported. Test suites generate executable files that can be easily run by launching the .EXE file where needed. Tests can be recorded by people with no programming skills, and logs are easy to navigate through. However, test execution is unstable at times, especially on remote or virtual machines. Also, the logs are not in common format, so they need to be additionally parsed to include in most CI/CD systems. Another drawback is that no additional plugins are supported.

J. *Oracle Application Testing Suite (OATS)*

OATS is a web-based comprehensive, integrated testing solution. It cooperates excellently with all Oracle applications and uses a functional testing module called OpenScript. The same script can be run on different instances. The generated report is quite detailed and useful but becomes too big. Performance is slower compared to most tools, the browser often runs out of memory, and significant programming knowledge is needed. Data-driven testing is supported using a feature called Data bank.

VII. Conclusion

There is no perfect GUI test automation tool. The fact that even the top scoring tool achieved only 26 out of 40 points shows that each of these tools has its drawbacks and room for improvement. Also, the difference between the first and the last of the finalist tools is just 10 points, which suggests that one should take all factors under consideration when selecting a GUI automation tool.

This paper can be complemented by adding more automation tools, adding more assessment factors and modifying the methodology for the existing ones, but the key points in creating a successful automated tool for software testing on GUI level are clear: such a tool needs to support both engineers with no programming skills (via Record/Replay features, understandable GUI, image-based recognition) and engineers with good programming skills (with Java and .NET being the most popular programming platforms). The tool should support additional plugins, CI/CD integration, reporting tools and high customization on different levels. The proper replaying of recorded scripts is a must, and the maintainability of test scripts is crucial. Last, but not least, tool maturity and popularity, good support, online documentation and big community are important additions for a complete product.

The findings of this paper may be valuable for the scientific community and the industry as a reference list for educational purposes or as baseline for picking the right testing tool. The initial list could produce completely different results if comparison is made according to different criteria, or according to the specific needs of individual or business, project, environment and budget.

ACKNOWLEDGMENT

This work is supported by the National Scientific Research Fund under the contract ДФНИ-И02/13.

REFERENCES

[1] M. Cohn, Succeeding with Agile: Software Development Using Scrum, Upper Saddle River, NJ: Addison Wesley, 2009, pp. 312-314.

[2] PractiTest, Tea Time with Testers, "State of Testing Report," PractiTest, Rehovot, Israel, 2016.

[3] Wikimedia Foundation, "Comparison of GUI testing tools," [Online]. Available: https://en.wikipedia.org/wiki/Comparison_of_GUI_testing_tools. [Accessed 14 01 2017].

[4] Y. Ben-Hur, "QA Testing Tools: All About Software Testing Tools," [Online]. Available: http://qatestingtools.com/compare-gui-testing-tools. [Accessed 14 01 2017].

[5] A. B. C. Brahim, "Evaluation of Tools of automated testing for Java/Swing GUI," Paris, 2014.

[6] Google Inc., "Google Search," Google Inc., [Online]. Available: https://www.google.com. [Accessed 14 01 2017].

[7] Google Inc., "Google Scholar," Google Inc., [Online]. Available: https://scholar.google.com/. [Accessed 14 01 2017].

[8] ResearchGate, "ResearchGate," researchgate.net, [Online]. Available: https://www.researchgate.net/home. [Accessed 14 01 2017].

[9] Alexa Internet, Inc. , "Find Website Traffic, Statistics, and Analytics," Alexa Internet, Inc. , [Online]. Available: http://www.alexa.com/siteinfo. [Accessed 14 01 2017].

[10] Wikimedia Foundation, "Wikipedia:Web statistics tool," Wikipedia, [Online]. Available: https://en.wikipedia.org/wiki/Wikipedia:Web_statistics_tool. [Accessed 14 01 2017].

[11] Wikimedia Foundation, "Comparison of continuous integration software," Wikipedia, [Online]. Available: https://en.wikipedia.org/wiki/Comparison_of_continuous_integration_software. [Accessed 15 01 2017].

[12] International Organization for Standardization, ISO/DIS 9241-11.2: Ergonomics of human-system interaction - Part 11: Usability: Definitions and concepts, Geneva: ISO, 2016.

[13] J. Brooke, "SUS-A quick and dirty usability scale," Usability evaluation in industry, vol. 189, no. 194, pp. 4-7, 1996.

Chimera: A Distributed High-throughput Low-latency Data Processing and Streaming System

Pascal Lau, Paolo Maresca

Infrastructure Engineering, TSG
Verisign
1752 Villars-sur-Glâne, Switzerland
Email: {plau, pmaresca}@verisign.com

***Abstract*—On a daily basis, Internet services experience growing amount of traffic that needs to be ingested first, and processed subsequently. Technologies to streamline data target horizontal distribution as design tenet, giving off maintainability and operational friendliness. The advent of the Internet of Things (IoT) and the progressive adoption of IPv6 require a new generation of data streamline platforms, bearing in mind easy distribution, maintainability and deployment. Chimera is an ultra-fast and scalable Extract Transform and Load (ETL) platform, designed for distribution on commodity hardware, and to serve ultra-high volumes of inbound data while processing in real-time. It strives at putting together top performance technologies to solve the problem of ingesting huge amount of data delivered by geographically distributed agents. It has been conceived to propose a novel paradigm of distribution, leveraging a shared nothing architecture, easy to elastically scale and to maintain. It reliably ingests and processes huge volumes of data: operating at the line rate, it is able to distribute the processing among stateless processors, which can join and leave the infrastructure at any time. Experimental tests show relevant outcomes intended as the ability to systematically saturate the I/O (network and disk), preserving reliable computations (at-least-once delivery policy).**

Keywords–Distributed computing, High performance computing, Data systems.

I. Introduction

With the gigantic growth of information-sensing devices (Internet of Things) [1] such as mobile phones and smart devices, the predicted quantity of data produced far exceeds the capability of traditional information management techniques. To accommodate the left-shift in the scale [2], [3], new paradigms and architectures must be considered. The big data branch of computer science defines these big volumes of data and is concerned in applying new techniques to bring insights to the data and turn it into valuable business assets.

Modern data ingestion platforms distribute their computations horizontally [4] to scale the overall processing capability. The problem with this approach is in the way the distribution is accomplished: through distributed processors, prior to vertically move the data in the pipeline (i.e., between stages), they need coordination, generating horizontal traffic. This coordination is primarily used to accomplish reliability and delivery guarantees. Considering this, and taking into account the expected growth in compound volumes of data, it is clear that the horizontal exchanges represent a source of high pressure both for the network and infrastructure: the volumes of data supposed to flow vertically is amplified by a given factor due to the coordination supporting the computations, prior to any movement. Distributing computations and reducing the number of horizontal exchanges is a complex challenge. If one was to state the problem, it would sound like: *to reduce the multiplicative factor in volumes of data to fulfill coherent computations, a new paradigm is necessary and such paradigm should be able to i. provide lightweight and stateful distributed processing, ii. preserve reliable delivery and, at the same time, iii. reduce the overall computation overhead, which is inherently introduced by the distributed nature.*

An instance of the said problem can be identified in predictive analytics [5], [6] for monitoring purposes. Monitoring is all about: *i.* actively produce synthetic data, *ii.* passively observe and correlate, and *iii.* reactively or pro actively spot anomalies with high accuracy. Clearly, achieving correctness in anomaly detection needs the data to be ingested at line rate, processed on-the-fly and streamlined to polyglot storage [7], [8], with the minimum possible delay.

From an architectural perspective, an infrastructure enabling analytics must have a pipelined upstream tier able to *i.* ingest data from various sources, *ii.* apply correlation, aggregation and enrichment kinds of processing on the data, and eventually *iii.* streamline such data to databases. The attentive reader would argue about the ETL-like nature of such a platform, where similarities in the conception and organization are undeniable; however, ETL-like kind of processing is what is needed to reliably streamline data from sources to sinks. The way this is accomplished has to be revolutionary given the context and technical challenges to alleviate the consequences of exploding costs and maintenance complexity.

All discussed so far settled a working context for our team to come up with a novel approach to distribute the workload on processors, while preserving determinism and reducing the coordination traffic to a minimum. Chimera (the name Chimera has been used in [9]; the work presented in this paper addresses different aspects of the data ingestion) was born as an ultra-high-throughput processing and streamlining system able to ingest and process time series data [10] at line rate, preserving a delivery guarantee of at least once with an out of the box configuration, and exactly once with a specific and tuned setup. The key design tenets for Chimera were: *i.* low-latency operations, *ii.* deterministic workload sharding, *iii.* backpropagated snapshotting acknowledgements, and *iv.* traffic persistence with on-demand replay. Experimental tests proved the effectiveness of those tenets, showing promising performance in the order of millions of samples processed per second with an easy to deploy and maintain infrastructure.

The remainder of this paper is organized as follows. Section II focuses on the state-of-the-art, with an emphasis on the current technologies and solutions meanwhile arguing why those are not enough to satisfy the forecasts relative to the advent of the IoT and the incremental adoption of IPv6. Section III presents Chimera and its architectural internals, with a strong focus on the enabling tiers and the most relevant communication protocols. Section IV presents the results from the experimental campaign conducted to validate Chimera and its design tenets. Section V concludes this work and opens to future developments on the same track, while sharing a few lessons learned from the field.

II. RELATED WORK

When it comes to assessing the state of the art of streamline platforms, a twofold classification can be approached: 1. *ETL* platforms originally designed to solve the problem (used in the industry for many years, to support data loading into data warehouses [11]), and 2. *Analytics* platforms designed to distribute the computations serving complex queries on big data, then readapted to perform the typical tasks of ingestion too. On top of those, there are *hybrid platforms* that try to bring into play features from both categories.

The ETL paradigm [12] has been around for decades and is simple: data from multiple sources is transformed into an internal format, then processed with the intent to correlate, aggregate and enrich with other sources; the data is eventually moved into a storage. Apart of commercial solutions, plenty of open-source frameworks have been widely adopted in the industry; it is the case of Mozilla Heka [13], Apache Flume and Nifi [14], [15], [16]. Heka has been used as a primary ETL for a considerable amount of time, prior to being dismissed for its inherent design pitfalls: the single process, multi-threaded design based on green threads (Goroutines [17] are runtime threads multiplexed to a small number of system threads) had scalability bottlenecks that were impossible to fix without a re-design. In terms of capabilities, Heka provided valid supports: a set of customizable processors for correlation, augmentation and enrichment. Apache Flume and Nifi are very similar in terms of conception, but different in terms of implementation: Nifi was designed with security and auditing in mind, as well as enhanced control capabilities. Both Flume and Nifi can be distributed; they implement a multi-staged architecture common to Heka too. The design principles adopted by both solutions are based on data serialization and stateful processors. This require a large amount of computational resources as well as network round trips. The poor overall throughput makes them unsuited solutions for the stated problem.

On the other hand, analytics platforms adapted to ETL-like tasks are Apache Storm, Spark and Flink [18], [19]; all of them have a common design tenet: a task and resource scheduler distributes computations on custom processors. The frameworks provide smart scheduling policies that invoke, at runtime, the processing logic wrapped into the custom processors. Such a design brings a few drawbacks: the most important resides in the need of heavyweight acknowledgement mechanisms or, complex distributed snapshotting to ensure reliable and stateful computations. This is achieved at the cost of performance and throughput [20]. From [21], a significant measure of the message rate can be extrapolated from the first benchmark. Storm (best in class) is able to process approx. 250K messages/s with a level of parallelism of eight, meaning 31K messages/s per node with a 22% message loss in case of failure.

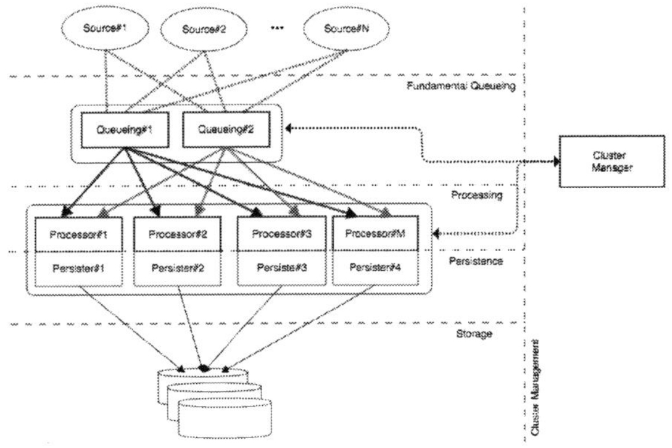

Figure 1. Chimera 10K feet view. Architectural sketch capturing the main tiers, their interactions, as well as relationships.

The hybrid category consists of platforms that try to bring the best of the two previous categories into sophisticated stacks of technologies; exemplar of this category is Kafka Streams [22], [23], a library for stream processing built on top of Kafka [24], which is unfortunately complex to setup and maintain. In distributed, Kafka heavily uses ZooKeeper [25] to maintain the topology of brokers. Topic offset management and parallel consumers balancing relies on ZooKeeper too; clearly, a Kafka cluster needs at least a ZooKeeper cluster. However, Kafka Stream provides on average interesting levels of throughput.

As shown, three categories of platforms exist, and several authoritative implementations are provided to the community by as many open-source projects. Unfortunately, none of them is suitable to the given context and inherent needs.

III. ANATOMY OF CHIMERA

Clearly, a novel approach able to tackle and solve the weaknesses highlighted by each of the categories described in Section II is needed. Chimera is an attempt to remedy those weaknesses by providing a shared nothing processing architecture, moving the data vertically with the minimum amount of horizontal coordination and targeting *at-least-once delivery guarantee*. The remainder of this section presents Chimera and its anatomy, intended as the specification of its key internals.

A. High Level Overview

Figure 1 presents Chimera by its component tiers. Chimera isolates three layers: *i.* queuing, *ii.* processing and *iii.* persistence. To have Chimera working, we would therefore need at least three nodes, each of which assigned to one of the three layers. Each node is focused on a specific task and only excels at that task. Multiple reasons drive such a decision. First, the separation of concerns simplifies the overall system. Second, it was a requirement to have something easy to scale out (by distributing the tasks into independent nodes, scaling out only requires the addition of new nodes). Finally, reliability: avoiding a single point of failure was a key design aspect.

B. Fundamental Queuing Tier

The fundamental queuing layer plays the central role of consistently sharding the inbound traffic to the processors. Consistency is achieved through a cycle-based algorithm, allowing dynamic join(s) and leave(s) of both queue nodes and processors. To maintain statelessness of each component, a coordinator ensures coordination between queue nodes and processors. Figure 2 gives a high-level view of a queue node.

Let $X = \{X_1, X_2, \dots, X_N\}$ be the inbound traffic, where N is the current total number of queue nodes. X_n denotes the traffic queue node n is responsible to shard. Let $Y = \{y_{11}, y_{12}, \dots, y_{1M}, y_{21}, \dots y_{2M}, \dots, y_{NM}\}$, with M the current total number of processors, be the data moving from queue node to processors. It follows that $X_n = \{y_{n1}, y_{n2}, \dots, y_{nM}\}$, where y_{nm}, $n \in [1, N]$ and $m \in [1, M]$, is the traffic directed at processor m from queue node n. Note that Y_m is all the traffic directed at processor m, i.e., $Y_m = \{y_{1m}, y_{2m}, \dots, y_{Nm}\}$.

As suggested above, the sharding operates at two levels. The first one operates at the queue nodes. Each node n only accounts for a subset X_n of the inbound data, reducing the traffic over the network by avoiding sending duplicate data. X_n is determined using a hash function on the data d (data here means a sample, a message, or any unit of information that needs to be processed), i.e., $d \in X_n \iff hash(d) \mod N = n$. The second sharding operates at the processor level, where $\forall d \in X_n$, $d \in Y_m \iff hash(d) \mod M$ = m. See Algorithm 1.

N and M are variables maintained by the coordinator, and each queue node keeps a local copy of these variables (to adapt the range of the hash functions). The coordinator updates N and M whenever a queue node joins/leaves, respectively a processor joins/leaves. This triggers a watch: the coordinator sends a notification to all the queue nodes, with the updated values for N and/or M. However, the local values in each queue node is not immediately updated, rather it waits for the end of the current cycle. A cycle can be defined as a batch of messages. This means that each y_{nm} belongs to a cycle. Let us denote y_{nm_c} the traffic directed to processor m by queue node n during cycle c. Under normal circumstances (no failure), all the traffic directed at processor m during cycle c (i.e., Y_{m_c}) will be received. Queue node n will advertise the coordinator that it has completed cycle c (see Algorithm 2). Upon receiving all the data and successfully flushing it, processor m will also advertise that cycle c has been properly processed and stored. As soon as all the processors advertise that they have successfully processed cycle c, the queue nodes move to cycle $c + 1$ and start over.

Let us now consider a scenario with a failure. First, the failure is detected by the coordinator, which keeps track of live nodes by the mean of heartbeats. Let us assume the case of a processor m failing. By detecting it, the coordinator adapts $M = M - 1$, and advertises this new value to all the queue nodes. The latter do not react immediately, but wait for the end of the current cycle c. At cycle $c + 1$, the data that has been lost during cycle c ($\forall d \in Y_{m_c}$) are resharded and sent over again to the new set of live processors. This is possible because all the data has been persisted by the journaler. This generalizes easily to more processors failing. See Algorithm 3.

Secondly, let us consider the case where a queue node

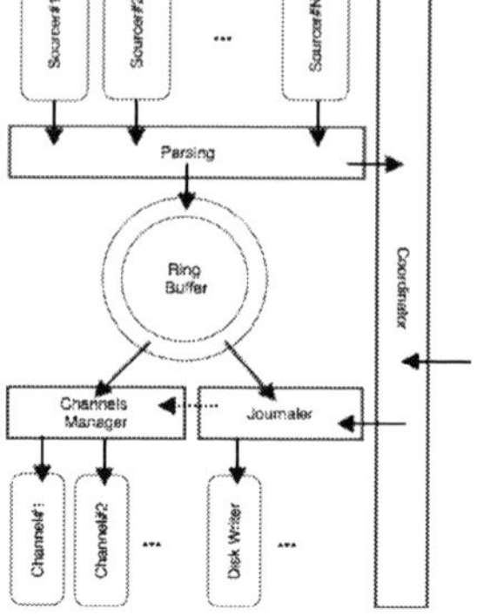

Figure 2. Fundamental queuing internals. A ring buffer disciplines the low-latency interactions between producers and consumers, respectively the sourcers that pull data from the sources, and the channels and journalers that perform the I/O for fundamental persistence and forwarding for processing.

fails during cycle c. A similar process occurs: the coordinator notices that a queue node is not responsive anymore, and therefore adapts $N = N - 1$, before advertising this new value to the remaining queue nodes. At cycle $c = c + 1$, $\forall d \in X_{n_c}$ are resharded among the set of live queue nodes, and the data sent over again. Similarly, this generalizes to multiple queue nodes failing. The case of queue node(s) / processor(s) joining is trivial and will therefore not be discussed here.

Note that the approach described above ensures that the data is guaranteed to be delivered at least once. It however does not ensure exactly-once delivery. Section III-E3 complements the above explanations.

Byzantine failures [26] are out of scope and will therefore not be treated. It is worth emphasizing that introducing resiliency to such failures would require a stateful protocol, which is exactly what Chimera avoids. Below, details about the three main components of the fundamental queuing tier are given.

1) Ring Buffer: The ring buffer is based on a multi-producers and multi-consumers scheme. As such, its design resolves around coping with high concurrency. It is an implementation of a lock-free circular buffer [27] which is able to guarantee sub-microsecond operations and, on average, ultra-high-throughput.

2) Journaler: The journaler is a component dealing with disk I/O for durable persistence. In general, I/O is a known bottleneck in high performance applications. To mitigate performance hit, the journaler uses memory-mapped file (MMFs) [28].

3) Channel: Communications between fundamental queuing and processors is implemented via the channel module, which is a custom implementation of a push-based client/server raw bytes asynchronous channel, able to work at line rate. It is a point to point application link and serves as an unidirectional pipe (queuing tier to one instance of processor). Despite the efforts in designing the serialization and deserialization from scratch, the extraction module in the processor will prove to be the major bottleneck (refer to Section IV).

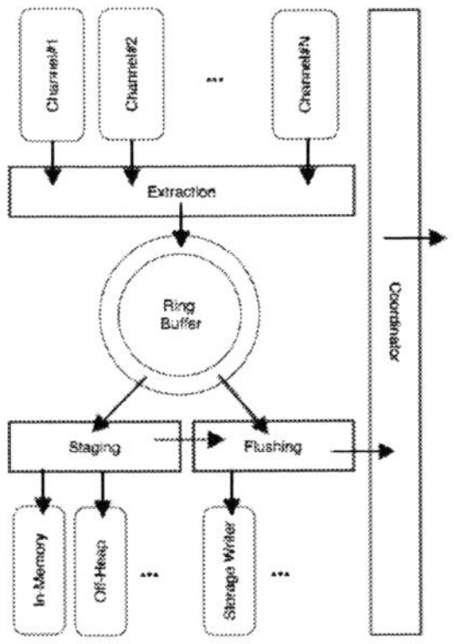

Figure 3. Processor internals. A ring buffer disciplines the interactions between producers and consumers, respectively the inbound channels receiving the data samples to process, and the staging and flushing sub-stages that store the data either for further processing or for durable persistence.

C. Shared-nothing Processing Tier

A processor is a shared-nothing process, able to perform a set of diversified computations. It is composed of three major components, which are the extractor, the stager and the flusher, as depicted on Figure 3. A processor only needs to advertise itself to the coordinator in order to start receiving traffic at the next cycle. Being stateless, it allows indefinite horizontal scaling. Details about the two main components of the processing tier are given below.

1) Extractor: The extractor module is the component that asynchronously rebuilds the data received from the queue nodes into Chimera's internal model. It is the downstream of the channel (as per Section III-B3).

2) Staging: The warehouse is the implementation of the staging area in Figure 3. It is an abstraction of an associative data structure in which the data is staged for the duration of a cycle; it is pluggable and has an on-heap and off-heap implementation. It supports various kinds of stateful processing, i.e., computations for which the output is function of a previously stored computation. As an example, the processor used for benchmarking Chimera has the inbound data aggregated on-the-fly for maximum efficiency; at the end of the cycle, all the data currently sitting in the warehouse gets flushed to the database. However, partial data is not committed, meaning that unless all the data from a cycle c is received (i.e., Y_{m_c}), the warehouse will not flush.

D. Persistence Tier

The persistence tier is a node of the ingestion pipeline that runs a database. This is the sole task of such kind of nodes. Chimera makes use of a time series database (TSDB) [29] built on top of Apache Cassandra. At design time, the choice was made considering the expected throughput and the possibility to horizontally scale this tier too.

E. Core Protocols

The focus of this section is on the core protocols, intended as the main algorithms implemented at the fundamental queuing and processor components; their design targeted the

Algorithm 1: Cyclic ingestion and continuous forwarding in the fundamental queuing tier.

```
Data: queueNodeId, N, M
Result: continuous ingestion and sharding.
while alive do
    curr = buffer.next();
    n = hash(current) mod N;
    if n == queueNodeId then
        m = hash(curr) mod M;
        send(curr, m);
    end
    if endOfCycle then
        c = c+1;
        advertise(queueNodeId, c);
    end
end
```

Algorithm 2: Cyclic reception, processing and flushing.

```
Data: processorId, data
Result: continuous processing and cyclic flushing.
initialization;
while alive do
    extracted = extract(data);
    processed = process(extracted);
    if to be staged then
        stage(processed);
    else
        flush();
        c = c+1;
        advertise(processorId, c);
    end
end
```

distributed and shared nothing paradigm: coordination traffic is backpropagated and produced individually by every processor. The backpropagation of acknowledgements refers to the commit of the traffic shard emitted by the target processor upon completion of a flush operations. This commit is addressed to the coordinator only. To make sense of these protocols, the key concepts to be taken into consideration are: *ingestion cycle* and *ingestion group*, as per their definitions.

1) Cyclic Operations: The ingestion pipeline works on ingestion cycles, which are configurable batching units; the overall functioning is independent of the cycle length, which may be an adaptive time window or any batch policy, ranging from a single unit to any number of units fitting the needs, context and type of data. Algorithm 1 presents the pseudo-code for the cyclic operations of Chimera on the fundamental queuing tier, and Algorithm 2 presents the pseudo-code for the processing tier.

2) On-demand Replay: On-demand replay needs to be implemented in case of any disruptive events occurring in the ingestion group, e.g., a failed processor or queue node. In order to reinforce reliable processing, the shard of data originally processed by the faulty member needs to be replayed, and this has to happen on the next ingestion cycle. The design of the cyclic ingestion with replay mechanism allows to mitigate the effect of dynamic join and leave: the online readaptation only

Algorithm 3: Data samples on-demand replay, upon failures (processor(s) not able to commit the cycle).

```
Data: cycleOfFailure, queueNodeId, prevM, M,
      failedProcessorId
Result: replay traffic according to the missing
        processor(s) commit(s).
initialization;
while alive do
    data = retrieve(cycleOfFailure);
    while data.hasNext() do
        current = data.next();
        if hash(current) mod N == queueNodeId then
            if (hash(current) mod prevM) ==
             failedProcessorId then
                m = hash(current) mod M;
                send(curr, m);
            end
        end
    end
end
```

happens in the next cycle, without any impact on the actual one.

Algorithm 3 presents the main flow of operations needed to make sure that any non committed shard of traffic is first re-processed consistently, and then properly flushed onto the storage. Note that this process of replaying can be nested in case of successive failures. It provides eventual consistency in the sense that the data will eventually be processed.

3) Dynamic Join/Leave: Any dynamic join(s) and leave(s) are automatically managed with the group membership and the distribution protocol. Join means any event related to a processor/queue node advertising itself to the cluster manager (or coordinator); instead, leave means any event related to a processor leaving the ingestion group and stop advertising itself to the cluster manager. Upon the arrival of a new processor, nothing happens immediately. Instead at the beginning of the next cycle, it is targeted with its shard of traffic; whenever a processor leaves the cluster (e.g., a failure), a missing commit for the cycle is detected and the on-demand replay is triggered to have the shard of traffic re-processed and eventually persisted by one of the live processors.

IV. Experimental Campaign

In order to assess Chimera performance with a focus to validate its design, a test campaign has been carried out. In this section, the performance figures are presented, notes are systematically added to give context to the figures and to share with the reader the observations from the implemented campaign.

A. Testbench

Performance testing has been conducted on a small cluster of three bare metal machines, each of which runs on CentOS v7. Machines were equipped with two CPUs of six cores each, 48 GB of DDR3 and a HDD; they were connected by the mean of a 1 Gbit switched network.

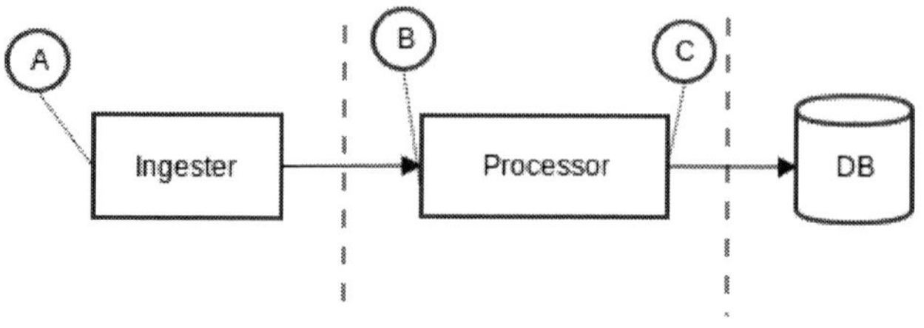

Figure 4. Graphical representation of the experimental methodology used to assess the performance of Chimera, tier by tier.

B. Experiments

The synthetic workloads were generated randomly. The data was formatted to reflect the expected traffic in a production environment. For each test scenario, twenty iterations were run; the results for each iteration were then averaged and summarized.

Figure 4 presents the testbench organization: probes were put in points A, B and C to capture relevant performance figures. As evident, the experiments were carried out with a strong focus on assessing the performance of each one of the composing tiers, in terms of inbound and outbound aggregated traffic.

The processor used for the tests performs a statistical aggregation of the received data points on per cycle basis; this was to alleviate the load on the database, which was not able to keep up with Chimera's average throughput.

The remainder of this section presents the results with reference to this methodology.

C. Results

1) Fundamental Queuing Inbound Throughput:

a) Parsing: At the very entrance of any pipeline sits the parsing submodule, which is currently implemented following a basic scheme. This is mostly because the parsing logic highly relates to the kind of data that would be ingested by the system. As such, parsing optimization can only be carried out when actual data is pumped into Chimera. Nevertheless, stress testing has been conducted to assess the performance of a general purpose parser. The test flow is as follow: synthetic workloads is created and loaded up in memory, before being pumped into the parsing module, which in turns pushes its output to the ring buffer. The results summarized in Table I are fairly good: a single threaded parsing submodule was able to parse 712K messages per second, on average. Clearly, as soon as the submodule makes use of multiple threads, the parser was able to saturate the ring buffer capacity.

b) Ring Buffer: The synthetic workload generator simulated many different sources pushing messages of 500 byte (with a slight variance due to randomness) on a multi-threaded parsing module. In order to push the limits of the actual implementation, the traffic was entirely loaded in memory and offloaded to the ring buffer. The results were fair, the ring buffer was always able to go over 4M data samples ingested per second; a summary of the results as a function of the input bulks is provided in 5(a);

TABLE I. Summary of the experienced throughputs in millions per second. This table provides a quantitative characterization of Chimera as composed by its two main stages and inherent submodules. Parsing and Extraction were multi-threaded, using a variable pool of cached workers (up to the limit of $(N * 2 + 1)$ where N was the number of CPUs available). Tests were repeated with a local processor to overcome the 1 Gbit network link saturation problem. The results involving the network are shown in the light gray shaded rows.

	Queuing [M/s]		*Processing [M/s]*			
Direction	Parsing	Ring Buffer	Journaler	Channel	Extraction	Staging
Inbound	6	4.3	4.3	0.2	0.2	0.2
Outbound	4.3	4.3	3.7	0.2	0.2	0.2
Inbound	6	4.3	4.3	4.3	0.9	0.9
Outbound	4.3	4.3	3.7	4.2	0.9	0.9

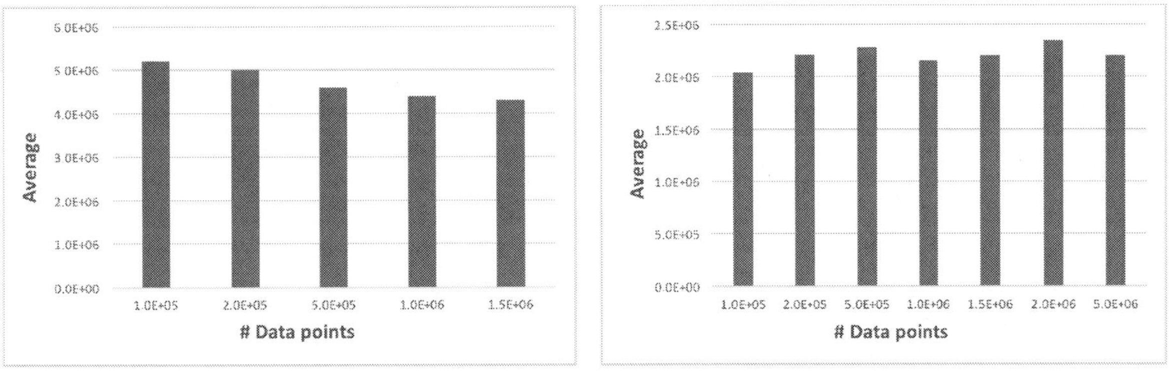

(a) Ring buffer stress test results. Synthetic traffic was generated as messages of average size 500 Byte.

(b) Journaler stress test results. Synthetic traffic was as per ring buffer.

Figure 5. Performance of the ring buffer and journaler.

c) Journaler: As specified in Section IV, the testbench machines were equipped with HDDs, clearly the disk was a bottleneck, which systematically induced backpressure to the ring buffer. Preliminary tests using the HDD were confirmed the hypothesis: the maximum I/O throughput possible was about 115 MByte/s. That was far too slow considering the performance Chimera strives to achieve. As no machine with a Solid State Drive (SSD) was available, the testing was carried out on the temporary file system (`tmpfs`, which is backed by the memory) to emulate the performance of an SSD. Running the same stress tests, a write throughput of around 1.6 GByte/s has been registered. By the time of writing, the latter is a number achieved by a good SSD [30], and which is perfectly in line with ring buffer experienced throughput (approx. 2 GByte/s of brokered traffic data). Figure 5(b) gives a graphical representation of the results.

2) Fundamental Queuing Outbound Throughput:

a) Channel: Results from channel stress testing are shown in Figure 6(a). The testbench works on bare metal machines on a 1 Gbit switched network, which is, as for the case of the HDD, a considerable bottleneck for Chimera. Over the network, 220K data points per second were transferred (approx. 0.9 Gbit/s), maxing out the network bandwidth. Stress tests were repeated with a local setup, approaching the same reasoning as per the case of journaler. The results are reported in Figure 6(b), which demonstrate the ultra high-level of throughput achievable by the outbound submodule of the fundamental queuing tier: the channel keeps up with the ring buffer, being able to push up to 4M data points per second.

3) Processor Inbound Throughput:

a) Channel: The channel is a common component, which acts as sender on the queuing side, and as receiver on the processor side. The performance to expect has already been assessed, so for the inbound throughput of the processor the focus would be on the warehouse, which is a fundamental component for stateful processing. Note that processors operate in a stateless way, meaning that they can join and leave dynamically, but, of course, they can perform stateful processing by staging the data as needed and as by design of the custom processing logic.

b) Staging Area: Assessing the performance of this component was critical to shape the expected performance curve for a typical processor. The configuration under test made use of an on-heap warehouse (see Section III-C2), which guarantees a throughput of 3.5M operations per second, as shown on Figure 7(a). Figure 7(b) shows the result obtained from a similar test, but under concurrent writes; going off-heap was proven to be overkilling as further serialization and deserialization were needed, clearly slowing down the entire inbound stage of the processor to 440K operations per second.

c) Extractor: This module was proven to be the bottleneck of Chimera. It has to deserialize the byte stream and unmarshal it into a domain object. The multi-threaded implementation was able to go up to 0.9M data points rebuilt per second: a high backpressure was experienced on the channels pushing data at the line rate, producing high GC overhead on long runs.

4) Processor Outbound Throughput:

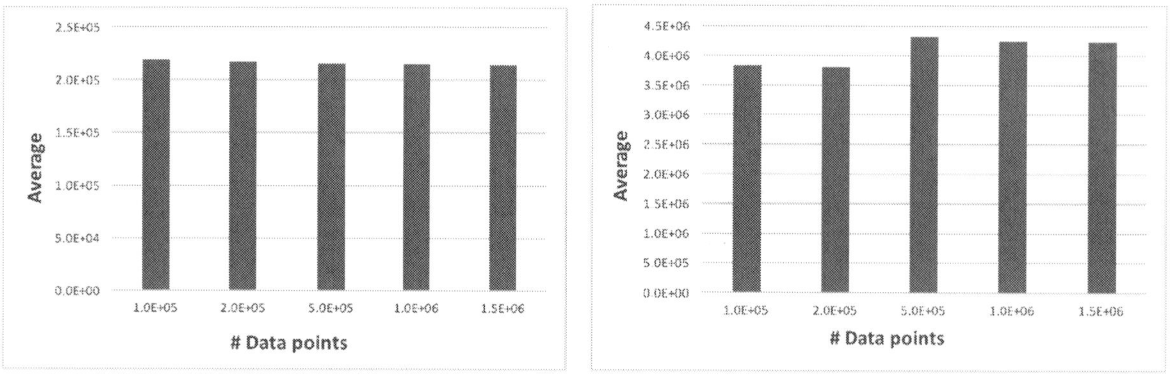

(a) Channel stress test results. Synthetic traffic was pulled from the ring buffer and pushed on the network, targeting the designated processor.

(b) Channel stress test results. Synthetic traffic was pulled from the ring buffer and pushed on the network, targeting the designated localhost processor.

Figure 6. Performance of the channel.

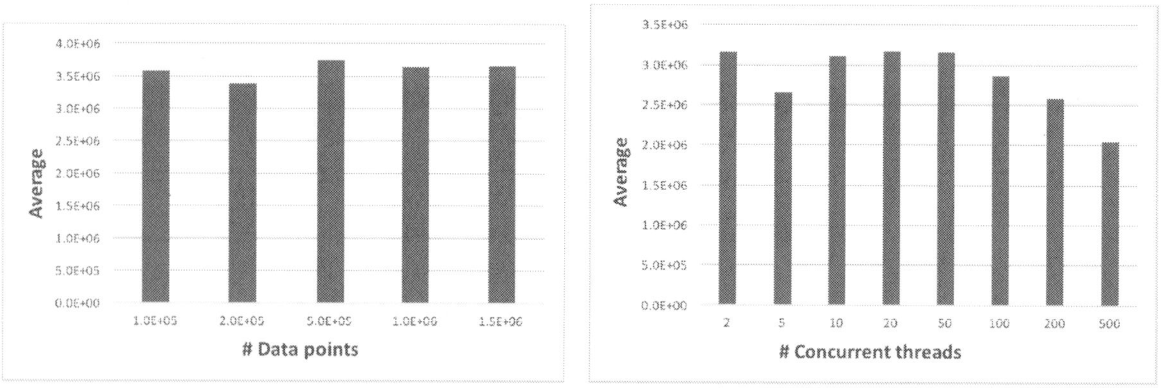

(a) Warehouse (i.e., staging area) stress test results. Scenario with non-concurrent writes.

(b) Warehouse (i.e., staging area) stress test results. Scenario with concurrent writes.

Figure 7. Performance of the staging area.

a) Flusher: It was very related to the specific aggregating processor and it was assessed to be approx. 85 MByte/s, which is reasonable considered the aggregation performed on the data falling into a batching on the cycle. The characteristic of this tier may variate with the support used for the storage.

D. Discussion

The test campaign was aimed at pushing the limits of each single module of the staged architecture. The setup put in place was single process both for the fundamental queuing and processor tiers, so the performance figures showed in the previous sections were referring to such setup.

The experimental campaign has confirmed the ideas around the design of Chimera. As per Table I, Chimera is a platform able to handle millions of data samples flowing vertically in the pipeline, with a basic setup consisting of single queuing and processing tiers. No test have been performed with scaled setups (i.e., several queuing components and many processors), but considered the almost shared nothing architecture targeted for the processing tier (slowest stage in the pipe having the bottleneck in the extraction module), a linear scalability is expected, as well as a linear increase of the overall throughput as the number of processors grows up.

During the test campaign, resource thrashing phenomenon was observed [31]. The journaler pushed the write limits of the HDD, inducing the exhaustion of the kernel direct memory pages. The HDD was only able to write at a rate of 115 MByte/s, and therefore, during normal runs, the memory gets filled up within a few seconds, inducing the operating system into a continuous swapping loop, bringing in and out virtual memory pages.

Figure 8 presents a plot of specific measurements to confirm the resource thrashing hypothesis. The tests consisted in writing over several ingestion cycles a given amount of Chimera data points to disk, namely one and three millions per cycle. The case of one million data points per batch shows resource thrashing after seven cycles: write times to HDD bump up considerably, the virtual memory stats confirmed pages being continuously swapped in and out; the case of three millions data points per batch shows resource thrashing after only two cycles, which is expected. High response times were caused by the cost of flushing the data currently in memory to

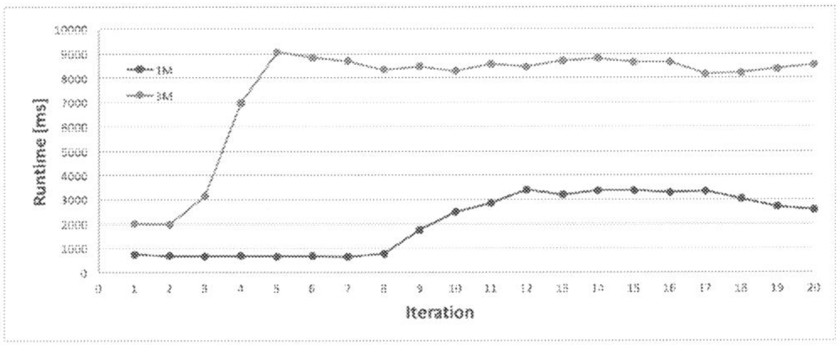

Figure 8. Experimented HDD-induced thrashing phenomenon. The I/O bottleneck put backpressure on the kernel, inducing high thrashing, which was impacting the overall functioning of the machine.

the slow disk, meanwhile the virtual direct memory was filled up and swapped in and out by the kernel to create room for new data, as confirmed in [32].

V. Conclusion

Chimera is a prototype solution implementing the proposed ingestion paradigm, which is able to distribute the queuing (intended as traffic persistence and replay) and processing tiers into a vertical pipeline, horizontally scaled, and sharing nothing among the processors (control flow is vertical, from queuing to processors, and from processors to queuing). The innovative distribution protocols allow to implement the backpropagated incremental acknowledgement, which is a key aspect for the delivery guarantee of the overall infrastructure: in case of failure, a targeted replay can redistribute the data on the live processors and any newly joining one(s). This same mechanism allows to redistribute the load, in case of backpressure, on newly joining members with a structured approach: the redistribution is implemented on a cyclic basis, meaning that a newly joined processor, once bootstrapped, start receiving traffic only during the next useful ingestion cycle. This innovative approach solves the problems highlighted with the solutions currently adopted in the industry, keeping the level of complexity of the overall infrastructure very low: the decoupled nature of the queuing and processing tiers, as well as the backpropagation mechanism are as many design tenets that enable easy distribution and guarantee reliability despite the very high level of overall throughput.

From a performance standpoint, experimental evidences demonstrate that Chimera is able to work at line rate, maxing out the bandwidth. The queuing tier outperforms the processing tier: on average a far less number of CPU cycles is needed to first transform and second persist the inbound traffic, and this is clear if compared to the kind of processing described as example from the experimental campaign.

A. Lessons Learned

The journey to design, implement and validate experimentally the platform was long and arduous. A few lessons have been learned by engineering for low-latency (to strive for the best from the single process on the single node) and distributing by sharing almost nothing (coordinate the computations on distributed nodes, by clearly separating the tasks and trusting deterministic load sharding). First lesson might be summarized as: *serialization is a key aspect in I/O (disk and network)*, a slow serialization framework can compromise the throughput of an entire infrastructure. Second lesson might summarized as:*memory allocation and deallocation are the evil in managed languages*, when operating at line rate, the backpressure from the automated garbage collector can jeopardize the performances, or worse, kill nodes (in the worst case, a process crash can be induced). Third lesson might be summarized as: *achieving shared nothing architecture is a chimera (i.e., something unique) by itself*, meaning that it looks almost impossible to let machines collaborate/cooperate without any sort of synchronization/snapshotting. Forth and last lesson might be summarized as: *tiering vertically allows to scale but it inevitably introduces some coupling*, this was experienced with the backpropagation and the replay mechanism in the attempt to have ensure stateless and reliable processors.

B. Future Work

The first step into improving Chimera would be to work on a better serialization framework. Indeed, as shown in the test campaign, bottlenecks were found whenever data serialization comes into play. Existing open-source frameworks are available, such as Kryo [33] for Java. Secondly, in order to further assess the performance of Chimera, it would be necessary to run a testbench where multiple queue nodes and processors are live. Indeed, the test campaign has only been focused on one queue node and one processor. This would also allow to further assess Chimera's resiliency to failures, and recovery mechanisms. Indeed, Byzantine failures have been excluded from the scope of this work, but resiliency with respect to such failures are necessary to enforce robustness and security.

VI. Acknowledgement

This work has been carried out in collaboration with the École Polytechnique Fédérale de Lausanne (EPFL) as partial fulfillment of the first author master thesis work. A special thank goes to Prof. Katerina Argyraki for her valuable mentoring and her continuous feedback.

References

[1] D. Evans, "The Internet of Things," Cisco, Inc., Tech. Rep., 2011.

[2] L. Atzori, A. Iera, and G. Morabito, "The internet of things: A survey," Computer networks, vol. 54, no. 15, 2010, pp. 2787–2805.

[3] J. Gubbi, R. Buyya, S. Marusic, and M. Palaniswami, "Internet of things (iot): A vision, architectural elements, and future directions," Future generation computer systems, vol. 29, no. 7, 2013, pp. 1645–1660.

[4] B. Gedik, S. Schneider, M. Hirzel, and K.-L. Wu, "Elastic scaling for data stream processing," IEEE Transactions on Parallel and Distributed Systems, vol. 25, no. 6, 2014, pp. 1447–1463.

[5] H. Chen, R. H. Chiang, and V. C. Storey, "Business intelligence and analytics: From big data to big impact." MIS quarterly, vol. 36, no. 4, 2012, pp. 1165–1188.

[6] P. Russom et al., "Big data analytics," TDWI best practices report, fourth quarter, 2011, pp. 1–35.

[7] M. Fowler and P. Sadalage, "Nosql database and polyglot persistence," Personal Website: http://martinfowler. com/articles/nosql-intro-original. pdf, 2012.

[8] A. Marcus, "The nosql ecosystem," The Architecture of Open Source Applications, 2011, pp. 185–205.

[9] K. Borders, J. Springer, and M. Burnside, "Chimera: A declarative language for streaming network traffic analysis." in USENIX Security Symposium, 2012, pp. 365–379.

[10] D. R. Brillinger, Time series: data analysis and theory. SIAM, 2001.

[11] R. Kimball and J. Caserta, The Data Warehouse? ETL Toolkit: Practical Techniques for Extracting, Cleaning, Conforming, and Delivering Data. John Wiley & Sons, 2011.

[12] P. Vassiliadis, "A survey of extract–transform–load technology," International Journal of Data Warehousing and Mining (IJDWM), vol. 5, no. 3, 2009, pp. 1–27.

[13] "Introducing Heka," https://blog.mozilla.org/services/2013/04/30/introducing-heka/, 2017, [Online; accessed 3-March-2017].

[14] D. Namiot, "On big data stream processing," International Journal of Open Information Technologies, vol. 3, no. 8, 2015, pp. 48–51.

[15] C. Wang, I. A. Rayan, and K. Schwan, "Faster, larger, easier: reining real-time big data processing in cloud," in Proceedings of the Posters and Demo Track. ACM, 2012, p. 4.

[16] J. N. Hughes, M. D. Zimmerman, C. N. Eichelberger, and A. D. Fox, "A survey of techniques and open-source tools for processing streams of spatio-temporal events," in Proceedings of the 7th ACM SIGSPATIAL International Workshop on GeoStreaming. ACM, 2016, p. 6.

[17] R. Pike, "The go programming language," Talk given at Googles Tech Talks, 2009.

[18] P. Carbone, S. Ewen, S. Haridi, A. Katsifodimos, V. Markl, and K. Tzoumas, "Apache flink: Stream and batch processing in a single engine," Data Engineering, 2015, p. 28.

[19] S. Kamburugamuve and G. Fox, "Survey of distributed stream processing," http://dsc.soic.indiana.edu/publications, 2016, [Online; accessed 3-March-2017].

[20] S. Chintapalli, D. Dagit, B. Evans, R. Farivar, T. Graves, M. Holderbaugh, Z. Liu, K. Nusbaum, K. Patil, B. J. Peng et al., "Benchmarking streaming computation engines: Storm, flink and spark streaming," in Parallel and Distributed Processing Symposium Workshops, 2016 IEEE International. IEEE, 2016, pp. 1789–1792.

[21] M. A. Lopez, A. Lobato, and O. Duarte, "A performance comparison of open-source stream processing platforms," in IEEE Global Communications Conference (Globecom), Washington, USA, 2016.

[22] "Kafka Streams," http://docs.confluent.io/3.0.0/streams/, 2017, [Online; accessed 3-March-2017].

[23] "Introducing Kafka Streams: Stream Processing Made Simple," http://bit.ly/2nASDDw, 2017, [Online; accessed 3-March-2017].

[24] J. Kreps, N. Narkhede, J. Rao et al., "Kafka: A distributed messaging system for log processing," in Proceedings of the NetDB, 2011, pp. 1–7.

[25] P. Hunt, M. Konar, F. P. Junqueira, and B. Reed, "Zookeeper: Wait-free coordination for internet-scale systems." in USENIX annual technical conference, vol. 8, 2010, p. 9.

[26] L. Lamport, R. Shostak, and M. Pease, "The byzantine generals problem," ACM Transactions on Programming Languages and Systems (TOPLAS), vol. 4, no. 3, 1982, pp. 382–401.

[27] M. Thompson, "Lmax disruptor. high performance inter-thread messaging library."

[28] S. T. Rao, E. Prasad, N. Venkateswarlu, and B. Reddy, "Significant performance evaluation of memory mapped files with clustering algorithms," in IADIS International conference on applied computing, Portugal, 2008, pp. 455–460.

[29] "KairosDB," https://kairosdb.github.io/, 2015, [Online; accessed 3-March-2017].

[30] "Intel SSD Data Center Family," http://intel.ly/2nASMqy, 2017, [Online; accessed 3-March-2017].

[31] P. J. Denning, "Thrashing: Its causes and prevention," in Proceedings of the December 9-11, 1968, fall joint computer conference, part I. ACM, 1968, pp. 915–922.

[32] L. Wirzenius and J. Oja, "The linux system administrators guide," versión 0.6, vol. 2, 1993.

[33] "Kyro Serialization Framework," https://github.com/EsotericSoftware/kryo, 2017, [Online; accessed 5-April-2017].

Integrating Static Taint Analysis in an Iterative Software Development Life Cycle

Thomas Lie and Pål Ellingsen
Department of Computing, Mathematics and Physics
Western Norway University of Applied Sciences
Bergen, Norway
Email: thomas.lie@student.hib.no, pal.ellingsen@hvl.no

Abstract—**Web applications expose their host systems to the end-user. The nature of this exposure makes all Web applications susceptible to security vulnerabilities in various ways. Two of the top problems are information flow based, namely injection and cross-site scripting. A way to detect information flow based security flaws is by performing static taint analysis. The idea is that variables that can directly or indirectly be modified by the user are identified as tainted. If a tainted variable is used to execute a critical command, a potential security flaw is detected. In this paper, we study how to integrate static taint analysis in an iterative and incremental development process to detect information flow based security vulnerabilities.**

Keywords–Taint Analysis; iterative development; software security; injection attacks.

I. Introduction

The Open Web Application Security Project (OWASP) analyses data from software security firms and periodically publishes a report about the top 10 most common security vulnerabilities found in Web applications. The data analysed covers over 500,000 vulnerabilities over thousands of applications making this list a well documented ranking of the most common vulnerabilities present in Web applications today [1]. Two of the types of vulnerabilities at the top of the OWASP top 10 list are information flow based, namely injection and cross-site scripting. Being information flow based means that in order for an attacker to successfully exploit the type of vulnerability, untrusted data must enter the application. This untrusted data then bypasses the validation due to a poor validation routine or a complete lack of validation. When the untrusted data eventually reaches the critical command the attacker aimed for, the vulnerability is exploited. In the category of injection based vulnerabilities reside numerous exploitable implementations, such as queries for SQL (Structured Query Language), LDAP (Lightweight Directory Access Protocol), Xpath, NoSQL and command injection in the form of operating system commands or program arguments. Due to the widespread use of database access based on SQL in Web applications, the most common injection vulnerability is therefore SQL injection. Two other types of information flow vulnerabilities that are worth briefly mentioning are path traversal and HTTP (Hypertext Transfer Protocol) response splitting. Path traversal allows an attacker to access or control files that are not intended by the application. This can happen if the application fails to restrict access to the file system. Path traversal belongs in the category of insecure direct object references in the OWASP top 10 [1] [2].

Numerous approaches for detecting SQL injection and cross-site scripting are documented. Some of them are briefly described in the following paragraphs. *SQLUnitGen* is a tool to detect SQL injection vulnerabilities in Java applications. First, the tool traces input values that are used for an SQL query. Based on this analysis, test cases are generated in the form of unit tests with attack input. Lastly, the test cases are executed and a test result summary showing vulnerable code locations is provided [3]. Fine-grained access control is more of a way of eliminating the possibility for SQL injection rather than detecting it. The concept is to restrict database access to information only the authenticated user is allowed to view. This is done by assigning a key to the user, which is required in order to successfully query the database. Access control is in fact moved from the application layer to the database layer. Any attempt to execute SQL injection cannot affect the data of different users [4].

SQLCHECKER is a runtime checking algorithm implementation for preventing SQL injection. It checks whether an SQL query matches the established query grammar rules, and the policy specifying permitted syntactic forms in regards to the external input used in the query. This means that any external input is not allowed to modify the syntactic structure of the SQL query. Meta-characters are applied to external input functioning as a secret key, for identifying which data originated externally [5]. Brower-enforced embedded policies is a method for preventing cross-site scripting vulnerabilities. The concept is to include policies about which scripts are safe to run in the Web application. Two types of policies are supported. A whitelisting policy is provided by the Web application as a list of valid hashes of safe scripts. Whenever a script is detected in the browser, it is passed to a hook function hashing it with a one-way hashing algorithm. Any script whose hash is not in the provided list is rejected [6]. The second policy, Document Object Model (DOM) sandboxing, is used to enable the use of unknown scripts. This could be a necessary evil for a Web site that, for example, requires scripts in third-party ads. Contrary to the first policy, this is a blacklisting policy. The Web page structure is mapped, and any occurrences of the noexecute keyword within a <div> or <span> element enables sandbox mode in that element, disallowing running scripts [6]. The methods covered in the preceding paragraphs for both detecting and/or preventing SQL injection and cross-site scripting have one thing in common. All approaches present detection solutions limited to their respective vulnerability, being it either SQL injection or cross-site scripting. Since both types of vulnerabilities belong to the same category of vulnerabilities, information flow vulnerabilities, a mutual approach is desirable to explore. Such an approach should also be able to detect all forms of information flow vulnerabilities. *FindBugs* [7] is a popular static analysis tool for Java. It has a plugin architecture allowing convenient adding of bug detectors presently detecting both SQL injection and cross-site scripting. The bug detectors analyse the Java bytecode in order to detect occurrences of bug patterns. Up to 50% false warnings may be acceptable if the goal of the analysis is just to get a general idea of where to do coding improvements in a development process. Having a much more precise analysis reporting none or low false warnings saves the developers time. Therefore, finding a method with a much higher accuracy is preferable. The approach that is explored in this paper in order to detect information flow vulnerabilities, is the approach called taint analysis.

In the following, we want to study how taint analysis can be integrated in the development process, and how suitable the existing implementations are for this kind of integration. To carry out this study, we have applied the analysis to the development of a Java Enterprise Edition (Java EE) application throughout the development process. The outline of the rest of this paper is as follows. Section II describes the principles of taint analysis, and some implementations of this technique. In Section III, the methodology used in this study is presented. Based on this, the results and an analysis of these is presented in Section V. Finally, our findings are summed up in Section VI.

II. Taint Analysis

Taint analysis resides within the domain of information flow analyses. Essentially, this means that tracking how variables propagate throughout the application of analysis is the core idea. In order to detect information flow vulnerabilities, entry points for external inputs in the application need to be identified. The external inputs could be data from any source outside the application that is not trusted. In other words, it must be determined where there is a crossing in the applications established trust boundary. In a Web application context, this is typically user input fetched from a Web page form, but would also include, e.g., URL parameters, HTTP header data and cookies. In taint analysis, the identified entry points are called sources. The sources are marked as tainted, and the analysis tracks how these tainted variables propagate throughout the application. A tainted variable rarely exclusively resides in the original assigned variable, and thus it propagates. This means that it affects variables other than its original assignment. This can happen directly or indirectly. Directly in that, e.g., a tainted string object is assigned either fully or partly to a new object of some sort. An example of indirect propagation is when a tainted variable that contains an id is used to determine what data is assigned to a new variable, see Figure 1 [8].
A tainted variable in itself is not harmful to an application. It is

```
HashMap map = ...;
String id = request.getParameter("id"); //Source
User user = (User) map.get(id);
```

Figure 1: A tainted source variable containing an id to fetch data from a HashMap indirectly induces taint on an object.

when a tainted variable is used in a critical operation without proper sanitization, that vulnerabilities could be introduced. Sanitizing a variable means to remove data or format it in such a way that it will not contain any data that could exploit the critical command in which it will be used. An example is when querying a database with a tainted string, it could open for SQL injection if the string contains characters that either change the intended query, or split it into additional new queries. Proper sanitization would remove the unwanted characters, eliminating the possibility of unintended queries and essentially preventing SQL injection. Contrary to input data being assigned as sources, methods that executes critical operations are called sinks in taint analysis. When a tainted variable has the possibility to be used within a sink, a successful taint analysis implementation would detect this as a vulnerability. Taint analysis can be divided into two approaches, dynamic taint analysis and static taint analysis. The dynamic taint analysis approach analyses the different executed paths in an application specific runtime environment. Tracking the information flow between identified source memory addresses and sink memory addresses is generally how this kind of analysis is carried out. A potential vulnerability is detected if an information flow between a source memory address and a sink memory address is detected. Static taint analysis is a method that analyses the application source code. This means that, ultimately, all possible execution paths can be covered in this type of analysis, whereas in a dynamic taint analysis context, only those paths specifically included in the analysis are covered.

Dynamic taint analysis can be used in test case generation to automatically generate input to test applications. This is suitable for detecting how the behaviour of an application changes with different types of input. Such an analysis could be desirable as a step in the development testing phase of a deployed application since this could also detect vulnerabilities that are implementation specific. Dynamic taint analysis can also be used as a malware analysis in revealing how information flows through a malicious software binary [9]. Taking this analysis one step further enables malicious software detection of, e.g., keyloggers, packet sniffers and stealth backdoors. The concept is to mark input from keyboard, network interface and hard disk tainted, and then track the taint propagation to generate a taint graph. By using the taint graph in automatically generating policies through profiling on a malicious software free system, detection of anomalies is possible. E.g., in the case of detecting keyloggers, the profile includes which modules would normally access the keyboard input on a per application basis. When a keylogger is trying to access a specific profiled application, this could be detected [10]. In both static and dynamic taint analysis implementations, the precision of the analysis is important for it to be trustworthy. Generally, two outcomes can affect the analysis precision. The first scenario is when the analysis for some reason marks a variable as tainted that has not propagated from a tainted variable. This is called over tainting and leads to false positives, which means that the reported error is not truly an error. The second outcome is when the analysis misses an information flow from a source to a sink. Thus, the analysis does not report an error that actually is present. This is called under tainting, and the term false negative describes the absence of an actual error [9]. Dynamic taint analysis has, as shown in previous paragraphs, several types of applications. However, static taint analysis may be a better fit for integration within the development process due to the direct analysis of source code. There are different ways to implement static taint analysis, and we have considered three different implementations for Java, which are elaborated in the following.

A. *Implementations of taint analysis*

An implementation of taint analysis for Java, described by Tripp et al. [11], consists of two analysis phases. The first phase performs a pointer analysis and builds a call graph. Pointer analysis, also called points-to analysis, enables mapping of what objects a variable can point to. A call graph in this context is static, which means that it is an approximation of every possible way to run the program in regards to invoking methods. Tripp et al. describe an implementation of specific algorithms, but the analysis design is flexible in that using any set of desired algorithms is feasible [11]. The second phase takes the results of the first phase as input and uses a hybrid thin slicing algorithm to track tainted information flow. Thin slicing is a method to find all the relevant statements affecting the point of interest, which is called the seed. In comparison to a traditional program slicing algorithm, thin slicing is lightweight in that it only includes the statements producing the value at the seed. This means that the statements that explain why producers affect the seed are excluded in a thin slice [12]. Thin slicing works well with taint analysis because the statements most relevant to a tainted flow are captured. Hybrid thin slicing essentially produces a Hybrid System Dependence Graph (HSDG) consisting of nodes corresponding to load, call and store statements. The call statements represent source and sink methods. The HSDG has two types of edges, direct edges and summary edges, that represent data dependence. The data dependence information is computed in the first phase by pointer analysis. Tainted flows are found by computing reachability in the HSDG from each source call statement, adding the necessary data dependence edges on demand [11]. The way this implementation defines sources and sinks is through security rules. Security rules exist in the form $(S1, S2, S3)$. $S1$ is a set of sources. A source is a method having a return value which is considered tainted. $S2$ is a set of sanitizers. A sanitizer is a method that takes a tainted input as parameter and returns that parameter in a taint-free form. $S3$ is a set of sinks. Each sink is defined as a pair (m, P), where m is the method performing the security sensitive operation and P defines the parameters in m that are vulnerable when assigned with tainted data [11]. This implementation of taint analysis for Java includes ways to incorporate Web application frameworks in the analysis. External configuration files often define how the inner workings of a framework is laid out. Therefore, a conservative approximation of possible behaviour is modelled. For the Apache Struts framework, which is an implementation of the Model View Controller (MVC) pattern, the Action and Action Form classes are treated as sources. These classes contain execute methods taking an ActionForm instance as a parameter. This instance contains fields which are populated by the framework based on user input meaning it should be considered tainted. Thus, the analysis implements a model treating the Action classes as entry points.

An alternative static taint analysis implementation is similar to Taint Analysis for Java in that it is based on pointer analysis and construction of a call graph. However, this implementation depends on pointer analysis and call graph alone in detecting tainted flows. The analysis uses binary decision diagrams in the form of a tool called *bddbddb* (BDD-Based Deductive DataBase), which includes pointer analysis and a call graph representation [2]. Binary decision diagrams can be utilized in adding compression to a standard binary decision tree based on reduction rules. In the context of this analysis, the compression of the representation of all paths in the call graph makes it possible to efficiently represent as many as 10 contexts. This allows the analysis implementation to scale to applications consisting of almost 1000 classes [2]. In order to detect vulnerabilities, specific vulnerability patterns need to be expressed by the user. A pattern consists of source descriptors, sink descriptors and derivation descriptors. Source descriptors specify where user input enters the application, e.g., `HttpServletRequest.getParameter(String)`. Sink descriptors specify a critical command that can be executed, e.g., `Connection.executeQuery(String)`. Lastly, derivation descriptors specify how an object can propagate within the application, e.g., through construction of strings with `StringBuffer.append(String)` [2]. Tainted Object Propagation Analysis does not implement any handling of Web application frameworks.

A third implementation, Type-based Taint Analysis, differs from the preceding approaches in that a type system is the basis of the analysis. The implemented type system is called SFlow, which is a context-sensitive type system for secure information flow. SFlow has two basic type qualifiers, namely tainted and safe. Sources and sinks are identified in these methods, and fields are annotated using these type qualifiers. A type system is a system that intends to prove that no type error can occur based on the rules established. This is done by assigning a type to each computed value in the type system, and the flow of these values is then examined. This concept is called subtyping [8]. The subtyping hierarchy is defined as *safe* <: *tainted*. This means that a flow from tainted sources to safe sinks is disallowed. The other way around, assigning a safe variable to a tainted variable is allowed. A third type of qualifier, *poly*, is included in order to correctly propagate tainted and safe variables through object manipulation, e.g., with `String` methods `append` and `toString`. All object manipulation methods, such as `String append` and `toString`, would be annotated as $poly$. The $poly$ qualifier in combination with viewpoint adaptation rules ensures that the implementation is context-sensitive. This means that parameters returned from such methods inherit the manipulated inbound parameters type qualifier (tainted or safe). As a result, the subtyping hierarchy becomes *safe* <: *poly* <: *tainted* [8]. Another benefit with the *poly* qualifier implementation is that tainted variables properly propagate in third-party libraries. As a result all application code is included in the analysis. Type-based Taint Analysis also supports Web application frameworks in the same way as the regular Java API is supported, namely by annotating the relevant fields and methods. An example of this is that for the Apache Struts framework, the Action class containing the execute method is what needs to be annotated. This method takes an ActionForm instance as a parameter, that contains fields which are populated by the framework based on tainted user input. Simply annotating the ActionForm parameter as

Figure 2: The Software Development Life Cycle [13].

tainted would include the framework in the analysis [8]. Type inference implies identifying a valid typing based on the subtyping rules defined in the SFlow type system. A succeeded inference means that there are no flows from sources to sinks. If the type inference fails, a type error is evident meaning that a flow from a tainted source to a safe sink is present.

III. Methodology

When developing software, a common approach is to establish a Software Development Life Cycle (SDLC). The SDLCs function is to cover all processes associated with the software developed. Different types of SDLC models exist. However, whether it being Waterfall, Agile or some other model, the processes in the SDLC can be partitioned into different phases. In this paper, the phases are named according to Merkow and Raghavan [13] as Requirements, Design, Development, Test and Deployment, see Figure 2. Developing software requires planning of both functional requirements and non-functional requirements in order to deliver an acceptable end product. The functional requirements refer to the functionality of the software, whereas non-functional requirements refer to quality attributes, e.g., capacity, efficiency, performance, privacy and security. The Requirements phase addresses the gathering and analysis of requirements regarding the environment in which the software is going to operate. Non-functional requirements based on security policies and standards, and other relevant industry standards that affect the type of software developed, are included in this phase. The Design phase is where the functional requirements of the software developed are planned, based on the mapping of requirements in the first phase. This phase also includes architectural choices that determine the technologies used in the development of the software. The Development phase contains the actual coding of the software developed. Both functional requirements and non-functional requirements from the earlier planning phases are being addressed. A common approach is to develop the functional requirements in small programs called units. These units are then tested for their functionality, a methodology called Unit Testing. The Test phase is where test cases are built, based on requirements criteria from earlier phases. Both test cases for functional requirements and non-functional requirements are included. The test phase is iterative in nature meaning that the problems found would need to be addressed and fixed in the development phase. After the problems are fixed, the system would need to go through the test phase once again. The deployment phase is the final phase in the cycle, and the main activity is to install the software and make it ready to run in its intended environment, or released into the market. At this point, both testing of functional requirements and non-functional requirements are finished [13].

The problem description (see Section I) states that we will study how to integrate static taint analysis in the development process of a Java EE Web application. Given the tools proposed in Section I for detecting information flow vulnerabilities, static taint analysis is explored in this experiment. This choice is based on the fact that this type of analysis embraces the detection of the whole domain of information flow vulnerabilities. Static taint analysis may also have significantly fewer false warnings compared to e.g., analyses depending on code patterns such as the FindBugs static analysis tool. The research approach regarding the problem description is to carry out a case study in two main parts. The first part is to develop a prototype Java EE Web application of an acceptable size so that it is not too small with regard to performing taint analysis on it. This means that the prototype application should preferably have multiple modules interacting with external processes, i.e., at a minimum implementing a database connection. Further, the user interaction would naturally be done through a website utilizing specific Java EE technologies. The goal of the last part in the case study is to architect a solution to the taint analysis integration. Many aspects regarding this integration would need to be clarified. Based on the experiences with the implementation of taint analysis in the specific prototype application, general conclusions regarding the problem description can be drawn. Some important approaches to implementing static taint analysis for Java are given in [2], [8], [10] and [14]. From these approaches, summarized in Section II-A, the Type-based Taint Analysis from [8] was selected. This choice was convenient in that the analysis platform is available as an open source project and Type-based Taint Analysis also looks promising with regard to how Web application frameworks are handled. Analysing frameworks are especially relevant in Java EE Web applications, e.g., in the form of the Java Server Faces (JSF) framework managing the applications front-end. Based on how this analysis method is described in [8], it would seem that the implementation is feasible as an integrated step in a Java EE Web application development context.

IV. Integrating Taint Analysis in the SDLC

Considering that modern development practices are team based, and in fact multi-team based on big projects, it is important to include this observation in assessing whether static taint analysis can efficiently be integrated in the SDLC. An agile development methodology including an iterative and incremental workflow leads to developing a piece of software in numerous modules. Being able to properly test both a single module and a set of modules for detecting information flow vulnerabilities is preferable. According to Huang et al. [8], the taint analysis implementation is modular, meaning that a whole program is not necessary for analysis. This is promising considering the modern development practice described in the previous paragraph. Additionally, the taint analysis implementation should be included in the development phase along with other testing activities (see Section III) describing the different phases in the SDLC [8]. In addition to the development phase, the testing phase could include static taint analysis. However, the reason to avoid integration within the testing phase is that anything added to that phase adds unnecessary overhead. Even if the overhead of running the analysis is eliminated by making it fully automated, a system for countering the output in form of requested fixes for the next development phase iteration needs some resources. Also, a known concept is that the earlier vulnerabilities are found in the SDLC, the cheaper it is to get them fixed. The aim is therefore to craft a solution to integrate static taint analysis into the development phase. Some methods for detecting and/or preventing information flow vulnerabilities are listed in Section I. Most of these methods focus exclusively on either SQL injection or cross-site scripting rendering detection of other information flow attacks uncovered. Although FindBugs is an example of a static analysis covering most, if not all, the information flow vulnerabilities, its detecting algorithm is prone to have a high percentage of false positives. The choice of type-based taint analysis in the form of SFlow was done because it can detect a high number of vulnerabilities and also has a low number of false positives.

For the case study, a Java EE based Web application for remotely controlling an automated production system was developed. The size of the project was determined to be sufficiently large to do a realistic study on the integration of static taint analysis in the development process, while at the same time being sufficiently small to focus on the research question at hand. The development resources for the case study application amounted to one developer limited to roughly three months development time. As in one man team, a natural SDLC approach to adopt is the Big Bang Model. This is simply a term made to cover an SDLC, which contains no or little planning and does not follow any specific processes [15]. Although a complete SDLC methodology was not followed during the case study project, several key activities were integrated in the SDLC in order to ensure delivery of an acceptable end product. Enabling development of the prototype application iteratively and incrementally was done by applying continuous delivery. This means that the functionality was split up and developed in smaller tasks and delivered in predefined iteration cycles of, e.g., two weeks. The prototype application was developed in iterations with an integrated static taint analysis as a part of the SDLC. While the prototype application has a limited size with a moderate number of iterations of development, we consider taint analysis conducted during the development cycle to be adequate in order to draw conclusions. The bigger the application the more value of frequent analysis. This is because the issues found earlier in a big application environment would contribute knowledge to prevent making the same mistakes over and over as the application progresses, thus saving developer resources.

V. Analysis

A main challenge during the implementation was to properly annotate external libraries, e.g., frameworks, in order to enable a working analysis without developer intervention. Adding annotations manually was not an option because, in addition to creating extra work for the developer, it is prone to errors. For SFlow to be a successful security analysis tool, we found that the annotation process needs to be improved. One approach in changing the annotation process could be to use a strategy from the paper by Sridharan et al. [14]. This paper describes a framework as a solution for adding Web application frameworks to a taint analysis implementation. In a similar way, a framework for adding annotations to the SFlow annotated Java Development Kit (JDK) could be developed easing the work of figuring out how to conduct the process of annotation. This framework could also include verification routines for testing that the annotations are working correctly [14]. Another change SFlow must undergo is the way the analysis is conducted. In its current form, SFlow exists as a manual command-line tool. For this tool to exist in the development phase without unnecessary overhead, an automatic integration of the analysis is required. Therefore, integrating SFlow as a plugin in an IDE (Integrated Development Environment) by utilizing this support by The Checker Framework could be a good solution. This would make the taint analysis convenient and seamless for the developer enabling analysis whenever the developer builds the application and/or desires to run it. However, deciding if the integration is not creating too much overhead for the developer boils down to the running time of the taint analysis implementation. Results from Huang et al. [8] state that analysing 13 relatively large applications resulted in running times of less than four minutes for all applications except one. The analysis ran on a server with Intel Xeon X3460 2.8GHz processor and 8GB RAM. As for the smaller prototype application, the running time is about 30 seconds on a laptop with Intel Core i5-3210M 2.5GHz processor and 6GB RAM [8]. Even though the running time of the taint analysis is done within minutes and may not introduce a significant overhead for the developer running the analysis in the background, implementation in a different way could be advantageous. This solution is to incorporate taint analysis in a continuous integration tool, e.g., Jenkins, by integrating SFlow in the build system it uses, e.g., Maven. By doing this, the taint analysis will automatically run on every build. The errors will then show up as compiler errors and warnings in the continuous integration tool for the developers to address. SFlow needs to undergo at least two significant changes in order to become a powerful taint analysis security tool for integration in the development phase in the SDLC. First, the annotation process for adding Web application frameworks and external libraries must become more user-friendly in order to be practical. As suggested, a solution to this would be to develop a framework for easing the annotation process. And secondly, the analysis should be integrated either in the developers development environment, or preferably within the build system of the continuous integration tool.

VI. Conclusion

Information flow vulnerabilities can occur when applications handle untrusted data. SQL injection and cross-site scripting are the most common information flow vulnerabilities. There are numerous methods presented in countering these vulnerabilities. One method, static taint analysis, looks promising in that it has the ability to cover detection of all kinds of information flow vulnerabilities. Out of three static taint analysis implementations presented in this paper, Type-based taint analysis was chosen as the preferred implementation. This approach looked promising in the way Web application frameworks are handled. The implementation is also freely available as an open-source project. A proposed solution in integrating this taint analysis approach in an iterative and incremental development process was presented. The proposed solution used the developed prototype application as a manageable sized concept application for implementing taint analysis. Annotations of sources and sinks are needed to detect information flow vulnerabilities. Some libraries are already annotated in the taint analysis implementation, referred to as the annotated JDK. To properly analyse an application, all libraries containing sources and sinks in a developed application need to be included in the annotated JDK. The development of the prototype application gave a good technical understanding of the inner workings of the application. This was advantageous in order to identify what needed to be annotated. The approach of mapping the attack surface of the prototype application turned out to be an effective way to identify the libraries containing sources and sinks.

Preparing the taint analysis implementation for analysis is mostly about making sure the libraries that are used are included in the annotated JDK and are also working properly. The experiences with annotation indicates that this is not a straight forward process, and could need many resources in order to get it right. A framework for easing the process of annotation, including verification that the annotation works correctly, is proposed as a solution to this challenge. Multiple approaches to conducting the taint analysis are possible. Running the taint analysis manually in command line, integrating it in the developers IDE and integrating it in the continuous integration tool are all possibilities. The latter suggestion is proposed as the most effective solution; implementing taint analysis in the continuous integration tools build system. This is considered an effective approach because an analysis could take several minutes to complete depending on application size. Also, processes done automatically and by an external instance will not be a distraction for the developer. When to counter any detected type errors is then up to when the developer monitors the notifications given in the continuous integration tool.

VII. Further Work

In order to support static taint analysis during the development process, the next step would be to get the annotations of the application's classes to work properly. A course worth researching, as suggested, could be to develop a framework for easing the process of annotating. Further work could also include more research in the area of how to best integrate taint analysis in a development process. The proposed solution of integrating the analysis in a continuous integration tools build system is probably worth exploring. An actual proof-of-concept implementation could be using Jenkins continuous integration tool with the Maven build system.

References

[1] OWASP Foundation, "OWASP top 10 - 2013: The ten most critical web application security risks," 2013, Accessed: 2017-04-13. [Online]. Available: https://www.owasp.org/images/f/f8/OWASP_Top_10_-_2013.pdf

[2] V. B. Livshits and M. S. Lam, "Finding security vulnerabilities in java applications with static analysis." in Usenix Proceedings of the 14th Conference on USENIX Security Symposium, vol. 2013, 2005, pp. 271–286.

[3] Y. Shin, L. Williams, and T. Xie, "Sqlunitgen: Test case generation for sql injection detection," North Carolina State University, Raleigh Technical report, NCSU CSC TR, vol. 21, 2006, p. 2006.

[4] A. Roichman and E. Gudes, "Fine-grained access control to web databases," in Proceedings of the 12th ACM symposium on Access control models and technologies. ACM, 2007, pp. 31–40.

[5] Z. Su and G. Wassermann, "The essence of command injection attacks in web applications," in ACM SIGPLAN Notices, vol. 41, no. 1. ACM, 2006, pp. 372–382.

[6] T. Jim, N. Swamy, and M. Hicks, "Defeating script injection attacks with browser-enforced embedded policies," in Proceedings of the 16th international conference on World Wide Web. ACM, 2007, pp. 601–610.

[7] The FindBugs Project, "Findbugs," 2015, Accessed: 2017-04-13. [Online]. Available: http://findbugs.sourceforge.net/

[8] W. Huang, Y. Dong, and A. Milanova, "Type-based taint analysis for java web applications," in International Conference on Fundamental Approaches to Software Engineering. Springer, 2014, pp. 140–154.

[9] E. J. Schwartz, T. Avgerinos, and D. Brumley, "All you ever wanted to know about dynamic taint analysis and forward symbolic execution (but might have been afraid to ask)," in 2010 IEEE Symposium on Security and Privacy. IEEE, 2010, pp. 317–331.

[10] H. Yin and D. Song, "Whole-system fine-grained taint analysis for automatic malware detection and analysis," 2007, Accessed: 2017-04-13. [Online]. Available: http://bitblaze.cs.berkeley.edu/papers/malware-detect.pdf

[11] O. Tripp, M. Pistoia, S. J. Fink, M. Sridharan, and O. Weisman, "Taj: effective taint analysis of web applications," in ACM Sigplan Notices, vol. 44, no. 6. ACM, 2009, pp. 87–97.

[12] M. Sridharan, S. J. Fink, and R. Bodik, "Thin slicing," ACM SIGPLAN Notices, vol. 42, no. 6, 2007, pp. 112–122.

[13] M. S. Merkow and L. Raghavan, Secure and Resilient Software Development. CRC Press, 2010.

[14] M. Sridharan, S. Artzi, M. Pistoia, S. Guarnieri, O. Tripp, and R. Berg, "F4F: taint analysis of framework-based web applications," ACM SIGPLAN Notices, vol. 46, no. 10, 2011, pp. 1053–1068.

[15] T. Bhuvaneswari and S. Prabaharan, "A survey on software development life cycle models," Journal of Computer Science and Information Technology, Vol2 (5), 2013, pp. 263–265.

Method for Automatic Resumption of Runtime Verification Monitors

Christian Drabek, Gereon Weiss

Fraunhofer ESK
Munich, Germany
e-mails: {christian.drabek,gereon.weiss}@esk.fraunhofer.de

Bernhard Bauer

Department of Computer Science
University of Augsburg, Germany
e-mail: bauer@informatik.uni-augsburg.de

***Abstract*—In networked embedded systems created with parts from different suppliers, deviations from the expected communication behavior often cause integration problems. Therefore, runtime verification monitors are used to detect if observed communication behavior fulfills defined correctness properties. However, in order to resume verification if unspecified behavior is observed, the runtime monitor needs a definition of the resumption. Otherwise, further deviations may be overlooked. We present a method for extending state-based runtime monitors with resumption in an automated way. This enables continuous monitoring without interruption. The method may exploit diverse resumption algorithms. In an evaluation, we show how to find the best suited resumption extension for a specific application scenario and compare the algorithms.**

***Keywords*–resumption; runtime verification; monitor; state machine; networked embedded systems; model-based.**

I. INTRODUCTION

In-car infotainment systems are an example for the increasing complexity of software services in networked embedded systems. Common basic architectures are utilized to enable faster development cycles, reuse, and shared development of non-differentiating functionality. Interoperable standards enable the integration of software components from multiple vendors into one platform. However, the integration of such services remains a challenge, since not only static interfaces have to be compatible but also the interaction behavior.

Even though single functions are tested thoroughly for their compliance to the specification, deviations in the behavior occur often when new functions are integrated into a complete system, e.g., caused by side-effects on timing by other functions, misconfiguration or incomplete specifications. Further, isolated testing is not feasible for all functionality, because of the exhaustive and sometimes unknown test-contexts that would be required. In these situations, it is vital to be able to monitor the interactions of the integrated system at runtime to detect deviations from the expected behavior. Nevertheless, a robust system continues its work after a non-critical failure or deviation from its specification; therefore, its monitors must also be able to resume verification after an observed deviation.

A finite state machine (FSM) can be used to specify the communication behavior in the networked embedded system. Such a reference model can also be generated from observed behavior and is quite versatile. It can be used as reference for development, but may also serve as basis for a restbus simulation, or the generation of test cases. Further, a reference model can be used as a monitor [1]. It is run in parallel to the system under test (SUT) and cross-checks the observed interactions with its own modeled communications (cf. Figure 1). As this

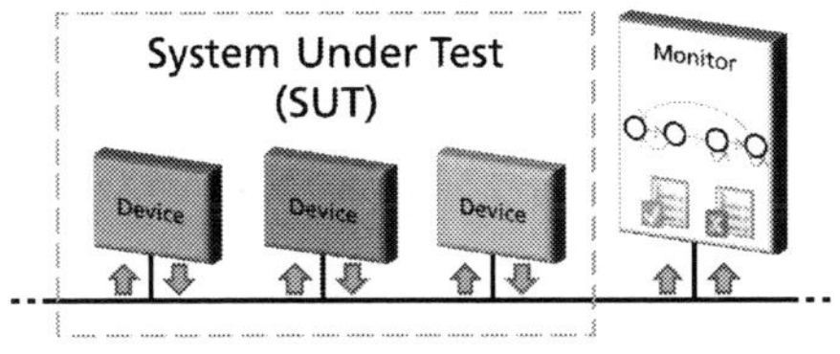

Figure 1. Monitor using a reference model to verify communication behavior.

model is directly derived from the specification, the monitor effectively compares the observation with the specification.

However, specifications often leave room for interpretation, in particular concerning handling of errors. Hence, it is undefined how a monitor based on such a specification should continue after a deviation. The adaptation to make the monitor resilient is usually done manually and needs to be maintained.

To reduce the effort and room for mistakes, we promote using a specification-based monitor and automating the process of making it resilient. We introduce a method that completes the transition function of such a monitor. Thereby, the extended monitor is granted the ability to resume its observation after deviations. The same monitor instance can be used to find multiple deviations. We call this resumption. When using a resumption extension, the same model can be used to define valid behavior in the specification and to verify its implementation, i.e., no separate verification model needs to be created. Moreover, resumption eliminates the need to split the specification into multiple properties. If available, we suggest to use the reference model of the specification as basis for the monitor. Thereby, it is easier to understand deviations, as they can be presented in the context of the whole specification. Further, the reuse of the specification guarantees compliance of the monitor. By exchanging the resumption algorithm ($\mathcal{R}$) generating the extension, the monitor's resilience can be optimized for the current application scenario.

This work introduces the general method of resumption and how resumption algorithms can be evaluated. To demonstrate the evaluation, we also present and compare different algorithms. They recreate patterns that we found to be commonly used when manually improving the resilience of a FSM. The evaluation framework and metrics help to find the best suited extension for individual systems.

The rest of this paper is structured as follows. After discussing related work in Section II, Section III describes the concept of specification-based monitors and the necessary notation. Section IV introduces the method of resumption and the algorithms considered in this paper. In Section V, we present the evaluation and discuss the findings. Section VI concludes the paper and gives an outlook on future work.

II. Related Work

Various areas address the problem of detecting differences between a SUT's behavior and its specification model. This section gives a brief overview of how existing approaches match specified model and observed behavior.

Conformance checking compares an existing process model with event logs of the same process to uncover where the real process deviates from the modeled process [2]. It is used offline, i.e., after the SUT finished its execution, because the employed data mining techniques to match model and execution are computationally intensive and can only be used efficiently once the complete logs are available. In contrast, the presented resumption uses assumptions on the expected deviations to provide lean algorithms that work at runtime.

Model-based testing aims to find differences between the behavior of a SUT and a valid behavior model [3]. An environmental [4] or embedded [5] test context stimulates the SUT with test sets, i.e., selected input sequences. The SUT's outputs are then compared with the expected output from the behavior model. Before each test set, the SUT is actively maneuvered into a known state using a homing sequence. Generally, these sequences reduce the current state uncertainty by utilizing separating or merging sequences [6]. Former assure different outputs for two states, latter move the machine into the same state for a given set of initial states. Minimized Mealy machines are guaranteed to have a homing sequence [6]. However, a passive monitor should not influence the SUT. Therefore, the presented resumption cannot actively force the system to a known state. Nevertheless, occurrences of separating and merging sequences can be tracked during observation to reduce the number of possible candidates for the current state.

In general, *runtime verification* can be seen as a form of passive testing with a monitor, which checks if a certain run of a SUT satisfies or violates a correctness property [7]. The observation of communication is well suited for black box systems, as no details about the inner states of the SUT are needed. Further, the influence on the SUT by the test system is reduced by limiting the intrusion to observation. In case the deviations are solely gaps in the observation, a Hidden Markov Model can be used to perform runtime verification with state estimation [8]. Runtime verification frameworks, such as TraceMatches [9] or JavaMOP [10], preprocess and filter the input before it is passed to a monitor instance. Thereby, each monitor only sees relevant events. A property-based monitor checks if a certain subset of the specification is fulfilled or violated. Unless extended with resumption, it will only report a single deviation. Nevertheless, if the properties are carefully chosen, the respective monitor can match an arbitrary slice of the input trace. Then, the monitor is instantiated and matched against different slices of the trace. However, this requires that the complete specification is split into multiple of such properties and implies additional design work. Thereby, or if the properties are extracted by data mining techniques from a running system or traces [11][12], a secondary specification is created that needs to be kept in sync. In contrast, resumption enables the reuse of an available

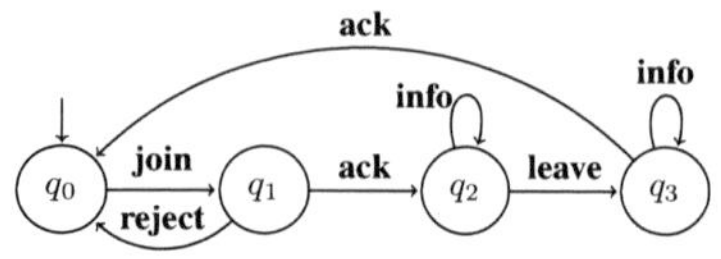

Figure 2. FSM of the communication behavior related to a subscription service.

specification by automatically augmenting its robustness for verification.

III. Specification-based Runtime Monitors

A monitor is "a system that observes and analyses the behavior of another system" [13]. The core of a monitor is an analyzer which is created from the requirements and different languages can be used to specify the analyzer [14], e.g., linear temporal logic [7]. However, without loss of generality, such a description can be mapped to a set of states and a set of transitions between the states [15], i.e., a (finite) state machine.

In diverse embedded system domains like automotive, state machines are often used for the specification of communication protocols or component interactions. We call such a state machine a reference model and a monitor that uses the reference model to check conformance of observed interactions a specification-based monitor. Reference models usually focus on capturing the valid behavior and include only critical or exemplary deviations. Therefore, they only describe a partially defined transition function and a subset of all possible error states. The respective specification-based monitor reports an accepting verdict ($\top$) for valid behavior and a rejecting verdict ($\bot$) or another associated verdict for deviations. The FSM in Figure 2 shows a FSM that specifies the communication behavior related to a subscription service. It has only accepting transitions; a possible resolution of implicit transitions is shown in Figure 3a. If an event without transition in the original FSM occurs, $q_\bot$ is entered. However, such a monitor will only detect the first deviation. To overcome this, the next section introduces resumption and how the resolution can be performed to overcome this.

Beforehand, we introduce the necessary notation. A monitor $M : \langle \mathbb{D}, \mathbb{A}, \mathbb{Q}, q_0, \delta, \gamma \rangle$ consists of a verdict domain $\mathbb{D}$, an observation alphabet $\mathbb{A}$, a set of states $\mathbb{Q}$, an initial state $q_0 \in \mathbb{Q}$, a transition function $\delta : \mathbb{A} \times \mathbb{Q} \to \mathbb{Q}$ and a verdict function $\gamma : \mathbb{A} \times \mathbb{Q} \to \mathbb{D}$. For a specification-based monitor, M is identical to the reference model and, thereby, identical to the specification. The observation alphabet $\mathbb{A}$ and the verdict domain $\mathbb{D}$ of the monitor are the input and output sets of the state machine. The latter is a set of verdicts, at least containing $\top$ and $\bot$. The former is a set of semantic events used to distinguish the different interactions of the SUT relevant for the monitor. At runtime, there are various ways to extract the semantic events by preprocessing and slicing the observed interactions, e.g., [9][10][15][1]. In the following, we will refer to them in general as events.

Let $\mathrm{dom}(\delta)$ be the domain of a partial function, such as δ, i.e., the set of elements with a defined mapping. Let $\mathbb{A}^q$ be the set of events with a defined transition in state q (1), $\mathbb{Q}^e$ be the set of states with a defined transition for event e (2) and $\mathbb{Q}^{e,\delta}$ be the set of defined target states for event e (3).

$$\mathbb{A}^q = \{e \in \mathbb{A} \mid \langle e, q \rangle \in \mathrm{dom}(\delta)\} \tag{1}$$

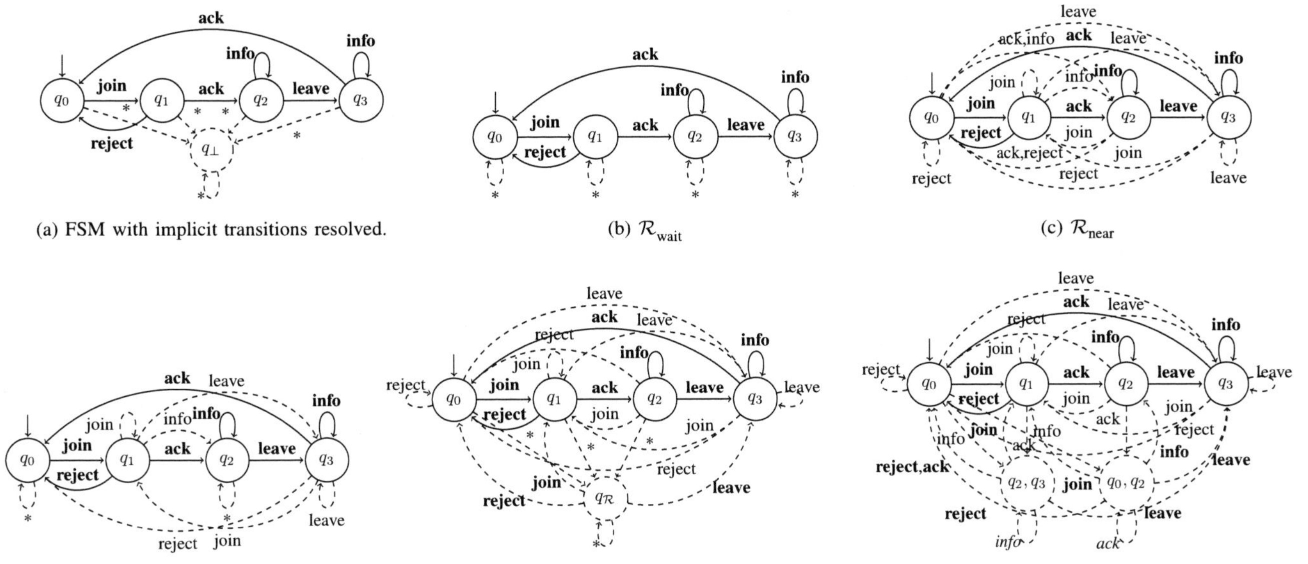

(a) FSM with implicit transitions resolved.
(b) $\mathcal{R}_{\text{wait}}$
(c) $\mathcal{R}_{\text{near}}$
(d) $\mathcal{R}_{\text{n-o-w}}$
(e) $\mathcal{R}_{\text{u-e}}$
(f) $\mathcal{R}_{\text{u-s}}$

Figure 3. FSMs with states and transitions (dashed) added by the implicit error assumption (a) and different $\mathcal{R}$ (b)-(f). **Bold** labels indicate an accepting, regular labels a rejecting, and *italic* labels an inconclusive verdict. The wild-card '*' matches all events that have no other transition in the state.

$$\mathbb{Q}^e = \{q \in \mathbb{Q} \mid \langle e, q\rangle \in \text{dom}(\delta)\} \tag{2}$$

$$\mathbb{Q}^{e,\delta} = \{q_t \in \mathbb{Q} \mid \exists q_s \in \mathbb{Q}^e : \delta(e, q_s) \mapsto q_t\} \tag{3}$$

IV. Resumption

A specification-based monitor, such as shown in Figure 3a, will only be able to find the first deviation from the specification, since it enters the final state $q_\perp$ at this point. Different techniques can be applied in order to create resilient monitors and to find deviations beyond the first. Up to now this is usually done manually and requires additional design work, e.g., to repeatedly add additional transitions and triggers or to artificially split the specification into multiple properties that can be checked separately. However, we suggest using a generic definition for how the monitor can resume its duty.

This section presents the method for *resumption* that enables a monitor to analyze the trace for additional deviations with respect to the same property. This can be used to resume the operation of the monitor, e.g., after a deviation was detected or for initialization, and is especially useful when the system under test cannot be forced into a known state.

Example 1 (Resumption): Let's assume M in state q observes event $\chi \in \mathbb{A} \setminus \mathbb{A}^q$, i.e., the specification defines no transition for χ in the active state. By the definition of a specification-based monitor, a deviation is reported. However, as the event is undefined for this state in the specification, additional information is required for the monitor to continue observation. If the application scenario allows to ignore the deviating event, the monitor can stay in the same active state and continue its work.

A. Resumption Extension

Any specification-based monitor may be extended with the help of a resumption extension. Even a monitor that has a complete transition function may have need for resumption, if it has unrecoverable states like $q_\perp$ in Figure 3a. To distinguish between the original monitor, the extension, the extended monitor and their components the sub-scripts $\mathcal{L}$, $\mathcal{R}$ and $\mathcal{E}$ are used respectively. $M_\mathcal{E}$ is created by combining the sets and functions of $M_\mathcal{L}$ with $M_\mathcal{R}$, where $M_\mathcal{L}$ is preferred. However, $\delta_\mathcal{R}$ may override $\delta_\mathcal{R}$ for choosable verdicts, e.g., $\perp$.

Example 2 (Resumption Extension): Figure 3b shows a possible extensions of the FSM given in Figure 2. Instead of entering a final rejecting state for unexpected events, the extended monitor ignores the event and stays in the currently active state. The resulting FSM has a complete transition function and can continue to monitor after reporting deviations. Thereby, the original monitor is extended with resumption.

While a resumption extension can be created in an arbitrary way, we suggest to use a resumption algorithm ($\mathcal{R}$) to create the extension. The algorithm's core function (4) takes an event and a set of (possible) active states as input. It returns the set of states that are candidates for resumption. The $\mathcal{R}$-based resumption extension can be easily exchanged to adjust the monitor to the current application scenario. Let $\mathbb{Q}_C = \mathbb{Q}_\mathcal{L} \cup \{q_\mathcal{R}\}$ and $\mathcal{P}(\mathbb{Q}_C)$ be the set of all subsets of $\mathbb{Q}_C$.

$$\mathcal{R} : \mathbb{A} \times \mathcal{P}(\mathbb{Q}_C) \rightarrow \mathcal{P}(\mathbb{Q}_C) \tag{4}$$

Using $\mathcal{R}$, the additional states and transitions that are needed for the extension of the original monitor can be derived. For finite sets $\mathbb{Q}_\mathcal{L}$ and $\mathbb{A}$, a preparation step creates the states $\mathcal{P}(\mathbb{Q}_C) \setminus \mathbb{Q}_C$. The transitions are derived by evaluating $\mathcal{R}$ to find the target state. If $\mathcal{R}(e, q)$ returns an empty set or solely states that cannot reach any state in $\mathbb{Q}_C$, it reached a finally non resumable state. The existence of such states depends on $\mathcal{R}$ and the specification. All states not reachable from a state in $\mathbb{Q}_C$ can be pruned.

An alternative is using $\mathcal{R}$ at runtime as transition function during resumption. If $\mathcal{R}$ returns solely a single state in $\mathbb{Q}_\mathcal{L}$, $M_\mathcal{L}$ can resume verification in that state. Otherwise, the set of candidates is stored and given to $\mathcal{R}$ with the next event.

$\gamma_\mathcal{R}$ is defined as follows: it accepts the transitions from $\mathbb{Q}_\mathcal{R}$ to $\mathbb{Q}_\mathcal{L}$, rejects transitions from $\mathbb{Q}_\mathcal{L}$, and returns an inconclusive verdict otherwise. Thereby, the resulting $\gamma_\mathcal{E}$ reports the specified verdicts, rejects unexpected deviations and accepts events as soon as it has resumed verification.

B. Resumption Algorithms

This section introduces algorithms that can be used for resumption. Often, these algorithms are mimicked to extend specifications manually to create resilient monitors. Based on an observed event and a set of candidates for the active state $\mathcal{R}$ will determine the possible states of the SUT with respect to the observed property. The results of applying the algorithms on the FSM from Figure 2 are shown in Figure 3. The presented algorithms can generally be categorized into local and global algorithms. The former are influenced by the state that was active before the deviation, while the latter look at all states equally.

The local algorithm *Waiting* (5) resumes verification with the next event accepted by the previously active state q, i.e., it stays in q and skips all events not in $\mathbb{A}^q$. $\mathcal{R}_{\text{wait}}$ assumes that a deviation was caused by a superfluous message that may be ignored. It is expected to perform bad for other deviations.

$$\mathcal{R}_{\text{wait}}(e, \mathbb{Q}_{in}) = \mathbb{Q}_{in} \tag{5}$$

An obvious danger is, the SUT may never emit an event that is accepted by the active state. Therefore, the next algorithms also look at states around the active state. The used distance measure $\|q_s, q_t\|$ is the number of transitions $\in \delta_\mathcal{L}$ in the shortest path between a source state q_s and a target state q_t. The extension $\|\mathbb{Q}_s, \mathbb{Q}_t\|$ is the transition count of the shortest path between any state in $\mathbb{Q}_s$ and any state in $\mathbb{Q}_t$.

The algorithm *Nearest* (6) resumes verification with the next event accepted by any state reachable from the active state. If multiple transitions match, it chooses the transition reachable with the fewest steps from the previously active state.

$$\mathcal{R}_{\text{near}}(e, \mathbb{Q}_{in}) = \underset{q_t \in \mathbb{Q}_C^{e,\delta_\mathcal{L}}}{\operatorname{argmin}} \min_{q_s \in \mathbb{Q}_{in}} \|q_s, q_t\| \tag{6}$$

$\mathcal{R}_{\text{near}}$ assumes that the deviations will be caused by skipped messages. It will resume on the next matched event unless the two closest valid states require the same number of steps. As it only looks forward, superfluous or altered messages may cause it to errantly skip ahead.

The algorithm *Nearest-or-Waiting* (7) resumes verification like *Nearest*, except if the selected state is more steps away from the active state than the active state is from any other state that could match the event. The idea is to ignore superfluous messages and identify them by looking as far back as was required to look forward to find a match. $\mathcal{R}_{\text{n-o-w}}$ is a combination of the previous two algorithms and shows how algorithms can be combined to create new ones.

$$\mathcal{R}_{\text{n-o-w}}(e, \mathbb{Q}_{in}) = \begin{cases} \mathcal{R}_{\text{wait}}, & \text{if } \|\mathbb{Q}_C^e, \mathbb{Q}_{in}\| < \|\mathbb{Q}_{in}, \mathcal{R}_{\text{near}}\| \\ \mathcal{R}_{\text{near}}, & \text{otherwise} \end{cases} \tag{7}$$

Global algorithms assume that you need to consider the whole specification to identify the current communication state. Therefore, they look at all states equally to keep all options open for resumption.

Unique-Event (8) resumes verification if the event is unique, i.e., the event is used on transitions to a single state only. $\mathcal{R}_{\text{u-e}}$ is the only examined $\mathcal{R}$ that ignores all input states. As there is only one target state of a unique event in the state machine, the algorithm considers this a synchronization point.

$$\mathcal{R}_{\text{u-e}}(e, \mathbb{Q}_{in}) = \begin{cases} \mathbb{Q}_C^{e,\delta_\mathcal{L}}, & \text{if } |\mathbb{Q}_C^{e,\delta_\mathcal{L}}| = 1 \\ \{q_\mathcal{R}\}, & \text{otherwise} \end{cases} \tag{8}$$

Unique-Sequence (9) extends the previous algorithm to unique sequences of events as unique events may not be available or regularly observable in every specification. $\mathcal{R}_{\text{u-s}}$ follows all valid paths simultaneously and resumes verification if there remains exactly one target state for an observed sequence.

$$\mathcal{R}_{\text{u-s}}(e, \mathbb{Q}_{in}) = \begin{cases} \mathbb{Q}_{in}^{e,\delta_\mathcal{L}}, & \text{if } \mathbb{Q}_{in}^{e,\delta_\mathcal{L}} \neq \emptyset \\ \mathbb{Q}_C^{e,\delta_\mathcal{L}}, & \text{if } \mathbb{Q}_{in}^{e,\delta_\mathcal{L}} = \emptyset \wedge \mathbb{Q}_C^{e,\delta_\mathcal{L}} \neq \emptyset \\ \{q_\mathcal{R}\}, & \text{otherwise} \end{cases} \tag{9}$$

Similar to homing sequences used in model-based testing, $\mathcal{R}_{\text{u-s}}$ aims to reduce the current state uncertainty with each step. In each iteration of the algorithm, it evaluates which of the input states accept the event. If the observed event is part of a separating sequence, the non matching states are removed from the set. If a merging sequence was found, the following $\delta_\mathcal{L}$-step returns the same state for two input states and the number of candidates is further reduced. If there are homing sequences for $\mathcal{L}$ and the SUT emits one, $\mathcal{R}_{\text{u-s}}$ will detect it. Any deviation in the behavior causes $\mathbb{Q}_{in}^{e,\delta_\mathcal{L}}$ to be empty and therefore resets the set of possible candidates to any state accepting the event, i.e., the resumption is resumed.

V. Evaluation

This section presents an evaluation of the introduced method for automatic resumption of runtime verification monitors. Therefore, a framework is employed to compare the presented algorithms.

A. Evaluation Framework

An overview of the evaluation setup is depicted in Figure 4. A specific *Application Scenario* usually provides the specification and, thereby, a *Reference Model*. However, to make general statements about the algorithms, a generator creates the models. The resulting FSMs use global events across the whole machine and local groups. To classify the FSMs, different metrics of their structure are collected, e.g., number of states and uniqueness. *Uniqueness* is the likelihood of an occurring event being unique. It is approximated by the fraction of all transitions in the FSM that have a unique event.

For each reference model, multiple traces are generated by randomly selecting paths from the respective FSM. The *Deviation Generator* manipulates the FSM used by the trace-generator by adding new states and transitions. These transitions use undefined events ($\chi \notin \mathbb{A}^{q_s}$) of the source state q_s. This guarantees that deviations are detected at this event,

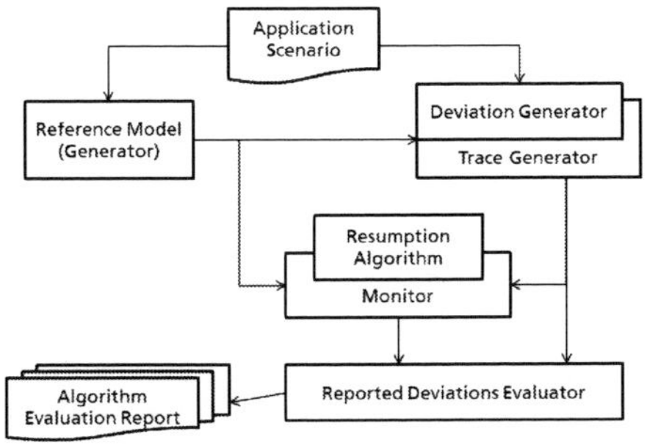

Figure 4. Overview of the evaluation framework for resumption algorithms.

if the monitor knows the current state. The added deviations are characterized by the different transition targets q_t: superfluous ($q_t = q_s$), altered ($\exists e : \delta_{\mathcal{L}}(e, q_s) \mapsto q_t$), skipped ($\exists e : \delta_{\mathcal{L}}(e, q_s) \mapsto q_i \wedge \delta_{\mathcal{L}}(\chi, q_i) \mapsto q_t$) and random events ($q_t \in \mathbb{Q}_{\mathcal{L}}$). Additionally, shuffled events are simulated by choosing a chain of two transitions and creating copies in inverse order with a new intermediate state. This is a special case of two altered events in sequence. If a scenario expects more complex deviations, they can be simulated by combining deviations. However, to evaluate the influence of each deviation kind, we apply only one kind of deviation per trace. For later analyses, the injected deviations are marked in the meta-data of the trace invisible to the monitor.

The traces are eventually checked using the original FSM extended with each $\mathcal{R}$. For the evaluation an Eclipse-based tool capable of using reference models as monitors [1] was used and extended. Using hooks in the tool's model execution runtime, resumption is injected if needed. Thereby, all introduced algorithms can easily be exchanged.

The goal of the evaluation framework is to measure how well a monitor is at finding multiple deviations in a given application scenario. Therefore, the *Reported Deviations Evaluator* rates each algorithm's performance by comparing the detected and the injected deviations. It calculates the well established metrics from information retrieval *precision* and *recall* [16] for each extended monitor. Precision (10) is the fraction of reported deviations (rd) that were true (td), i.e., injected by the deviation generator. Recall (11) is the fraction of injected deviations that were reported. Both values are combined to their harmonic mean, also known as F_1 score (12).

$$p = |td \cap rd| / |rd| \tag{10}$$

$$r = |td \cap rd| / |td| \tag{11}$$

$$F_1 = 2 \cdot \frac{p \cdot r}{p + r} \tag{12}$$

A monitor that reports only and all true deviations has a perfect precision $p = 1$ and recall $r = 1$. Up to the first deviation, all extended monitors exhibit this precision, as they work like regular monitors in this case. Regular monitors only maintain this precision by ignoring everything that follows. Extended monitors may loose precision as they attempt to find further deviations. Therefore, recall estimates how likely all true deviations are reported. A regular monitor's recall is $|td|^{-1}$ as it reports only the first deviation.

B. Comparison of Resumption Algorithms

The subscription service example evaluates to the F_1 scores: $\mathcal{R}_{\text{wait}} = 0.53$, $\mathcal{R}_{\text{near}} = 0.68$, $\mathcal{R}_{\text{n-o-w}} = 0.79$, $\mathcal{R}_{\text{u-e}} = 0.80$, $\mathcal{R}_{\text{u-s}} = 0.78$. For the general evaluation, traces with a total of 55 million deviations in 220 different FSMs with up to 360 states have been generated and were analyzed by monitors extended with the algorithms. Each trace included 20 injected deviations on average, so the recall for a regular monitor is 0.05 and its F_1 score 0.095. Figure 5 shows the precision and recall for each $\mathcal{R}$ per kind of deviation. While $\mathcal{R}_{\text{wait}}$ has the worst precision for most deviations, it shows very high recall scores overall and a perfect result for superfluous deviations. Besides that, each algorithm performs very similar for altered and superfluous deviations. When comparing $\mathcal{R}_{\text{near}}$ and $\mathcal{R}_{\text{n-o-w}}$, the former has slightly less precision, however, it provides a better recall. $\mathcal{R}_{\text{u-e}}$ has a low recall independent of deviation but also the best precision for shuffled and skipped deviations. $\mathcal{R}_{\text{u-s}}$ enables better precision for the other deviations, plus a very high recall.

Figure 6 compares the F_1 scores of the algorithms for different levels of uniqueness and numbers of states of the generated FSMs. The low overall score of $\mathcal{R}_{\text{wait}}$ is clearly visible for both metrics. For FSMs with low uniqueness, $\mathcal{R}_{\text{u-s}}$ outperforms the other algorithms. However, its F_1 score slightly drops with increased uniqueness. The other algorithms benefit from an increase of uniqueness, especially $\mathcal{R}_{\text{u-e}}$. For very high uniqueness, $\mathcal{R}_{\text{u-s}}$ and $\mathcal{R}_{\text{u-e}}$ are identical. Nevertheless, both $\mathcal{R}_{\text{n-o-w}}$ and $\mathcal{R}_{\text{near}}$ perform better, then. An increase of the state count leads to a declined performance for $\mathcal{R}_{\text{u-e}}$, $\mathcal{R}_{\text{n-o-w}}$ and $\mathcal{R}_{\text{near}}$. $\mathcal{R}_{\text{u-e}}$ even drops below $\mathcal{R}_{\text{wait}}$. $\mathcal{R}_{\text{wait}}$ and $\mathcal{R}_{\text{u-s}}$ are hardly affected by the state count.

C. Discussion

The perfect precision and recall of $\mathcal{R}_{\text{wait}}$ for superfluous deviations were as expected, since this deviation matches exactly the resumption behavior of the algorithm. This shows

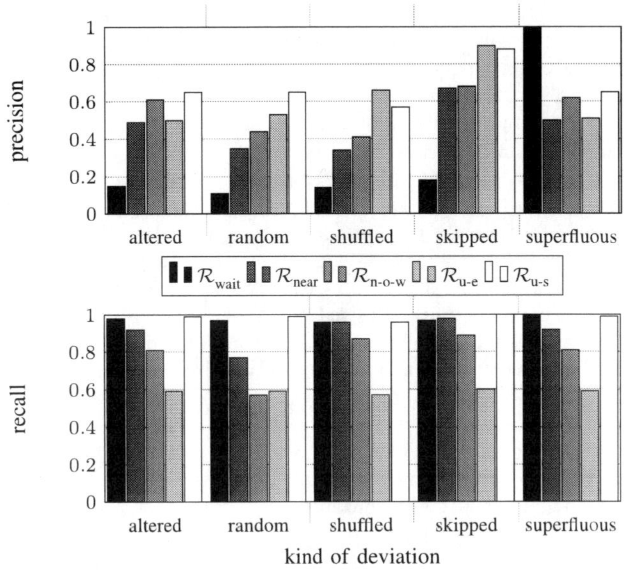

Figure 5. Precision and recall of $\mathcal{R}$ compared for different kinds of deviations.

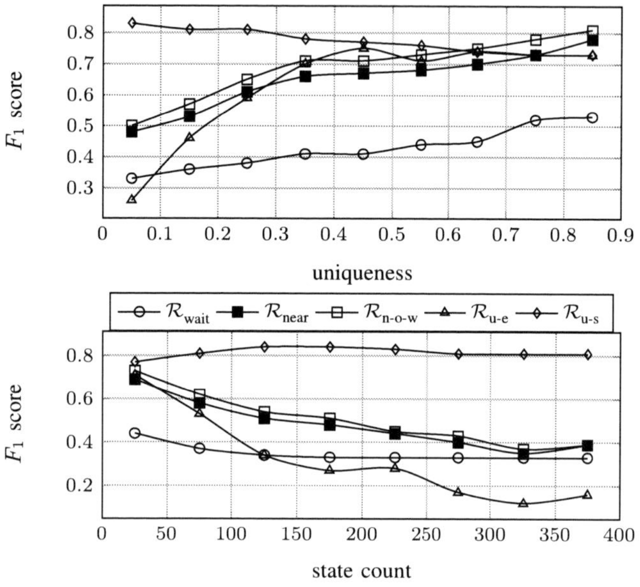

Figure 6. F_1 scores of $\mathcal{R}$ compared for metrics uniqueness and state count.

that knowing which deviations are expected can help formulate specialized algorithms. However, $\mathcal{R}_{\text{wait}}$ performs worst for all other kinds of deviations, as the SUT transitioned internally to a different state already and would have to return to the original state. It benefits from unique events as they prevent taking wrong transitions in the meantime.

The metric uniqueness helps to decide the class of algorithm that is needed for a scenario. For low values, the algorithm needs to combine multiple events in order to reliably synchronize model and SUT. Of the examined algorithms, only $\mathcal{R}_{\text{u-s}}$ takes multiple events into account and, therefore, should be preferred in this case. However, $\mathcal{R}_{\text{u-s}}$ slightly drops its precision with increasing uniqueness, as the chance increases to overeagerly synchronize with an erroneous unique event. For example, if all events are unique, any observed deviation is an unique event and the algorithm will resume with the associated state. As the next valid event is unique again, the monitor will jump back. However, it registered two deviations when there actually was only one. The same holds for $\mathcal{R}_{\text{u-e}}$. Therefore, especially with a high uniqueness, it may be desirable to limit the options for which an algorithm may resume and use a local resumption algorithm. The choice between $\mathcal{R}_{\text{near}}$ and $\mathcal{R}_{\text{n-o-w}}$ depends on the desired precision and recall. According to the F_1 score, $\mathcal{R}_{\text{n-o-w}}$ is slightly favorable. However, as these algorithms may maneuver themselves into dead-ends, they are less suited for higher state counts. A bias towards lower uniqueness for higher state counts in the sample set severs the impact on $\mathcal{R}_{\text{u-e}}$. Nevertheless, in all cases, the F_1 scores of the extended monitors are always better than what can be calculated for a regular monitor.

The results for the subscription service example (uniqueness 0.43, 4 states) and the respective results from Figure 6 match well. While the evaluation framework can be used to identify the best suited algorithm, this example shows that the metrics state count and uniqueness can be used as an estimation.

VI. Conclusion

In this paper, we introduce a method for extending runtime monitors with resumption. Such an extension allows a specification-based monitor to find subsequent deviations. Thereby, an existing reference model of the system can be used directly without creating a secondary specification for test purposes only. Each of the presented resumption algorithms has its strength and weaknesses. The presented framework and metrics help to find the best suited algorithm for an application scenario. Future work includes improving the method for resumption, e.g., by taking event parameters into account and by handling partially-independent behavior. Moreover, enhanced algorithms that target specific real world scenarios will be examined.

Acknowledgment

The project was funded by the Bavarian Ministry of Economic Affairs, Infrastructure, Transport and Technology.

References

[1] C. Drabek, A. Paulic, and G. Weiss, "Reducing the Verification Effort for Interfaces of Automotive Infotainment Software," SAE Technical Paper 2015-01-0166, 2015.

[2] W. van der Aalst, A. Adriansyah, and B. van Dongen, "Replaying history on process models for conformance checking and performance analysis," Wiley Interdisciplinary Reviews: Data Mining and Knowledge Discovery, vol. 2, no. 2, 2012, pp. 182–192.

[3] A. Pretschner and M. Leucker, "Model-Based Testing A Glossary," in Model-Based Testing of Reactive Systems. Springer Heidelberg, 2005, pp. 607–609.

[4] T. Herpel, T. Hoiss, and J. Schroeder, "Enhanced Simulation-Based Verification and Validation of Automotive Electronic Control Units," in Electronics, Communications and Networks V, ser. LNEE. Springer Singapore, 2016, no. 382, pp. 203–213.

[5] A. Kurtz, B. Bauer, and M. Koeberl, "Software Based Test Automation Approach Using Integrated Signal Simulation," in SOFTENG 2016, Feb. 2016, pp. 117–122.

[6] S. Sandberg, "Homing and Synchronizing Sequences," in Model-Based Testing of Reactive Systems. Springer Heidelberg, 2005, pp. 5–33.

[7] M. Leucker and C. Schallhart, "A brief account of runtime verification," The Journal of Logic and Algebraic Programming, vol. 78, no. 5, May 2009, pp. 293–303.

[8] S. D. Stoller et al., "Runtime Verification with State Estimation," in Runtime Verification. Springer Berlin Heidelberg, 2012, pp. 193–207.

[9] C. Allan et al., "Adding Trace Matching with Free Variables to AspectJ," in OOPSLA '05. ACM, 2005, pp. 345–364.

[10] P. O. Meredith, D. Jin, D. Griffith, F. Chen, and G. Rou, "An overview of the MOP runtime verification framework," Int J Software Tools Technology Transfer, vol. 14, no. 3, Apr. 2011, pp. 249–289.

[11] A. Danese, T. Ghasempouri, and G. Pravadelli, "Automatic Extraction of Assertions from Execution Traces of Behavioural Models," in DATE '15, 2015, pp. 67–72.

[12] F. Langer and E. Oswald, "Using Reference Traces for Validation of Communication in Embedded Systems," in ICONS 2014, pp. 203–208.

[13] D. K. Peters, "Automated Testing of Real-Time Systems," Proc. Newfoundland Electrical and Computer Engineering Conference, 1999.

[14] N. Delgado, A. Gates, and S. Roach, "A taxonomy and catalog of runtime software-fault monitoring tools," IEEE Transactions on Software Engineering, vol. 30, 2004, pp. 859–872.

[15] Y. Falcone, K. Havelund, and G. Reger, "A Tutorial on Runtime Verification," Engineering Dependable Software Systems, vol. 34, 2013, pp. 141–175.

[16] D. M. W. Powers, "Evaluation: From Precision, Recall and F-Measure to ROC, Informedness, Markedness and Correlation," Journal of Machine Learning Technologies, vol. 2, no. 1, 2011, pp. 37–63.

Quality Evaluation of Test Oracles Using Mutation

Ana Claudia Maciel, Rafael Oliveira and Márcio Delamaro
ICMC/USP
University of São Paulo
São Carlos, BRA
anamaciel@usp.br, rpaes@icmc.usp.br, delamaro@icmc.usp.br

***Abstract*—In software development, product quality is directly related to the quality of the development process. Therefore, Verification, Validation & Test (VV&T) activities performed through methods, techniques, and tools are needed for increasing productivity, quality, and cost reduction in software development. An essential point for the software testing activity is its automation, making it more reliable and less expensive. For the automation of testing activities, automated test oracles are crucial, representing a mechanism (program, process, or data) that indicates whether the output obtained for a test case is correct. In this paper, we use the concept of program mutation to create alternative implementations of oracles and evaluate their quality. The main contributions of this paper are: (1) propose specific mutation operators for oracles; (2) present a useful support tool for such mutation operators; and (3) establish an alternative to evaluate assertion-based test oracles. Through an empirical evaluation, our main finding is that mutations may help in assessing and improving the quality of test oracles, generating new oracles and/or test cases and decreasing the rate of test oracles errors.**

Keywords–Test Oracles; Mutation Testing; Mutation Operators;

I. INTRODUCTION

Automated test oracles are essential components in software testing activities. Defining a test oracle involves synthesizing an automated structure that is able to offer the tester an indicative verdict of system accuracy [1]. Thus, oracle is the mechanism that defines and gives a verdict about the correctness of a test execution [2]. Despite the importance of the oracle mechanisms, there is no systematic way to evaluate their quality [3].

In some cases, the results of running a test suite may have unwanted results, not due to problems in test data or program under test, but because of errors in the oracle implementation. Accordingly, test oracles correctness is as important as the selection of test inputs and, therefore, should be systematically implemented according to well-defined requirements [2].

This study aims to provide an alternative to improve the quality of test oracles, proposing an automated strategy for assessing quality of oracles, inserted in the cost amortization of realization of software testing. We extended the idea of mutation testing, applying it to evaluate the quality of test oracles implemented using the JUnit framework [4], a test framework which uses annotations to identify methods that specify a test. The main idea is to use test oracles to verify whether the oracles with mutations may contribute to reveal defects in programs.

We designed and created mutation operators to assertion-based test oracles written in JUnit format, based on the method assert signatures and its parameters. Operators have been developed to generate assertions that the tester did not create, or to correct oracles that have been written in the wrong way. Following the concepts of mutation test, oracles can be evaluated automatically. Thus, this work provides specific mutation operators to test oracles in order to systematize the evaluation of oracles.

The main contributions of this paper are related to the context of automation of processes associated with software engineering. In view of this, four contributions are provided through the following work:

- The definition and evaluation of mutation operators specific to assertion-based test oracles;
- MuJava 4 JUnit: a tool to generate the mutant oracles;
- Using the approach and tools with real programs of different functions, showing main operating characteristics and limitations of the proposed strategy; and
- Discussion on automated quality assessment of automated oracles and its importance for the improvement of automated tests.

The remainder of this paper is organized as follows: In Section II, we present the background with the main concepts related to this research. In Section III, we describe our mutation operators for JUnit assertion-based test oracles and our tool: MuJava 4 JUnit. In Section IV, we explain our empirical evaluation by describing the experiment design, research questions, research design and our experiment procedure. In Section V and Section VI we discuss the results of the experiment and threats to validity, respectively. Finally, we present the final remarks of our study in Section VII.

II. BACKGROUND

This section presents and discusses the concepts related to test oracles and mutation testing.

A. Test Oracles

Test oracles can be defined as a tester ("human oracle") or an external mechanism that can decide whether the output produced by a program is correct [5]. Typically, a test oracle is composed of two parts: (1) the expected behavior that is used to check the actual behavior of the System Under Test (SUT); and (2) a procedure to check if the actual result matches the expected output [2]. In this context, one can define that test oracle is a software testing technology, which can be associated with different processes and test techniques [6].

The "oracle problem" happens in cases when, depending on the SUT, it is extremely difficult to predict expected behaviors to be compared against current behaviors [5]. Depending on the oracle, problems like false positives and false negatives may occur:

- False positive: a test execution is identified as failing when in reality it passed, or the functionality works properly; and
- False negative: a test execution is identified as passing when in reality it failed, or there is some problem in functionality.

In this work, we use oracles in JUnit classes format. In JUnit framework, test oracles are written in the form of assertions [7] and tests are units, contributing to expose flaws in the current version of the program or regression faults introduced during maintenance.

B. *Mutation Testing*

Mutation [8] is a fault-based testing technique. The program being tested is changed several times, generating a set of alternative versions with syntactic changes. This technique measures the fault-finding effectiveness of test suites, on the basis of induced faults. The general principle underlying Mutation Testing is that the faults used by Mutation Testing represent the mistakes that programmers often make [9].

A transformation rule that generates a mutant from the original program is known as mutation operator [10]. Typical mutation operators are designed to modify variables and expressions by replacement, insertion or deletion operators [9].

III. MUTATION OPERATORS FOR ASSERTION-BASED TEST ORACLES

This section presents the mutation tool and a novel mutation operators set, which is specifically designed for test oracles written as JUnit classes.

A. *MuJava 4 JUnit - a mutation testing tool for JUnit test oracles*

We have adapted MuJava [11] to create a tool (MuJava 4 JUnit) to include our new mutation operators to test oracles, in order to systematize the evaluation of the oracles written using JUnit assertions. Operators were included in MuJava, using the existing code structure. The tool MuJava 4 JUnit is publicly available in [12].

B. *Definition of "MuJava 4 JUnit's" operators*

We defined generic mutation operators to introduce changes in the most common types of assertions of JUnit. Signature variations of the statements were created adding, removing, modifying, or replacing some setting values. In order to automate and systematize the evaluation of test oracles, we establish four classes of operators:

- **Adding:** parameters are added to the method `assert`;
- **Modifying:** parameters from the method `assert` are changed;
- **Replacing:** the method `assert` is replaced with another method `assert`; and
- **Removing:** parameters are removed from the method `assert`.

The mutation operators for assertion-based test oracles were classified in two levels:

- **Signature level:** changes are made on the type of method assert, or on the parameters received by the `assert` method; and
- **Annotation level:** changes are applied by replacing annotations, removing, or replacing its parameters.

1) Signature-based mutation operators: These mutation operators to test oracles were defined by combining the signatures of assert methods adding or removing parameters, or replacing the assert method by other assert method, improving the quality of test oracles through the creation of new oracles, or even adding new test cases.

The operators of this level are described in Table I. These operators were created according to the JUnit's specifications and can simulate problems, made by the tester, at the coding test oracles.

TABLE I. SIGNATURE LEVEL MUTATION OPERATORS.

Signature Level			
#	Class	Description	Acronym
1	Adding	Adding Threshold Value	ATV
2	Modifying	Decrement Constant from Threshold Value	DCfTV
3	Modifying	Increment Constant to Threshold Value	ICtTV
4	Replacing	Replace Boolean Assertion	RBA
5	Removing	Removing Threshold Value	RTV

2) Annotation-based mutation operators: We created the operators at the level of annotation changing or removing the timeout value, and adding possible exceptions that may occur in the execution of the oracles which were not previously thought by the tester. The operators from annotation level are presented in Table II.

TABLE II. ANNOTATION LEVEL MUTATION OPERATORS.

Annotation Level			
#	Class	Description	Acronym
1	Adding	Adding Expected Class	AEC
2	Modifying	Decrement Constant from Timeout	DCfT
3	Modifying	Increment Constant to Timeout	ICfT
4	Removing	Removing Timeout	RTA

C. *Discussion analysis of each individual mutation operator*

Next, we present an individual analysis of the effect of each mutation operator. The operators and their effects are:

ATV: adds the delta parameter, which is the third parameter of *assertEquals(expected, actual, delta)* method and kills mutants in two situations: (i) deprecated assert; and (ii) depending on the test value and the constant value.

The purpose of the delta parameter is to determine the maximum value of the difference between the numbers *expected* and *actual* so that they are considered the same value.

The ATV operator is a signature-level operator and belongs to the addition class. It adds the delta parameter. With this, one has a mutated version of the original oracle, in which the result is accepted as correct, considering an error rate. However, it is not always easy to know the acceptable value for a particular application. Currently, only the value 0001 is used as delta, but other values could be considered, taking into account the actual expected value. For example: *expected*/2, *expected*/10, *expected*/100, *expected*/1000, etc.

Figure 1 calculates a function of the second degree by means of the Bhaskara formula in which the coefficients are 1, 2 and 1. Depending on the value of the coefficients, the roots can generate values with several decimal places, so it is important to add the delta value (Figure 1, Line 5). Implementations with and without the delta value may have the same or different results depending on the value of the delta and the coefficients in question. If the difference between oracles is never revealed, this may indicate that the fragility is in the test case or the error may be directly in the program being executed by the oracle.

```
@Test
public void testBhaskara() {
    Bhaskara B = new Bhaskara();
    double raiz = B.raiz(1,2,1);
    assertEquals(-1.0, raiz , 0.1);
}
```

Figure 1. ATV example.

DCfTV: decrements the delta parameter, which is the third parameter of the method *assertEquals(expected, actual, delta)*. It kills the mutant depending on the decrement value and the value obtained during testing. If the oracle is designed with a case such that changing the precision value will change the result by applying this operator, the mutant oracle will have different results from the original oracle.

Figure 2 uses the *assertEquals(expected, actual, delta)* method in line 7, and a calculation of a rate over the value of a given product is being tested. The DCfTV operator allows the tester to adjust the delta value, decrementing it, according to his/her needs.

```
1 @Test
2 public void taxValue() {
3     Product prod=new Product("TV",600,Product.
        ELETRONIC);
4     CalTaxs calculatorTax=new CalTaxs();
5     double tax=calculatorTax.getTax(prod);
6     double finalPrice=prod.getPrice()*(1+tax);
7     assertEquals(660, finalPrice , 0.001);
8 }
```

Figure 2. DCfTV example.

In the example, the tester should provide a test case that has an error less than the initial error, but near it, ie: $0.0001 < error \leq 0.001$. For one such case, the original oracle indicates that the test passes but the mutant oracle indicates a failure. Thus, the mutant helps the tester verify his oracle or plan new test cases that exercise his oracle.

As in the case of the ATV operator, it is difficult to define how much the delta value decreases. Thus, one can think of extending the DCfTV operator using values such as *error/*2, *error/*10, *error/*100, *error/*1000, etc.

ICfTV: increments the delta parameter, the third parameter of the method *assertEquals(expected, actual, delta)*. It kills mutants depending on the incremented value. If the oracle is designed in the sense of changing the precision value, it will affect the result by applying this operator, then the mutant oracle will have different results from the original oracle.

The ICfTV operator follows the same logic as the DCfTV operator. However, one increment the value of the delta (ICfTV) and another decrement the value of the delta (DCfTV). In Figure 3, the oracle is on line 4, where the *assertEquals* method checks the result of a multiplication with the value of delta 0.1. By applying the ICfTV operator, a mutant oracle is generated with this increased delta value. The two implementations, original oracle and mutant oracle, may have the same or different results depending on the incremental value, which is set by the tester. If the difference between oracles is never revealed, this indicates the fragility of the test oracle.

```
1 @Test
2 public void assertSum(){
3     Calculator c = new Calculator();
4     assertEquals(4.0,c.mult(2,2),0.1);
5 }
```

Figure 3. ICfTV example.

As in the case of the ATV and DCfTV operators, it is difficult to define how much the delta value decreases. Thus, one can think of extending the ICfTV operator using values as *error/*2, *error/*10, *error/*100, *error/*1000, etc.

RBA: replaces boolean assertions (`assertTrue`, `assertFalse`). It produces high rate of dead mutants. Useful to reveal defects in oracles designed to Boolean cases, the replacement of the statements, the mutant oracle can improve the quality of the original oracle.

In Figure 4, the oracle presented in line 4 with the `assertTrue` method checks whether the String "Dog's god" is a palindrome, by applying the RBA operator, the `assertFalse` will be executed. If the result of the mutant oracle is different from the original oracle, the mutant will be considered dead. If the mutant or original oracles present the same result, the tester should check the test case and/or the program being tested.

```
1 @Test
2 public void testPalindrome3(){
3  CheckPalindrome cp=new CheckPalindrome();
4  assertTrue(cp.isPalindrome("Dog's god"));
5 }
```

Figure 4. RBA example.

RTV: removes the delta value, kills mutants depending on the test oracle. If the oracle is designed with a case that changing the precision value it changes the result by applying this operator, the mutant oracle will have different results from the original oracle.

In Figure 5 the arithmetic mean between two numbers is performed, and the oracle in line 5 has the value 0.001 of delta. The RTV operator removes this delta value. The two implementations, with the delta value and no delta value, may have the same or different results depending on the incremental value, which is set by the tester. In this case, we can have two correct implementations, in which it will be up to the tester to perform the analysis of the mutant oracle's correctness.

```
1 @Test
2 public void testAverage(){
3     int x=10, y=7;
4     assertEquals(8.5,calcAverage(10,7),0.001);
5 }
```

Figure 5. RTV example.

It is not recommended that an oracle be designed depending on the delta value. Therefore, if removing this value changes the result of the oracle, this can suggest to the tester to design new test cases that do not depend on this error value. In practice, this operator corresponds to changing the delta value to zero.

AEC: adds an expected class in annotation `@Test`. Kills mutants depending on the executed exception and the oracle running.

The AEC operator assists the tester in handling the exceptions that may occur during oracle execution. For example, in Figure 6 the exception`NullPointerException` avoids a month that does not exist be called in the `getAllDays` method.

```
@Test(expected=NullPointerException.class)
public void testException() {
    int month = 4;
    Assert.assertNotNull(calendar.getAllDays(month
        ));
}
```

Figure 6. AEC example.

AEC operator can add the exceptions: *IOException, NullPointerException, IllegalArgumentException, ClassNot-FoundException, ArrayIndexOutOfBoundsException, Arith-meticException* and *Exception*.

The tester must add the exception according to the operation being performed, as well as done in Figure 6, where it is possible to avoid calling a null value.

DCfT: decrements a constant value of the timeout. Kills mutants depending on the decrement value and the value of the timeout. If the oracle depends on the previously established timeout value, using this operator, the mutant oracle will have different results from the original oracle;

Figure 7 is set to a value of timeout in 10 seconds. The DCfT operator can reduce this value, depending on the amount of records that are registered in the database, reducing this timeout is a good solution because it decreases the waiting time for the result. However, the tester must make a decision on how much to decrease in order to improve the performance of the test oracle.

```
@Test(timeout=10000)
public void searchEmployee(){
    Employee emp=empDAO.findEmployee("12345");
    Assert.assertEquals("JOHN",emp.getName());
    verify(transaction ,atMostOnce()).execute("
        12345");
}
```

Figure 7. DCfT example.

Deciding how much to decrease from this timeout value is not an easy decision, it is necessary to analyze how long it takes to process the method being tested. One solution is to use some predefined values: *timeout* − 10, *timeout* − 100, *timeout* − 1000, *timeout*/2, *timeout*/10, etc.

ICtT: increments a constant value of the timeout. Kills mutants depending on the increment value and the value of the timeout. If the oracle depends on the previously established timeout value, using this operator, the mutant oracle will have different results from the original oracle.

Figure 8 performs a test of a connection in the database, with the timeout of 1000 milliseconds. The mutant oracle generated by the ICtT operator may give a different result from the mutant oracle, causing the timeout value to be sufficient, or the mutant oracle may still live, giving the same result as the original oracle, showing that the problem may not be in the test program, but the program that performs the database connection. In this case, it is up to the tester to check the program and identify the error.

```
@Test(timeout=1000)
public void testGetConnection() {
        Connection con = Connection.getConnection();
        assertNull("Unable to connect!", con);
}
```

Figure 8. ICfT example.

In the example presented in Figure 8, the tester must define a test case whose runtime is higher than the original timeout value, but lower than the mutated value, ie $1000 < \textit{runtime} \leq 10000$.

RTA: removes the timeout value. Kills mutants depending on the value of the timeout. If the oracle depends on the previously established timeout value, using this operator, the mutant oracle will have different results from the original oracle.

In JUnit, it is possible for a test to have a maximum time to run. For example, if the tester wants the test to take no more than 500 milliseconds, the following operation can be performed (Figure 9). However, some operations may take longer than the time set in the timeout parameter, and for this, the RTA operator removes this parameter, causing the test run to use the default JUnit timeout time.

```
@Test(timeout=500)
public void fastTestCase() {
        assertEquals(1500, calendar.getSize());
}
```

Figure 9. RTA example.

This mutation operator causes the mutating oracle to not depend on the execution time of the test case and, in theory, could run for an infinite amount of time. In the case of the mutant being killed, that is, indicating that the test has passed, while the original oracle indicates that it has failed, there is an indication that the test case actually does not depend on the execution time and that the timeout clause was improperly used.

IV. EMPIRICAL EVALUATION

In this section, we present an empirical evaluation involving the mutation of test oracles and some subject programs. The idea of this study is to apply specific operators to assertion- based test oracles (written with JUnit) and generate mutants. The syntactic modifications provided by the mutant test oracles are minimal. They reproduce faults in the signatures or annotations of assertion methods, as described in the previous section.

The generation of mutated test oracles suggest some repairs in unit tests previously defined. Further, new test cases can be found to improve the quality of the original test set.

A. Experiment Design

The experiment was conducted in order to verify whether the mutated oracles are able to identify failures that were not identified by original oracles, and analyze mutated test oracles for the purpose of their evaluation with respect to effectiveness and efficiency from the point of view of the tester revealing defects in faulty programs.

Figure 10 illustrates the steps performed in the experiment, namely: (1) run the original oracle against the subject program; (2) apply MuJava 4 JUnit mutation operators in the test oracles, generating the mutant oracles; (3) run all mutant oracles against the original subject programs; and (4) analyze the results.

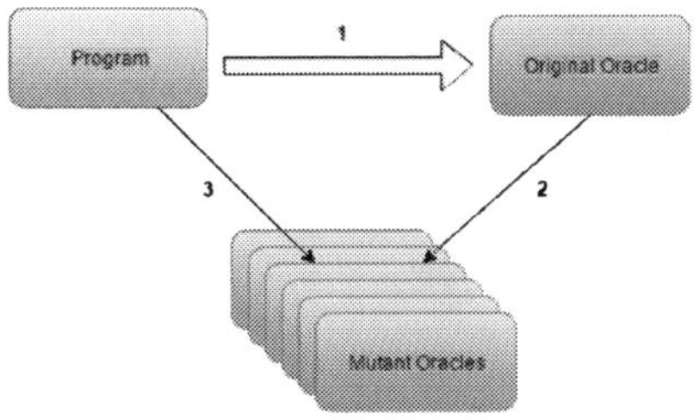

Figure 10. Step-by-step followed in this experiment.

B. Research Questions

The following Research Questions has been defined:

RQ1 Are the mutant test oracles able to improve the quality of the original oracle?

RQ2 Does the operator efficiency change depending on the program in test?

Aiming at answer these questions, we applied the mutation operators for test oracles in the assertion-based oracles of 5 subjects programs, which provided mutant oracles that are supposed to improve the original oracle.

C. Subject Programs

We selected five programs with different cyclomatic complexities, ranging from 1 to 6, to verify the effectiveness of the mutants in oracles, so revealing defects in the original oracles. The subject programs and their complexities are presented in Table III.

Each subject program has a test oracle written in JUnit form. Information about test oracles, including the number of failures in each test oracle used in the experiment are shown in Table IV.

TABLE III. SUBJECT PROGRAMS.

Program	#Cyclomatic Complexity	#Lines of code
Calculator	1	19
CheckPalindrome	3	16
BinarySearch	4	31
BubbleSort	4	66
ShoppingCart	6	117

TABLE IV. TEST ORACLES FROM SUBJECT PROGRAMS.

Oracle	#Cyclomatic Complexity	#Lines of Code	#Failures
TestingCalculator	1	58	7
TestingCheckPalindrome	1	61	2
TestingBinarySearch	1	114	2
TestingBubbleSort	1	146	3
TestingShoppingCart	1	212	13

D. Experimental Procedure

The experiment was divided in 3 steps (Figure 10). Five small programs were selected. Each original program had a correspondent testing class with some assertion-based oracle written through JUnit unit tests. Then, our mutation operators for test oracles were applied to each oracle, and the living and

V. RESULTS DISCUSSION

In total, MuJava 4 JUnit tool implements 10 mutation operators to oracles from which 5 are signature level and 5 are annotation level. In this section, we provided a detailed analysis on the effects of using slightly modified version of test oracles to improve the quality of the test class.

A. Answers to RQs

[RQ1] Are the mutant test oracles able to improve the quality of the original oracle?

Some operators generate more mutants than others. The generation of mutants will depend on the assertion used, the parameters used in this assertion and which annotation is being employed. In this experiment, we collect data about the mutants generated by each operator implemented in MuJava 4 JUnit.

The percentages of live and dead mutants by each operator of the MuJava 4 JUnit tool are summarized in Table V. It can be observed that some operators kill more mutants than others. It is also observed that the MuJava 4 JUnit tool operators worked well in the generation of the mutant oracles.

TABLE V. MUTANTS ALIVE AND DEAD BY OPERATOR.

	Alive(%)	Dead(%)
ATV	94,74	5,26
DCfTV	80,00	20,00
ICtTV	80,00	20,00
RBA	50,00	50,00
RTV	62,50	37,50
AEC	78,57	21,43
DCfT	87,50	12,50
ICtT	70,00	30,00
RTA	100,00	0,0

[RQ2] Does the operator efficiency change depending on the program in test?

Each operator generates mutants according to the Assert method and their parameters, or the annotations used. Therefore, when performing the experiment, we conclude that the type of data that the subject program is using is what will determine which operator is more efficient in that situation.

In the context of our experiment, `CheckPalindrome` program, for example, works with boolean values, so that the operators which use these values are more efficient, in this case, RBA. The `Calculator` program works with integer and double values, causing the ATV, DCfTV, ICtTV and RTV operators more efficient. The `BinarySearch`, `ShoppingCart`, and `BubbleSort` programs perform operations with boolean, integer and double values, thus using all operators of these genres. Table VI shows the number of mutants generated by each operator in each program used in the experiment.

TABLE VI. MUTANTS GENERATED IN EACH PROGRAM SEPARATED BY OPERATOR.

	Calculator	CheckPalindrome	BinarySearch	BubbleSort	ShoppingCart
ATV	4	0	0	0	34
DCfTV	5	0	5	5	5
ICtTV	4	0	5	5	6
RBA	0	14	14	0	28
RTV	5	0	0	0	3
AEC	78	90	72	78	102
DCfT	3	0	0	0	5
ICtT	4	0	0	0	6
RTA	3	0	0	0	4

The most interesting mutant oracles are those giving results equal to the original oracles. They can suggest new test cases, indicate weaknesses in the test case, and then identify errors in the program being tested.

In Table V, it is possible to observe that the generated mutants have a higher rate of live mutants compared to the dead mutants. Therefore, the answer to the QP1 research question in the context of this experiment is yes. However, in the future, a detailed analysis of mutants should be carried out for this result to be consolidated.

B. Pros and cons

In this first experiment, the operators performed well and we observed their behavior in different situations. We focused this experiment on operator's behavior, but we also collected some numbers about live mutants and dead mutants for further analysis.

ATV, DCfTV, ICtTV, and RTV are useful when a mutant is dead, because it indicates that the precision value that is making a difference in the outcome of the oracle. In practice, to obtain a mutant in this condition, the tester must pay attention to the fact that the test case is not necessary for the test case, and then change their oracle so that the precision value does not need to interfere to change the final value of the oracle's execution.

The AEC operator, in practice, to obtain a mutant in this condition, the tester must pay attention to the fact that the test case requires the exception added by the operator and it is interesting that the tester designed the oracle taking into account all the situations that may occur for the required exceptions.

DCfT, ICfT and RTA operators generate mutants that can be dead or alive. They are useful when a mutant is dead, because it shows that the timeout should be reconsidered by the tester when designing the test oracle.

VI. Threats to Validity

This section presents the threats of this study on four different perspectives:

Internal validity: Our study is designed with a narrow scope – assertion-based test oracles. The experiment was designed to answer our RQs. We believe that the results were consistent to answers our RQs, leading to a high and acceptable internal validity.

External validity: The study evaluates the effectiveness of the mutation operators for assertion-based test oracles in five small Java applications. However, our experiment does notprovide results to assume that the behavior of our technique will be the same in industrial-real-world systems. Further work is required in this context. In addition to that, our tool is designed only for Java applications, reducing the generalizations of our results.

Construct validity: The concept of mutation is useful in several contexts, making our construction validity higher. Hence, the size, and complexity, of the chosen applications are suitable to show the mutation operators effectiveness for JUnit-based test oracles.

Conclusion validity: We have presented our methodology in detail and we are providing the code of the tool we have developed. In this context, our results are associated with our results, and we therefore, claim that we have high conclusion validity.

VII. Conclusion

There were no systematic ways to assess the quality or accuracy of an automated test oracle. Thus, it is possible that in some cases, the results of running a test suite present unwanted results, not by problems in test data or test program, but because of errors in the implementation of the oracle. Therefore, this study designs mutation operators to oracles, until then, there was no work in this direction. Operators have been developed to test oracles written in JUnit format and defined replacing signatures of assert methods, adding parameters assert method, or removing parameters assert method.

Operators were implemented and included in MuJava tool. The experiment conducted in this study highlights the behavior of the operators when applied to simple programs and different ciclomatic complexities, data were collected from living and dead mutants, as well as detailed data for each operator in different cases.

We can conclude that using mutation test oracles collaborates in improving the quality of test oracles. The work also contributes presenting a systematic way of assessing the quality of oracles, which has not yet found in the literature.

Mutation operators to test oracles do not have a high rate of generation of dead mutants, however, they may reveal weaknesses in the original or even new test cases oracle, even not generating mutants dead. Therefore, the generated mutants should be scrutinized to make the actual operators.

As future work, we will carry out further experiments with real-world programs, seeking to affirm the results obtained with this work. In addition, we will design mutation operators to other oracle types.

Acknowledgment

Ana is supported by Fapesp (Grant Number 2014/09629-1).

References

[1] R. A. Oliveira, U. Kanewala, and P. A. Nardi, "Automated test oracles: State of the art, taxonomies, and trends," Advances In Computers, Vol 95, vol. 95, 2014, pp. 113–199.

[2] M. Pezz and C. Zhang, "Automated test oracles: A survey," Advances in Computers, vol. 95, 2014, pp. 1–48.

[3] K. Shrestha and M. Rutherford, "An Empirical Evaluation of Assertions as Oracles," in Proceedings of the 4th ICST, March 2011, pp. 110–119.

[4] E. Beck and K. Gamma, "JUnit: A cook's tour," Java Report, vol. 4, no. 5, May 1999, pp. 27–38.

[5] E. J. Weyuker, "On testing non-testable programs," The Computer Journal, vol. 25, no. 4, 1982, pp. 465–470.

[6] L. Baresi and M. Young, "Test oracles," Technical Report CISTR-01, vol. 2, 2001, p. 9.

[7] D. S. Rosenblum, "Towards a method of programming with assertions," in Proceedings of the 14th ICSE. ACM, 1992, pp. 92–104.

[8] R. A. DeMillo, R. J. Lipton, and F. G. Sayward, "Hints on test data selection: Help for the practicing programmer," IEEE Computer Society Press, vol. 11, no. 4, Apr. 1978, pp. 34–41.

[9] Y. Jia and M. Harman, "An analysis and survey of the development of mutation testing," IEEE Transactions on Software Engeneering, vol. 37, no. 5, 2011, pp. 649–678.

[10] R. Abraham and M. Erwig, "Mutation operators for spreadsheets," IEEE Transactions on Software Engineering, vol. 35, no. 1, January 2009, pp. 94–108.

[11] Y.-S. Ma, J. Offutt, and Y.-R. Kwon, "MuJava: A Mutation System for Java," in Proceedings of the 28th ICSE. New York, NY, USA: ACM, 2006, pp. 827–830.

[12] A. Maciel. MuJava 4 JUnit. [Online]. Available: https://goo.gl/ZGXqI5 (2016)

Visual Component-based Development of Formal Models

Sergey Ostroumov, Marina Waldén
Faculty of Science and Engineering
Åbo Akademi University
Turku, Finland
E-Mail: {Sergey.Ostroumov, Marina.Walden}@abo.fi

***Abstract*—Formal methods, such as Event-B provide a means for system-level specification and verification supported by correctness proofs. However, the formal Event-B specification of a system requires background knowledge, which prevents a fruitful communication between the developer and the customer. In addition, scalability and reusability are limiting factors in using formal methods, such as Event-B in complex system development. This paper presents an approach to facilitate scalability of formal development in Event-B. Our aim is to build a formal library of parameterized visual components that can be reused whenever needed. Each component is formally developed and proved correct by utilizing the advantages of Event-B. Furthermore, each component has a unique graphical representation that eases the rigorous development by applying the "drag-and-drop" approach and enhances the communication between a developer and a customer. We present a subset of components from the digital hydraulics domain and outline the compositionality mechanism.**

Keywords-Components Library; Visual Design; Event-B; Formal Components.

I. INTRODUCTION

Event-B [1] is a formal method that allows designers to build systems in such a manner that the correctness of the development process is supported by mathematical proofs. The specification (or the model) of a system in Event-B captures the functional behaviour, as well as the essential properties that must hold (invariants). The development process proceeds in a top-down fashion starting from an abstract (usually non-deterministic) specification. This specification is then stepwise refined by adding the details about the system until the implementable level is reached. The process of transforming an abstract specification into an implementable one via a number of correctness preserving steps is known as refinement [2]. It helps the designers to deal with the system requirements in a stepwise manner, which makes the correctness proof along the development easier. However, as more details are added to the system specification, it becomes complex and hard to handle. This limits the scalability and reusability of this approach. Moreover, as more details are added to the specification through refinement, it is harder to convince the stake holders about the fact that the system specification embodies all the necessary requirements.

This paper proposes an approach to visual system design whose aim is to enhance scalability and reusability, as well as to facilitate the communication between a developer and a customer. In addition, the visual design is aimed at making the rigorous development process easier. The idea behind our approach is to build a formal library of parameterized visual components. Each component is formally developed and proved correct by utilizing the Event-B engine. Moreover, each component is tied to a unique graphical representation. The development process then proceeds according to the "drag-and-drop" approach, where the developer picks the necessary components from the library and instantiates them. Since the components are parameterized and are in the library, they can be reused in various application domains depending on the requirements. The specification of a system is then twofold: a visual model whose correctness is supported by the underlying Event-B language. We present a pattern for the development of formal components and create a subset of components from the digital hydraulics domain. We also outline the compositionality mechanism.

The paper remainder is as follows. Section II outlines the Event-B notation and outlines proof obligations that provide the correctness proof. Section III presents the formal library of parameterized visual components. Section IV outlines the compositionality mechanism. Section V gives an overview of the existing approaches. Finally, Section VI concludes the paper and summarizes the directions of our future work.

II. PRELIMINARIES: EVENT-B

Event-B [1] is a state-based formalism that offers several advantages. First, it allows us to build system level models. Second, the development follows the top-down refinement approach, where each step is shown correct by mathematical proofs. Finally, it has a mature tool support extensible with plug-ins, namely the Rodin platform [3]. Currently, Event-B is limited to modelling discrete time, but the work on its extension to continuous models is on-going [4].

An Event-B specification consists of *contexts* and *machines*. A context can be *extended* by another context whereas a machine can be *refined* by another machine. Moreover, a machine can refer to the contents of the context via "*sees*" (see Figure 1).

A context specifies static structures, such as data types in terms of *sets*, *constants* and properties given as a set of *axioms*. One can also postulate and prove *theorems* that ease proving effort during the model development.

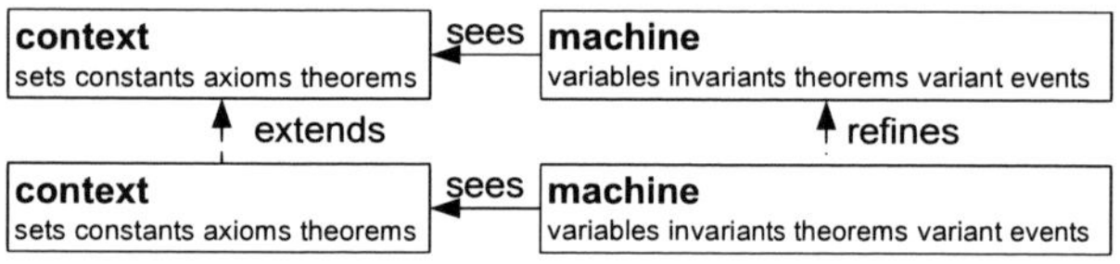

Figure 1. Event-B contexts, machines and relationship [1].

A machine models the behaviour of a system. The machine includes *state variables*, *theorems*, *invariants* and *events*. The invariants represent constraining predicates that define types of the state variables, as well as essential properties of the system. The overall system invariant is defined as the conjunction of these predicates. An event describes a transition from a state to a state. The syntax of the event is as follows:

E = **ANY** x **WHERE** g **THEN** a **END**

where x is a list of event local variables. The *guard* g stands for a conjunction of predicates over the state variables and the local variables. The *action* a describes a collection of assignments to the state variables.

We can observe that an event models a guarded transition. When the guard g holds, the transition can take place. In case several guards hold simultaneously, any of the enabled transitions can be chosen for execution non-deterministically. If none of the guards holds, the system terminates or deadlocks. Sometimes, the system should never terminate, i.e., it has to be deadlock free. To achieve this, one needs to postulate a machine theorem that requires the disjunction of the guards of all the events to hold.

When a transition takes place, the action a is performed. The action a is a parallel composition (||) of the assignments to the state variables executed simultaneously. An assignment can be either deterministic or non-deterministic. The deterministic assignment is defined as $v := E(w)$, where v is a list of state variables, E is a list of expressions over some set of state variables w (w might include v). The non-deterministic assignment that we use in this paper is specified as $v :\in Q$, where Q is a set of possible values.

These denotations allow for describing semantics of Event-B in terms of *before-after predicates* (BA) [5]. Essentially, a transition is a BA that establishes a relationship between the model state before (v) and after (v′) the execution of an event. This enables one to prove the model correctness by checking if the events preserve the invariants ($Inv \wedge g_E \Rightarrow [BA_E]Inv$) and are feasible to execute in case the event action is non-deterministic ($Inv \wedge g_E \Rightarrow \exists v' . BA_E$).

The refinement relation between the more abstract and more concrete specifications is also corroborated by the correctness proofs. Particularly, the more concrete events have to preserve the functionality of their abstract counter parts [6]. This paper however does not focus on this aspect.

The Rodin platform [3], tool support for Event-B, automatically generates and attempts to discharge (prove) the necessary proof obligations (POs). The best practices encompass the model development in such a manner that 90-95% of the POs are discharged automatically. Nonetheless, the tool sometimes requires user assistance provided via the interactive prover.

III. Library of Formal Components

Our idea is to create a formal library of visual components. Each component is developed formally within the Event-B formal framework and is tied to a unique graphical symbol. Moreover, the components in the library have to be parameterized whenever possible in order to be reusable during the development process. The system specification/development is then a process of picking, instantiating and connecting the needed components, so that the system is developed in the "drag-and-drop" fashion.

At present, the library contains components from the digital hydraulics and railway domains. The library also includes a generic component used to create a placeholder to be replaced by a specific one. Although our library consists of generic components parameterized for reuse, one can see that our approach is related to the work on domain specific languages, where the language is aimed at a specific problem domain [7][8]. Despite this, the formal language behind the components is Event-B and not domain specific.

Next, we present a pattern for the component development and overview some components from the digital hydraulics domain, namely an electro-valve and a cylinder. We focus on the crucial parts of the models whose details, as well as more examples can be found in our TR [9].

A. Component Functionality

We start by describing the generic functionality of a component. A component is a reactive device that updates its outputs according to the input stimuli. The component typically consists of two parts: an interface and a body (Figure 2, a). The interface is comprised of the set of inputs and outputs that are seen by the outside world whilst the body performs the component functions.

The operation of the component has to be deterministic in order to precisely determine the output result. That is, the same input stimuli must generate the same output results and the order of operations to compute these outputs according to the input stimuli is known a priori. To achieve this, we use a common pattern for control systems [10] in which the component first reads the inputs (environment) and then produces the outputs (control). In other words, a component has at least two indefinitely alternating modes: read of the inputs and production of the outputs (Figure 2, b)). Thus, the non-termination (deadlock freedom) is the main property of a component.

We model components as Event-B machines that contain shared variables and rely on the principle of shared variables

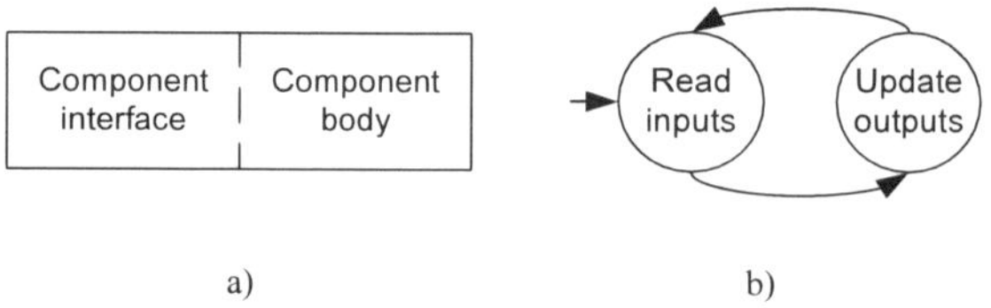

Figure 2. A component pattern: a) component structure, b) automaton.

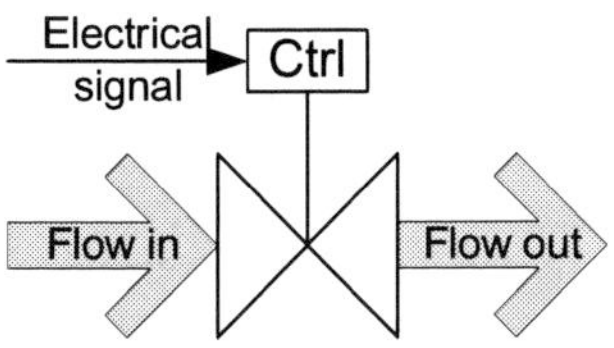

Figure 3. A symbolic representation of an electro-valve with the interface.

composition within Event-B when composing the components [11][12]. The variables that are local to a machine are considered private, while the shared variables are shared between machines and provide communication facilities in form of inputs and outputs. The inputs and the outputs of a component also form the interface of the component and are distinguished by the suffixes _I and _O (e.g., in Event-B we could have an input variable in_I and an output variable out_O).

B. *Hydraulic component: an electro-valve*

As an example of a parameterized visual component we develop and add to the library an electro-valve. Its visual symbol is shown in Figure 3 whereas the corresponding formal model is illustrated by Figure 4 and Figure 5.

The electro-valve is a physical device that transfers a flow of liquid from one port to another. It contains a plunger controlled by an electrical signal. The application of a positive control signal moves the plunger, so as to open the valve, whilst the negative signal closes it. If no signal is present on the control input, the plunger and therefore the valve keep the current position. Moreover, the valve opens and closes with some rate due to physical laws. The specification of a valve then has the following parameters (context Valve_parameters in Figure 4): the minimum (valve_flow_min) and the maximum (valve_flow_max) flow the valve can let trough and the rate (valve_rate) with which the valve opens and closes. The rate cannot be greater than the difference between the maximum and the minimum flow (valve_rate ≤ valve_flow_max − valve_flow_min). Assuming that when the valve is closed, so that the outlet is fully closed as well (no flow can come through), the minimum flow equals to zero and the rate cannot be greater than the maximum. Moreover, if the rate equals to the maximum, the valve is simply open or closed. The minimum flow, the maximum flow and the rate parameters, as well as the set of control signals (valve_CONTROL) are all captured by constants in the context Valve_parameters (Figure 4).

The interface of a valve consists of two inputs and one output, namely the control signal (valve_control_I), the input port (valve_flow_I) and the output port (valve_flow_O), respectively (see Figure 5). Additionally, the valve has a variable that shows the current position of the plunger (valve_position), as well as the mode variable (valve_mode) that models the deterministic order of the transitions between the inputs read and outputs production states.

The valve has the property that the flow from the output port cannot be greater than the flow on the input port (valve_mode = 0 ⇒ valve_flow_O ≤ valve_flow_I). Moreover, the position of the plunge regulates the output flow, so that the output flow cannot be stronger than allowed (valve_flow_O ≤ valve_position). Additionally, the output flow always has to be updated when the new inputs are read (i.e., the non-termination property as it was stated earlier). The former properties are captured as invariants. The latter is stated as a deadlock freedom theorem (see in Figure 5,

```
context Valve_parameters
constants
 valve_flow_min  valve_flow_max  valve_rate  valve_CONTROL
axioms
 valve_flow_min = 0 ∧ valve_flow_max ∈ ℕ1 ∧
 valve_CONTROL = {−1,0,1} ∧
 valve_rate ∈ ℕ1 ∧ valve_rate ≤ valve_flow_max – valve_flow_min
end
```

Figure 4. Parameters of a generic valve.

```
machine Valve_Behaviour sees Valve_parameters
variables valve_control_I  valve_flow_I  valve_flow_O
  valve_mode  valve_position
invariants
 valve_control_I ∈ valve_CONTROL ∧ valve_mode ∈ 0..1 ∧
 valve_flow_I ∈ valve_flow_min..valve_flow_max ∧
 valve_flow_O ∈ valve_flow_min..valve_flow_max ∧
 valve_position ∈ valve_flow_min..valve_flow_max ∧
// The output flow cannot be stronger than allowed nor input
 valve_flow_O ≤ valve_position ∧
 (valve_mode = 0 ⇒ valve_flow_O ≤ valve_flow_I)
// The property of non-termination
theorem (valve_mode = 0 ∨
 (valve_mode = 1 ∧ valve_control_I = 1 ∧
  valve_position + valve_rate ≤ valve_flow_max) ∨
 (valve_mode = 1 ∧ valve_control_I = −1 ∧
  valve_position − valve_rate ≥ valve_flow_min) ∨
 (valve_mode = 1 ∧ (valve_control_I = 0 ∨
  (valve_control_I = 1 ∧
   valve_position + valve_rate > valve_flow_max) ∨
  (valve_control_I = −1 ∧
   valve_position − valve_rate < valve_flow_min))))
events ...
 event valve_environment
  where  valve_mode = 0
  then  valve_mode := 1 || valve_control_I :∈ valve_CONTROL ||
    valve_flow_I :∈ valve_flow_min..valve_flow_max
 end

  event valve_opening
  any valve_flow_O_new
   where  valve_control_I = 1 ∧ valve_mode = 1 ∧
   (valve_position + valve_rate ≤ valve_flow_max) ∧
   (valve_position + valve_rate < valve_flow_I ⇒
        valve_flow_O_new = valve_position+valve_rate) ∧
   (valve_position + valve_rate ≥ valve_flow_I ⇒
       valve_flow_O_new = valve_flow_I)
  then  valve_flow_O := valve_flow_O_new || valve_mode := 0 ||
   valve_position := valve_position + valve_rate
  end
end
```

Figure 5. The excerpt of the machine of a generic valve.

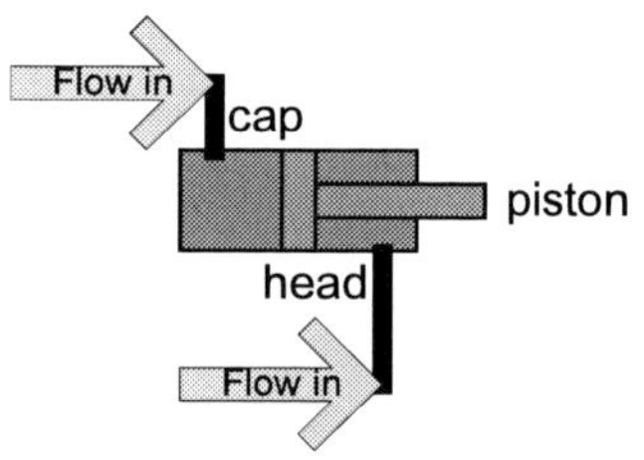

Figure 6. Visual representation of a cylinder.

theorem (valve_mode = 0 ∨ ...), which evaluates to true and supports the fact that the component always works.

The functionality of the valve includes: reading the control signal and the input flow, opening the valve, closing the valve and keeping the previous position (i.e., neither opening nor closing). Initially, the valve is idle. There might be some input flow, but the valve is closed. Hence, there is no output flow. The mode is set to reading the new inputs.

In order for a valve to produce the intended outputs, the valve first needs to read the inputs. This is captured by an environmental event that updates the inputs of the model. We assume that all inputs of the valve are updated simultaneously as shown in **event** valve_environment in Figure 5. The input flow is read non-deterministically bounded to the parameters of the valve.

Once the inputs are read (valve_mode = 1), the valve can perform the following operations: open with some rate, close with the same rate or keep the current position. These operations are modelled using the three events shown below.

The valve opening event (**event** valve_opening) can clearly take place when the control signal (the command) is to open the valve (valve_control_I = 1). However, the valve cannot open more than allowed, that is, it cannot exceed the maximum (valve_position + valve_rate ≤ valve_flow_max). When the valve is opening, the output flow increases according to the rate and the current position of the plunge (valve_position + valve_rate < valve_flow_I ⇒ *valve_flow_O_new* = valve_position + valve_rate). Notice however that if the diameter of the valve allows a flow stronger than the input flow to come through, the output flow is simply the same as the input one (valve_position + valve_rate ≥ valve_flow_I ⇒ *valve_flow_O_new* = valve_flow_I).

The valve closing event is specified similarly considering the fact that it is opposite to the opening of the valve. It can take place when the command is to close the valve (valve_control_I = −1) and proceeds as long as the valve is not completely closed (valve_position − valve_rate ≥ valve_flow_min).

```
context Cylinder_parameters
constants
  cylinder_input_flow_min  cylinder_input_flow_max
  cylinder_cap_pos  cylinder_head_pos
axioms
  cylinder_input_flow_min = 0 ∧ cylinder_cap_pos = 0 ∧
  cylinder_input_flow_max ∈ ℕ1 ∧ cylinder_head_pos ∈ ℕ1
end
```

Figure 7. Parameters of a cylinder.

Finally, if the command is neither open nor closed (valve_control_I = 0) or the valve is fully closed or open, it keeps its position. In other words, the valve is idle or stopped. Therefore, the output flow remains unchanged with respect to the current flow (valve_flow_I ≥ valve_flow_O ⇒ *valve_flow_O_new* = valve_flow_O) or the input flow (valve_flow_I < valve_flow_O ⇒ *valve_flow_O_new* = valve_flow_I).

The visual symbol and the specification of the electro-valve component extend the formal library of visual components. The specification was modelled and proved in the Rodin platform. The tool generated 24 POs out of which 20 were proved automatically.

C. *Hydraulic component: a cylinder*

Another example of a hydraulic component for the component library is a cylinder. The cylinder reacts on liquid flows only and does not have any electrical inputs. Nonetheless, it is a reactive device whose outputs are updated according to the input stimuli. The visual symbol of a cylinder is shown in Figure 6.

The cylinder contains a piston that can move forward and backward in the cylinder body depending on the differences between the liquid flows. The liquid flows via the cap and the head into the cylinder and is transformed into piston movement. The piston moves forward (extends) if the pressure of the flow coming into the cap is greater than the liquid flow coming into the head. In the opposite case, the piston moves backward. Clearly, if the pressure of both input flows is the same, the piston keeps the position. Due to physical laws, the piston moves with some rate. This rate is also determined by the difference in the input flows.

The cylinder specification has four parameters (Figure 7). Two of them define the minimum (cylinder_input_flow_min) and maximum (cylinder_input_flow_max) input flow of the liquid. We assume that both inputs are of the same size, so that the motion of the piston is proper. The other two parameters specify the limits of the piston motion (cylinder_head_pos and cylinder_cap_pos). The difference between cylinder_head_pos and cylinder_cap_pos sets the length that the piston can move.

The interface of the cylinder has two inputs (flows) (cylinder_flow_cap_I and cylinder_flow_head_I), as well as one output cylinder_piston_position_O (see Figure 8). The inputs allow the liquid to flow into the body of the cylinder via the cap and the head. The output of the cylinder is the piston that moves according to the difference in the input flows. Moreover, there is a variable that specifies the modes of the cylinder component, cylinder_mode (Figure 8). The main property of the cylinder is the deadlock freedom theorem. The theorem evaluates to true, which supports the fact that the cylinder is non-terminating.

Initially, there are no input flows, the piston is at some position within the cylinder body and the mode is set to read the inputs. In order for the piston to move, both of the inputs have to be updated (similar to the valve component).

There are three possible reactions to the input flows. The piston can move forward (extend), if the flow coming into

```
machine Cylinder_behaviour sees Cylinder_parameters
variables
  cylinder_flow_cap_I
  cylinder_flow_head_I
  cylinder_piston_position_O
  cylinder_mode
invariants
  // Current position of the piston in the cylinder
  cylinder_piston_position_O ∈
      cylinder_cap_pos..cylinder_head_pos ∧
  // Input to move the piston to the right
  cylinder_flow_cap_I ∈
      cylinder_input_flow_min..cylinder_input_flow_max ∧
  // Input to move the piston to the left
  cylinder_flow_head_I ∈
      cylinder_input_flow_min..cylinder_input_flow_max ∧
  cylinder_mode ∈ 0..1 ∧
  // Deadlock freedom – non-termination
theorem cylinder_mode = 0 ∨
  (cylinder_mode = 1 ∧
   cylinder_flow_cap_I > cylinder_flow_head_I ∧
   cylinder_flow_cap_I > cylinder_input_flow_min ∧
   cylinder_piston_position_O + cylinder_flow_cap_I –
   cylinder_flow_head_I ≤ cylinder_head_pos) ∨
   ... // Guards of other events
```

Figure 8. Variables and properties of a cylinder.

the cap is larger than the flow coming into the head (cylinder_flow_cap_I > cylinder_flow_head_I). Moreover, the flow must be present on the cap input (cylinder_flow_cap_I > cylinder_input_flow_min) and there has to be space for the piston to extend (cylinder_piston_position_O + *cylinder_rate* ≤ cylinder_head_pos). If these conditions are met, the piston extends with a rate equal to the difference between the input flows (Figure 9). The piston retracting is modelled in a corresponding manner.

Finally, if the flows are the same (cylinder_flow_head_I = cylinder_flow_cap_I) or there is no space for the piston to extend (cylinder_piston_position_O + cylinder_rate > cylinder_head_pos) nor to retract (cylinder_piston_position_O + cylinder_rate < cylinder_cap_pos), the piston keeps its position. In other words, the piston is stopped (Figure 10.). The complete formal model of a cylinder can be found in [9].

```
event cylinder_extending
  any cylinder_rate
  where
   cylinder_rate = cylinder_flow_cap_I – cylinder_flow_head_I ∧
   cylinder_mode = 1 ∧
   cylinder_flow_cap_I > cylinder_flow_head_I ∧
   cylinder_flow_cap_I > cylinder_input_flow_min ∧
   cylinder_piston_position_O + cylinder_rate ≤
                                          cylinder_head_pos
   then
    cylinder_mode := 0 || cylinder_piston_position_O :=
     cylinder_piston_position_O + cylinder_rate
 end
```

Figure 9. Forward motion of the piston (extend).

```
event cylinder_stop
  any cylinder_rate
  where
   cylinder_rate = cylinder_flow_cap_I–cylinder_flow_head_I ∧
   cylinder_mode = 1 ∧
   (cylinder_flow_head_I = cylinder_flow_cap_I ∨
    cylinder_piston_position_O + cylinder_rate >
     cylinder_head_pos ∨
    cylinder_piston_position_O + cylinder_rate <
     cylinder_cap_pos)
  then  cylinder_mode := 0
 end
```

Figure 10. Keep the position of the piston (stop).

IV. RIGOROUS DESIGN USING THE LIBRARY

Once the components are developed and added to the library, one can (re)use/instantiate them while designing a system. The idea behind rigorous design with the library is the use of the "drag-and-drop" approach. Specifically, the developer picks and instantiates the necessary components by providing specific values for the parameters, a component name and adds them to the system model (Figure 11).

A. Composition of decomposed machines

The components can be seen as sub-unit machines which can be composed via parallel composition (||) [11][13]. For example, the machines A and B are composed into the (system) machine A || B, where the variables, invariants and events of A and B are merged. Overlapping variable and event names are renamed before composition. Note that composition is associative and commutative, but it cannot be reversed.

A way of refining a system is to superpose a new feature on its existing model (specification). The existing model is left unchanged while new variables and events modifying them are added to the model. The superposed feature and the existing model can be seen as components that can be composed. All these components in form of features or existing models are here considered to form library components. In addition, the composed models can form new library components.

The library components to be composed are connected via a connector. A connector is represented as a shared variable of a system machine whose mission is to promote the value of the output from one component to the input of the other one. Figure 12 illustrates a generic composition of two machines Component_n and Component_m into a single system machine System_M. The system model embodies the parameters of the components, their interfaces (environment events) and the connections between them. The functional events of the components are stored in separate machines and are *included* in the system.

B. Composition of library components

To show the connectivity mechanism, we will use a part of the Landing Gear (LG) case study whose details and formal model are described in [14]. Here, we will only show the connectivity of the valve and cylinder components as

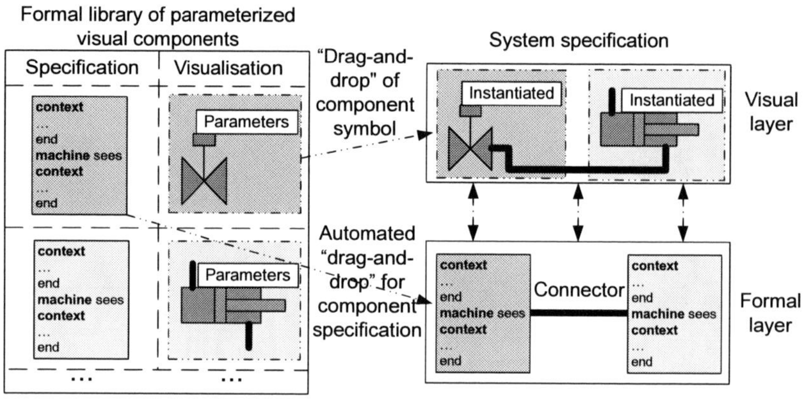

Figure 11. "Drag-and-drop" approach for visual system design in Event-B.

```
context SystemC
constants SYSTEM_CONTROL
  // Component n constants
  // Component m constants
axioms SYSTEM_CONTROL = {0,1,2}
  // Component n axioms
  // Component m axioms
end
machine System_M sees System_C
includes Component_n Component_m
variables Control connection_Comp_n_Comp_m
  // Shared variables of Component n
  // Shared variables of Component m
invariants Control ∈ SYSTEM_CONTROL ∧
  connection_Comp_n_Comp_m ∈ <COMPONENT_n_OUTPUT_TYPE>
  // Component n invariants
  // Component m invariants
variant max(SYSTEM_CONTROL) – Control
events
  event INITIALISATION extends INITIALISATION then
    Control := 0 || connection_Comp_n_Comp_m := <INIT_VALUE>
  end

  event Comp_n_environment refines Comp_n_environment
    where ... // Guards derived from component n
      ∧ Control = 0
    then ... // Actions derived from component n
      || Control := 1
  end

  convergent event system_connection_Component_i_Component_k
    where Control = 1 ∧ <Component_n_mode> = 0
      // Ensure that the component n has updated its outputs
    then Control := 2 ||
      connection_Comp_n_Comp_m:= <Comp_n_Out>
  end

  event Comp_m_environment refines Comp_m_environment
    where ... // Guards derived from the component m
      ∧ Control = 2
    then ... // Actions derived from the component m
      || Control := 0
  end
end
```

Figure 12. Composition of Component n and Component m machines.

visually depicted in Figure 11. More details about various components, connectivity mechanisms and refinement patterns, can be found in the technical reports [9][14].

The main purpose of the LG system is to extend the landing wheels (connected to the hydraulic cylinders) when an airplane is to be landed and to retract them during the flight. The extension/retraction of the cylinders is controlled by the valves. Thus, the valves are connected to the cylinders sequentially (see Figure 11, visual layer).

The formal layer of the visual representation of Figure 11 is shown in Figure 13 and Figure 14. The context machine contains the constants and axioms of the valve and the cylinder. The theorem supports the connectivity between the components. It shows that the output of the source component is compatible with the input of the target component. Generally, the maximum diameter of the valve output should be the same as the maximum input flow of the cylinder connected to it.

The system machine LG_System_M includes the library components valve (Valve_Behaviour) and cylinder (Cylinder_Behaviour) (see Figure 14). The connectivity between these components is represented by the variable connection_Valve_Cylinder_head. When the valve updates its

```
context LG_System_C
constants CONTROL_HEAD
  valve_0_flow_min valve_0_flow_max valve_0_CONTROL
  valve_0_rate cylinder_0_cap_pos cylinder_0_input_flow_min
  cylinder_0_input_flow_max cylinder_0_head_pos
axioms
  // valve_0
  valve_0_flow_min = 0 ∧ valve_0_flow_max = 10 ∧
  valve_0_CONTROL = {−1,0,1} ∧ valve_0_rate = valve_0_flow_max ∧
  // cylinder_0
  cylinder_0_input_flow_min = 0 ∧ cylinder_0_input_flow_max=10 ∧
  cylinder_0_cap_pos = 0 ∧ cylinder_0_head_pos ∈ ℕ1 ∧
  // system_1
  CONTROL_HEAD = {0,1,2}
  theorem // system_1
    cylinder_0_input_flow_max = valve_0_flow_max
end
```

Figure 13. The parameters of the LG system: a valve, a cylinder and system parameters.

output value (i.e., when its mode is 0), this value is then used to update the value of the connector (connection_valve_cylinder_head := valve_0_flow_O in **convergent event** Connection_Valve_Cylinder). This value is in turn used as the input to the cylinder (cylinder_0_flow_head_I := connection_valve_cylinder_head in **event** cylinder_0_environment). Hence, the overall scheme is as follows. First, the valve inputs are updated, so that the valve component can update its output. Then, the value of the connector is updated according to the valve output. Finally, the inputs of the cylinder are updated according to the value of the connector.

Several connectors can be added in one refinement step following the same pattern. The proof of the connectivity mechanism relies on the superposition refinement rule, where the machine of the composed system refines the machine of each component.

```
machine LG_System_M sees LG_System_C
includes  Valve_Behaviour  Cylinder_Behaviour
variables  Control_head  connection_valve_cylinder_head
  valve_0_control_I  valve_0_flow_I  valve_0_flow_O
  valve_0_mode  valve_0_position
  cylinder_0_piston_position_O  cylinder_0_flow_cap_I
  cylinder_0_flow_head_I  cylinder_0_mode
invariants
  ... // Valve_0 type definitions and main invariants
  ... // Cylinder_0 type definitions and main invariants
  control_head ∈ CONTROL_HEAD ∧
  connection_Valve_Cylinder_head ∈
   cylinder_0_input_flow_min .. cylinder_0_input_flow_max
variant  max(CONTROL_HEAD) - control_head

events
  ...
  event valve_0_environment refines valve_0_environment
   where
    mode = 0 ∧ control_head = 0
   then
    valve_0_mode := 1 || valve_0_control_I :∈ valve_0_CONTROL ||
    valve_0_flow_I := <INPUT> || control_head := 1
  end

  convergent event Connection_Valve_Cylinder
   where
    valve_0_mode = 0 ∧ control_head = 1
   then
    control_head := 2 ||
    connection_valve_cylinder_head := valve_0_flow_O
  end

  event cylinder_0_environment
   where
    cylinder_0_mode = 0 ∧ control_head = 2
   then
    cylinder_0_mode := 1 || cylinder_0_flow_cap_I := <NEW_VALUE>
   || cylinder_0_flow_head_I := connection_valve_cylinder_head
   || control_head := 2
  end
end
```

Figure 14. An instantiated valve connected with an instantiated cylinder.

V. RELATED WORK

BMotionStudio has been proposed as an approach to visual simulation of the Event-B models [15][16]. The idea behind BMotionStudio is that the designer creates a domain specific image and links it to the model using a "gluing" code written in JavaScript. The simulation is based on the ProB animator and model checker [17], so that whenever the model is executed the corresponding graphical element reacts is updated. The BMotionStudio tool also supports interaction with a user – the user can provide an input via visual elements instead of manipulating the model directly.

In contrast to the BMotionStudio approach, we aim for creating visual descriptions of models via a library of predefined components that have a formal, as well as a visual representation. The development of the specification is then a process of the instantiation of the necessary components and the connection of them into a system. That is, the developer does not need to redraw the graphical representation of the components, but simply to reuse them. Eventually, the designer obtains a graphical representation of the system whereas its specification is in fact written in Event-B and supported by correctness proofs. Certainly, our approach can be complemented by BMotionStudio in order to obtain visualisation of the model execution.

Snook and Butler [18] proposed an approach to merge visual UML [19] with B [20]. The latter is supposed to give a formal precise semantics to the former at the same time as the former is aimed at reducing the effort in training to overcome the mathematical barrier. This approach has then been extended to Event-B and is called iUML-B [21]. The authors define semantics of UML by translating it to Event-B. The use of the UML-B profile provides specialisation of UML entities to support refinement. The authors also present tools that generate an Event-B model from UML.

A component based reuse methodology for Event-B was presented by Edmunds et al. [22], where the composition is based on the shared events principle. Their idea is to have a library of Event-B components where the component instances and the relationships between them are represented diagrammatically using an approach based on iUML-B.

Instead of using UML as a visualisation tool as in both the above cases, we aim to create a formal library of parameterised components, each of which has its own graphical representation. The system specification is then a visual model that represents a composition of the instantiated versions of these components. Nevertheless, we target automated generation of the necessary data structures and Event-B elements whenever our approach is applied.

An approach to a component-based formal design within Event-B has been proposed by Ostroumov, Tsiopoulos, Plosila and Sere [23]. The aim of this work is the generation of a structural VHDL [24] description from a formal Event-B model. The authors present a one-to-one mapping between formal functions defined in an Event-B context and VHDL library components. The authors rely on an additional refinement step where regular operations are replaced with function calls. This allows for automated generation of structural VHDL descriptions.

Instead of focusing on code generation, we propose an approach to systems development in Event-B in a visual manner. This approach is not limited to VHDL descriptions and allows the designers to utilize various components from different application domains. Our goal is to create a formal library of parameterized Event-B specifications that capture the generic behaviour of these components. Our approach is to facilitate component reuse, where the developers can specify systems in a "drag-and-drop" manner.

VI. CONCLUSION AND FUTURE WORK

We have proposed an approach to the development of rigorous components augmented with unique graphical symbols. It is based on the pattern that allows seamless integration of components into a system. We have illustrated the proposed approach using components from the digital hydraulics domain, where each component has been formally developed and proved correct within Event-B. The components constitute the library, which captures the graphical representations, formal specifications and a one-to-one relation between them. The library enables components reuse and instantiation in various applications depending on the requirements. In addition, visual design structures the specifications and facilitates scalability of the rigorous development. Moreover, it is useful in the communication between developer and customer. This will need an evaluation via empirical studies comparing our approach to the traditional formal development. We believe that the proposed approach is applicable to other than Event-B formalisms as well considering their syntactical specifics.

The components connectivity outlined in this paper is an important element of systems development. We are currently extending this mechanism considering various types of connections and stepwise refinement. Moreover, the tool support is one of the key factors for facilitating an easy access to the proposed approach. Thus, our future work also includes providing the tool support, which will include an interface to "drag-and-drop" components, maintenance and extension of the library, as well as automated application of the connectivity patterns through instantiation in order to derive a composed system. The proofs will be conducted via the tool support for Event-B.

ACKNOWLEDGMENT

The authors would like to thank Dr. Marta Olszewska and Dr. Andrew Edmunds for the fruitful discussions. The work was done within the project ADVICeS funded by the Academy of Finland, grant No. 266373.

REFERENCES

[1] J.-R. Abrial, Modeling in Event-B: System and Software Engineering, Cambridge: Cambridge University Press, 2010.

[2] R. J. Back and J. Wright, Refinement Calculus: A Systematic Introduction, New York: Springer-Verlag, 1998.

[3] RODIN IDE. [Online]. Available from: http://sourceforge.net/projects/rodin-b-sharp/, February 2017.

[4] R. Banacha, M. Butler, S. Qinc, N. Vermad, and H. Zhue, "Core Hybrid Event-B I: Single Hybrid Event-B machines", Science of Computer Programming, vol. 105, Elsivier, pp. 92-123, 2015.

[5] C. Métayer, J.-R. Abrial, and L. Voisin, Event B language, vol. 3.2, RODIN Deliverables. [Online]. Available from: http://rodin.cs.ncl.ac.uk/deliverables/D7.pdf, May 2005.

[6] K. Robinson, System Modelling & Designing using Event-B. [Online]. Available from: http://wiki.event-b.org/images/SM%26D-KAR.pdf, October 2010.

[7] A. van Deursen, P. Klint, and J. Visser, "Domain-specific languages: An annotated bibliography", vol. 35(6), SIGPLAN Notices, pp. 26–36, 2000.

[8] P. Boström, Formal Verification and Design of Systems using Domain Specific Languages, TUCS Dissertations 110, 2008.

[9] S. Ostroumov and M. Waldén, Formal Library of Visual Components, TUCS TR, vol. 1147. [Online]. Available: http://tucs.fi/publications/view/?pub_id=tOsWa15a, May 2015.

[10] M. Butler, E. Sekerinski, and K. Sere, "An Action System Approach to the Steam Boiler Problem", Formal Methods For Industrial Applications, vol. 1165, LNCS: Springer-Verlag, pp. 129-148, 1996.

[11] J.-R. Abrial, Event Model Decomposition, ETH Zurich TR, vol. 626. [Online]. Available from: http://wiki.event-b.org/images/Event_Model_Decomposition-1.3.pdf, April 2009.

[12] T. S. Hoang, A. Iliasov, R. A. Silva, and W. Wei, "A Survey on Event-B Decomposition", Workshop on Automated Verification of Critical Systems, vol. 46, Electonic Communication of the EASST, pp. 1-15, 2011.

[13] R. J. Back, "Refinement calculus, part II: Parallel and reactive programs", Stepwise Refinement of Distributed Systems: Models, Formalisms, Correctness, vol. 430, LNCS: Springer-Verlag, pp. 67–93, 1990.

[14] S. Ostroumov and M. Waldén, Facilitating Formal Event-B Development by Visual Component-based Design, TUCS TR, vol. 1148. [Online]. Available from: http://tucs.fi/publications/view/?pub_id=tOsWa15b, September 2015.

[15] L. Ladenberger, J. Bendisposto, and M. Leuschel, "Visualising Event-B Models with B-Motion Studio", Workshop on Formal Methods for Industrial Critical Systems, vol. 5825, LNCS: Springer-Verlag, pp. 202-204, 2009.

[16] BMotion Studio for ProB Handbook. [Online]. Available from: https://www3.hhu.de/stups/handbook/bmotion/current/html/index.html, April 2015.

[17] M. Leuschel and M. Butler, "ProB: A Model Checker for B", Symposium of Formal Methods Europe, vol. 2805, LNCS: Springer-Verlag, pp. 855-874, 2003.

[18] C. Snook and M. Butler, "UML-B: Formal Modeling and Design Aided by UML", ACM Transactions on Software Engineering and Methodology, Vol. 15(1), pp. 92–122, 2006.

[19] G. Booch, I. Jacobson, and J. Rumbaugh, Unified modeling language Reference Manual, The (2nd edition), USA: Pearson Higher Education, 2004.

[20] S. Schneider, The B-method: An Introduction, Basingstoke: Palgrave, 2001.

[21] C. Snook and M. Butler, "UML-B and Event-B: an integration of languages and tools", IASTED Conference on Software Engineering, pp. 12-17, 2008.

[22] A. Edmunds, C. Snook, and M. Walden, "On Component-Based Reuse for Event-B", ABZ Conference on ASM, Alloy, B, TLA, VDM, and Z, vol. 9675, LNCS: Springer-Verlag, pp. 151-166, 2016.

[23] S. Ostroumov, L. Tsiopoulos, J. Plosila, and K. Sere, "Generation of Structural VHDL Code with Library Components From Formal Event-B Models", DSD Euromicro Conference, IEEE, pp. 111-118, 2013.

[24] IEEE Standard: VHDL Language Reference Manual, IEEE 1076, 2008.

Analysing the Need for Training in Program Design Patterns

An empirical exploration of two social worlds

Viggo Holmstedt
University College of South-East Norway
School of Business, Department of Business and IT
Horten, Norway
email: vh@usn.no

Shegaw A. Mengiste
University College of South-East Norway
School of Business, Department of Business and IT
Horten, Norway
email: sme@usn.no

Abstract- **This paper addresses the implications of design patterns knowledge in the social worlds of practitioners and managers from the context of Norwegian software companies. Although there are diverse perspectives on the role and importance of design patterns for object-oriented systems, many academic institutions believe in their relevance, particularly in improving software quality through reusable design. However, when invoking the topic of the relevance of Design Patterns (DP) in a software development process, the engagement varies from no interest to enthusiasm. It was this diverse perspective on the relevance of design patterns that drive us to explore this topic. The paper analyzed practitioners and managers perspectives and our findings revealed a convincing evidence for practitioners' confidence in pattern knowledge and its positive influence on their coding abilities. Our findings are relevant to software design and production, as it addresses methodological issues in software development.**

Keywords-design patterns; object oriented system;practitioner; perspective; manager.

I. INTRODUCTION

The success rate of global systems development was 29% in the year 2015 [41]. Such low rate of success indicates that systems development is a complex process and needs to be addressed with proper planning and guiding. In systems development, earlier design decisions can have a significant impact on software quality; they can also be the most costly to revoke [1]. Design Patterns (hereafter DP, used in plural form) constitute an important tool for improving software quality by providing reusable solutions for recurring design problems.

Design patterns are best practices of specifying and allocating responsibilities to program elements, like classes, packages and components. DP also support the construction of mechanisms based on patterns of class cooperation. Industrial usage and success over a long time typically establishes and confirms a specific design pattern, accepted as a guide to construct mechanisms in complicated systems development contexts.

As Shlezinger et al. [2] indicated, design patterns have over the years provided solutions to design problems with the goal of assuring reusable and maintainable solutions. As a result, DP now exist for a wide range of software development topics, from process patterns to code pattern at various levels of abstraction to maintenance patterns [3]. In the context of object-oriented programming, design patterns are used as building blocks of the architecture and to allow change to evolve in a way that prevents an erosion of the software design [4]. From a software implementation perspective, the value of a design pattern comes from the codification of its specification [5-6]. Regarding usage of DP, Subburaj [13] described the importance of aspects of searching, finding and applying specific patterns, and also convey how an incorrectly applied pattern poses disadvantages.

DP also transfer industrial experience about performing creation and allocating behavior to the internals of classes [7]. Separation of concerns, as between data, logic and presentation, is a success condition in almost all types of systems development [8-11]. Naming is an important characteristic of DP, enabling precise communication and query based search [12]. DP must be constructed and instantiated by developers with experience and ability to realize abstractions with success, including creating and customizing the DP instances.

In terms of usability of DP, a research conducted by Manolescu [14] also indicates that only half of the developers and architects in a software organization tend to use design patterns. The cost of finding and proving the right pattern for a specific mechanism can simply be too high. Despite the fact that there are successful and durable industrial experiences in using DP, as Subburaj [13] clearly noted, DP could be applied in wrong instances and contexts. This alone is a good reason to discuss possible impacts of DP [15], and the importance of training DP skills and knowledge.

Subburaj (ibid) refers to Rising [16], for a debate on formal DP training. Much work is done to construct and establish searchable libraries of DP, reducing the need for formal training. But, pattern catalogs have become too abstract to use for untrained practitioners. We assume that the formal training of classical DP and GRASP (General Responsibility Assignment Software Patterns), which is a methodological approach to learning basic object design [5], would give the practitioner necessary background to assess new in-house patterns, utilize pattern catalogs and correctly instantiate patterns from the practitioner's own knowledge base whenever needed. Formal training would reduce the impact of the abstraction level of pattern catalogs. The debate on the merits of formal training is minimal, and, in this paper, we would like to contribute to this research void.

To meet the huge challenges reported on the usability of DP in practice, academic institutions like our own are offering courses in DP for Object Oriented Systems. Campus students are often impressed by the relevance DP have to their system problems and solutions. Out of campus, we sometimes initiate informal talks with IT directors, developers, managers and other industry practitioners. When invoking the topic of the relevance of DP in a software development process, the engagement varies from no interest to enthusiasm. These informally observed opposites gave us motivation to explore what our own DP students have experienced after leaving school, and after having practiced for a while. We also approached IT employers and other relevant stakeholders without formal training on DP, to have their perception of the importance and relevance of trained DP developers in their respective companies. We acknowledge that many other researchers have investigated the power of DP training to improve the software produced under pattern rules. We appreciate the works of Khomh [15] and Wydaeghe [17] who study and evaluate DP quality attributes. The bottom-line for our investigation is to assess the value or relevance of DP to help software developers to produce better software by guiding them in code production. This will help in assessing the different perspectives on the relevance of running courses in DP, particularly in terms of the experience and minds of the social worlds of practitioners (software developers) and their employers (IT managers and other staff members). To address this research problem, we formulated the following research questions:

Q1: How, when and why do DP trained practitioners perceive relevance of DP knowledge?

Q2: How mutual is practitioners' and managers' understanding of the relevance of DP?

It is our conviction that by answering these research questions, we can contribute to the ongoing research debate between research of DP as a tool to improve software versus DP as a tool to improve thinking and the quality of the practitioner.

The paper is organized as follows: Section II provides an overview of the theoretical framework; and section III presents the research approach and methods, while section IV presents the findings. The last section presents analysis, discussion, and concluding remarks.

II. CONCEPTUAL FRAMEWORK : THE SOCIAL WORLDS FRAMEWORK

The social worlds framework is an analytical framework that has been used in many Science and Technology Studies (STS) [19], and has its roots in the American sociological tradition of symbolic interactionism. The framework focuses on meaning-making among groups of actors- collectives of various sorts – and on collective action – people doing things together and working with shared objects [19]. Strauss [19] citing Shibutani [20] noted that each social world is an arena in which there is some kind of organization; and each social world is a cultural area, where its boundaries are set neither by territory or formal membership but only by the limits of effective communication. The social worlds perspective, as such, conceptualizes organizations "...as being mutually constituted and constituting the systemic order of organizational actions and interactions kept together by individuals and groups commitment to organizational life and work [22]. The notion of groups in this description involves all collective actors (be it a formal organization or group of people) committed to act and interact within the specific social world [23]. In the social world, various issues are debated, negotiated, fought out, forced and manipulated by representatives of the participating social worlds [20].

Huysman & Elkjær [23] argued that organizations could be viewed as arenas where members of different social worlds take different positions, seek different ends, engage in contest and make or break alliances in order to do things they wish to do (ibid, p.8). Over time, social worlds typically segment into multiple worlds (sub-worlds), intersect with other worlds with which they share substantive/topical interests and commitments, and merge [19].

The social worlds perspective has also introduced the notion of agency as well as tension and conflict as triggers for learning among actors in different social worlds [23][25]. Agency is used to denote "various organizational actions and learning and how these are enacted by different kinds of agencies" [23]. Tension and conflict are results of different commitments to different interests, practices and values.

In the context of the study, we adopted the social world perspective as our theoretical framework. We identified two important social worlds: the social world of software developers (practitioners), and the social world of managers (practitioners' superiors). The agencies of both worlds are the production of software, including the learning of best practices to enhance the return on investments.

III. RESEARCH APPROACH AND METHODS

A. Research Approach

Our research approach is informed by the priciples of engaged scholarship which advocates a participative form of research to get the perspectives of key stakeholders to understand a complex social problem [25]. One of the main forms of the engaged scholarship research approach is the informed basic research. In this form of research, the researcher acts as a detached outsider of the social system being examined, but solicits advice and feedback from key stakeholders [25][26]. We adopted the informed basic research mainly as our role is detached outsiders, but also we wanted some of our informants in formulating the questionnaire. We already have prepared some grounding by educating a little more than half of the informants through the years 2000 to 2015. Having run DP courses those years, we trusted the benefits to be solid. However, in the research context, that would be like a research lab generated bias, as opposed to the Van de Ven's interactional view. In his view, both the professional and research practices contribute to their common growth of knowledge.

B. Data Collection Methods

We collected data from 28 informants (20 practitioners and 8 IT managers). Both groups contain former students and external contacts. The reason for having some of the former students in the managers' stakeholder group was to assure that most respondents should have at least some knowledge of DP. Van de Ven raises the important question "... why organizational professionals and executives want to participate in informed basic research" [26]. We held this question as an important factor in selecting our respondents. As such we approached only managers with some knowledge of DP, to ascertain their motivation to take part in our investigation.

Our second group of respondents is composed of former students who are now working as system developers in organizations in Norway. Getting the contact information was a challenge since our institution lacks a mechanism to trace former students. So, we relied on technologies like LinkedIn, acquaintances, and a data tool constructed for the purpose. We located about 110 of our former students from courses on DP. We also got a list of about 60 externally collected contacts. Then we used the list and managed to talk to nine of them by phone or face to face, to ascertain that our topic of investigation was relevant to them. During the conversations, we discussed the design of our questionnaire and our chances for having the actual interlocutor as respondent. Those nine helped us in preparing the questionnaires, by giving different comments and sharing their insights.

NVivo [42] is a tool for qualitative research that is specialized for coding and analyzing and for finding trends and interesting opinions. In preparing the questionnaire, we emphasized that all questionnaire items are open to any formulation. This is possible, because the NVivo tool lets us code and analyze the respondents' contributions independent of prior organizing. We let each respondent know that we wanted to learn how, when and why knowledge of design patterns had any importance on his/her professional life after the end of training. We also used each respondent as a possible source of contact information to relevant managers that might have opinions on the relevance of DP.

Finally, we distributed the questionnaire to 170 potential respondents, both managers and practitioners. Out of the 170 emails we sent, we received a total of 28 answered questionnaires that have been analyzed and used in this paper.

The data we got from the 28 respondents has been analyzed using NVivo. As NVivo has huge possibilities for automatic and semi-automatic text analyses, the tool labeled each answer with a code in the place of the full text instruction. The existence of tools for programming the docx format to filter out relevant content from complex structures, available for several programming languages, made this content transformation possible. The transferring of informant documents alleviated the NVivo analysis activities a lot. The filtering of questionnaire content also raised the analysis quality by assuring the non-existence of irrelevant text in the sources.

IV. FINDINGS

In this section, we present our findings. As our focus was to know the perspectives and views of the two social worlds (practitioners and managers) on the relevance and value of design patters in work settings, we present our findings accordingly for the two social worlds. Then, we make a comparison of our findings in the two stakeholder groups.

A. Relevance of DP from the practitioner's perspective

An important occasion for many people in their professional career is the job interview. Therefore, we asked our respondents to comment on what they really think about the relevance of DP knowledge when they apply for a new job in the IT industry. The typical response we received was that: "I hope and believe that it is mandatory to have a good knowledge of Software Design Patterns (SDP). I think SDP is one of the most important aspects of programming." An interesting finding was the distinction between junior and senior developers that reads as follows. "If you apply for a junior position it might not be that relevant because they wouldn't expect you to have knowledge about design patterns, but if you apply for a medium/senior development position it is very relevant." This evidence relies to a discussion concerning introductory training in DP. Some respondents also indicated that Knowledge of DP did not have quite a lot to say when they got their current job.

When we looked for the informants' general perception of DP, we found good evidence for positive perceptions like: "Whenever I need to work on new features / product development, I use design patterns". We also found typical evidence like "it helps with code structure". An interesting finding from respondents free comments is that: "if I have used a common SDP, it might have been easy to understand what I have coded", and "Also DP makes it easier for my colleagues to understand". More evidence for relevance is "I mostly use patterns to communicate intent behind non-trivial code structures."

We wanted to test the evidence material for any sign of enthusiasm, which we interpret as more than just a notion of relevance. We found formulations that we think conveys enthusiasm: "SDP had a big role in my evolution with object oriented programming", and one referring to training: "It has been a great year for me - From finishing school to this point in time I've become a much better coder and problem solver."

Some of the expressions from our respondents on the use of DP show us when and why DP is being used in work settings:

Practitioner 1: *"Yes, weekly, to solve problems."*

Practitioner 2: "Yes. I used it every day. The main purpose is to be able to understand the code faster and easier if it needs to be changed later on."

Practitioner 3: "Daily. ... . We use it in our own development, but it is also essential to understand different design patterns when debugging other developers code efficiently."

One informant also specify two relevant situations: "Yes, first under the design phase of the project and then in the implementation phase."

Much of the evidence refers to daily use: "Everyday, solving problems or reading code in an architectural way to find or create solutions at the right places keeping the code maintainable." There is also evidence in the context of how often, that add concern of code quality: "Most of the time, usually to handle complex situations that would otherwise result in spaghetti code".

As our findings reveal, most of the practitioners believe that DP usage and knowledge improve their code. Our findings also confirm that the improvement is in fact a distinct purpose for using DP as some of the practitioners use DP in order to improve the way they write the code so that to make it as clear and logical as possible.

Our findings also revealed the relevance of DP as a communication agent. As one of the informants indicated: "The software design patterns knowledge will give some help in having meaningful discussions with partners". DP is relevant as a knowledge framework in some situations, helping participants from both different and same social worlds discuss and elaborate solutions.

We specifically asked for informants' perception of the DP influence on time balance in projects. A typical answer for this group is "projects may take a longer time to finish. But it is usually worth it and may save time later." We summarized our findings in the following table (Table 1).

TABLE I. SUMMARY OF PRACTITIONERS' PERCEPTIONS.

Question	Practitioners' perception
How	• has a big role in practitioner's evolution • is a very important aspect of programming • studying DP has been great • makes much better coders and problem solvers • allows for architectural perspective • keeps code maintainable • is timesaver in the longer run • is a knowledge framework
When	• weekly • daily • needing to change existing code • debugging • applying for a job • applying for medium/senior development position • starting new features and product development
Why	• helps with code structure • easy to understand what is coded • communicate intent behind non-trivial code • solve problems • understand others code quickly • long term code maintainability • using DP is doing it right

B. Relevance of DP from Managers' perspective

It was important to have informant practitioners with sufficient knowledge of DP to make the questionnaire relevant. The relevance is for managers to have a stake in development. Again, the communication between management and practitioner profits on a mutual understanding of tools and methodologies. Relevant to this concern is evidence like "I think the application of design patterns are very useful for designing faster and more structured applications". More directly targeted at a mutual understanding between practitioners and managers is the following evidence: "Use SDP to increase effectivity in their daily work and to reuse code or methodology from project to project. "

Evidence also displays the relevance of new hires knowledge of DP as follows: "I think very much. It would help keep the number of code lines down overhaul in an application and in the long run perhaps save money".

Managers believe in the positive influence of DP on code improvement:

Manager 1: "Yes, absolutely."

Manager 2: "Yes, because for other people with the same design pattern knowledge, will make it much easier to understand and thereby perhaps much easier to improve upon later".

Manager 2 also confirms the communication and mutual understanding aspects of using DP as follows:

"The software design patterns knowledge will give some help in having meaningful discussions with partners". We also found an interesting reflection in "it makes me aware of need for pattern creation to create re-usability and standardization."

Interestingly we found more strong evidence of positive management perceptions of DP. Manger 3 stated the following:

"I want all employers to be as effective as possible, and in this regard use SDP."

Another informant (manager 4) formulated his perception even stronger: "Extremely important". In our material, the positive perception of DP has strong prevalence before any other alternative.

Managers' concern for DP knowledge and new hires are expressed in attitudes like:

"My understanding is that this influence them",

"I imagine it does make them more effective.", and

"This has not been on my criteria list (until now)."

The statement "Very relevant, most employers look for design patterns knowledge" represents the most prominent perception among managers. We also found variants of that statement, like "have a positive attitude to design patterns" and "In the current company it is high interest and positivity for it." Some informants thought company size decides level of interest, and stated accordingly: "In bigger companies where you have 100++ employees there is an interest and maintenance of this at a manager level."

A manager focus relevance like this: "It helps seeing pitfalls that has to be handled in the project." Our findings regarding managers' preceptions towards the relevance of DP are presented in the following table (Table 2).

TABLE II. SUMMARY OF MANAGERS' PERCEPTIONS

Question	Managers' Perception
How	• designing faster and more structured applications • opens for meaningful discussions • better communication between developers • positive outlook on SDP • reuse code or methodology • seeing pitfalls
When	• employing new hires • manager is reminded • daily work
Why	• makes hires more effective • code improvement • keeps the number of code lines down • perhaps saves money • has lower maintenance requirement • makes it easier to improve production software later • increases effectivity • create re-usability and standardization

V. ANALYSIS AND DISCUSSION

This section contains analysis of our findings and how they contribute to answering the research questions we set in the introduction. Our findings pointed out that the social world of IT managers have a mixed interest and knowledge about DP and its relevance towards enhancing software development practices. Our findings also demonstrated that the social world of practitioners had a more common interest towards DP with better engagement and knowledge; and even with good understanding of the positive influence of DP usage.

In our research, we wanted to find out how, when and why DP had relevance to practitioners. We constructed a questionnaire that aimed to reveal if DP had any relevance or not in work settings. As highlighted in our findings, most of the practitioners answered positively on the relevance of knowledge in DP to software development. There was only one feeble evidence on the irrelevance of DP among practitioners.

So, in the following subsections, we analyze and discuss our findings around the two research questions we set in the introduction.

A. How, when and why do DP trained practitioners perceive relevance of DP knowledge

We find that the study of DP has been a great personal satisfaction for some of the informants. They also generally think DP give important aspects of programming activities in themselves. DP infer better coding, keep the code maintainable and even give coders a view into architectural considerations. DP also affects problem-solving abilities, and is a timesaver in the long run. The timesaving aspect is especially important in terms of system change claims, which also answers the "when" question. Using DP also creates a knowledge framework to be used for the facilitation of communication between stakeholders. It can even be used to enhance program understanding through pattern reverse-engineering [40].

The reasons for DP's relevance to practitioners are close to the answers for "how" and "when". The understandability is important in multiple directions, that is when coders shall understand other's code, when other shall understand "my code", and even when the coder shall understand his own code. This aspect is also tied to intentions behind code that are difficult to understand without the DP references. The "why" aspect also reveals practitioner responsibility for future needs, as using DP is considered doing the right thing. The same responsibility is even deeper, as it emphasizes positive effect on long term maintainability. Practitioners who have concerns for long term effects of their work, do actually share managers perspectives and interests like return on investment (ROI), e.g. interest of ROI.

Based on our evidence, we assume that knowledge and use of DP is so advanced, that it infers a reinforced perception of ownership to the work. Even more interesting is whether advanced knowledge improves productivity through enhanced self-esteem, as some of our evidence indicated. Judge and Bono [28] pointed out the relevance of self-esteem for job satisfaction and performance. Pierce and Gardner [29] delve deep into these questions in their review of organization-based self-esteem literature. It is much more difficult to find literature on DP knowledge affecting self-esteem and practitioner productivity.

B. *How mutual is practitioners' and managers' understanding of the relevance of DP?*

The DP literature argues on the importance of IT managers to have insights, reasoning, and techniques to promote and implement design patterns in order to gain operational efficiency and provide strategic benefit for their IT organization. Learning and organizing DP provide an important step [31]. Fowler also state that developers should adapt design patterns to their own environment, and that implementing a pattern for a particular purpose is one of the best ways to learn about it. Cline [31] noted, as design patterns capture distilled experience, they could be used as a tool to improve communication between software developers and other stakeholders, including less experienced developers and managers. Moudam et al. [12] also referred to DP as a communication agent.

Our findings actually highlighted DP as a communication tool to facilitate the interaction between the social worlds of managers and practitioners. The social worlds of managers and practitioners are different, but importantly influenced by the limits of effective mutual communication. Generally, the communication between management and practitioners profits on a mutual understanding of tools and methodology. The hierarchical positions of each member makes the mutual understanding of methods and tools a critical factor. We wanted to gather evidence of the practitioner's perception of the management's and industry's general understanding and attitudes towards DP. Since managers have the model power [33, 34], their knowledge of DP is critical to the practitioners' access to DP and in creating mutual understanding between the two worlds. DP can create mutual understanding by providing a standard vocabulary among practitioners and managers. Under such circumstances, we assume that practitioners who want to use DP will suffer from a weak mutuality of DP understanding and interest.

Even more problematic are the possibilities of misunderstandings and errors induced by different understanding. Literature on this topic for other disciplines exists for example in Hantho et al. [33]. Much closer to our research is Margaret [34] who reports a study of the communication between systems analysts and clients to create requirements. Marne [35] actually construct a DP library as a communication tool. We differ from this by focusing the importance of communication between practitioners and their superiors. DP is by evidence depicted as a tool of communication between individuals of both our social worlds.

We have evidence that most managers have little knowledge of DP, but still express considerable confidence in their employees' usage of them. Managers naturally possess an economical mind-set. The practitioners' more technical mind-set actually has some commonalities with their superiors, which support the mutual understanding between the two social worlds. We found evidence of practitioners' concern for ROI, and also manager's concern for building faster applications more effectively. This is evidence of mutual interests, which is likely to infer a shared interest of communication.

Some managers appreciate relevance of DP based on their assumptions of faster and more structured applications, terms applied to faster designing and development, rather than meaning the application run faster. Still, the interesting part is that the evidence implies an interest for the practitioner's concerns. Besides a general positive appreciation of DP, managers also believe in reuse, enhanced communication between stakeholders in the software process. There is also evidence that managers find DP useful in detecting architectural and technical pitfalls.

There is convincing evidence of mutual understanding between our two social worlds. Even if the mind-sets and perspectives are different, we claim that the reasons mostly fall under the practitioners' concerns as well. DP increases effectivity, and more specifically makes hires more effective. The code improvement, as in lowered number of code lines, is in both stakeholder group's interest. Lower maintenance requirements and easier software improvement are also a concern of practitioners. Reusability is of course also in the practical interest of the coder, while standardization is a general interest of the growing software community that embrace open source solutions. Coherence in DP perceptions between the two social worlds, as well as self-confidence based on knowledge, likely enhance productivity in both social worlds.

Despite the fact that the DP community has been successful in promoting good software engineering practices [37], adoption rates are still low for IT organizations due to lack of discovery and limited education around how to apply design patterns to specific domain contexts [14]. This low adoption rate attributed to the fact that finding DP relevant to a particular problem isn't trivial [14]. This challenge is, in part, due to the nature of how patterns often match a problem domain and each domain needs a distinct approach [37].

When Khom et al. [15] considered criticism to DP; they discussed three GoF [7] examples. Patterns like Flyweight can be a topic of internal discussion, and thus act as social glue among participants. Classical patterns are important not only to infer high software quality, but also to let developers feel at home and find their way in complicated code. Confident and pattern-aware programmers can influence software quality positively, if they are comfortable with the specific pattern instance in use. If the developer finds that a pattern actually decreases the understanding of a software area, it might be because the wrong pattern is used, or that the pattern infers abstractions that decreases both learnability, understandability and the simplicity of debugging. Such abstractions may even amount to emotional resistance [38]. The quality of discussions is better when it is grounded in well-known DP topics, awakening the feel-good of being "at home", even at work. We would like to promote formal instruction and common knowledge of DP as a social glue between individuals from both the social worlds of practitioners and managers. We would also like to see the construction of meet-up arrangements for the discussion of DP, in order to strengthen the communication attributes of the topic.

Khom et al. [15] states "we consider reusability as the reusability of the piece of code in which a pattern is implemented". We oppose this, and stated earlier that DP must be constructed and instantiated on site. We find it important to apply the reusability term to the pattern and not the pattern instance code. A target for a specific pattern usage is to improve understandability. A misplaced or miscoded pattern might be the cause of reducing understandability. Internalized pattern knowledge can lead to creative solutions, as opposed to solutions searched by catalogue. The catalogue solutions have to be tested and found usable for the specific problem, and are often only partially understood. We therefore promote formal instruction of DP to internalize a small set of pattern repertoire in the minds of the social worlds' individuals.

VI. CONCLUSION

In this paper, we empirically assessed whether or not knowledge of DP is relevant for managers and practitioners in software development companies. Our findings revealed that there are differences between the social worlds of managers and practitioners in how they perceive DP as a vehicle to enhance performance of development teams. Practitioners expressed high level of relevance for the knowledge of DP, while managers put a lower level of relevance to DP. However, our findings also revealed that both social worlds believed in DP's ability to act as a communication tool, and that the quality of mutuality in DP perceptions between the two social worlds is good.

Several works focus on measurable characteristics by inspecting collections of code. Hegedus et. al. [39] inspect the quantitative grounding for evaluating the effect of DP on software maintainability. In contrast, we wanted to investigate the effect on human thinking and courage in software building. Meaningful naming of components, like classes, fields and enum type items, is an example of less measurable code characteristics that still may have huge effect on software maintainability, because of its ability to guide human understanding.

We do not focus DP's characteristics as a direct software improving tool, but indirect as a human helper. DP help humans think, and thereby help humans improve design and program code. Tahvildari et al. [40] focus on their own classification schemas to help designers understand relationships between patterns, but do not connect DP directly to the assistance to think, or to the user's attitudes towards DP. Even if the correct usage of DP reduces risk, the adoption rates are still low. Manolescu [14] claimed low discovery and education to be important factors, which makes it interesting to investigate the present attitudes of employers and former students of DP, and detect any importance for their professional life. If practitioners' knowledge and usage of DP enhance them as coders, it is of great significance when their managers find positive relevance in their usage of DP. The practitioners will feel support and encouragement to continue their good work.

Measuring attributes of software created with patterns would oversee all the varying ways of instantiation, all the varying machine and OS variants and escape future changes in OS/machine dependencies. We therefore and alternatively suggest the discussion of practitioners' self-confidence and its effect on productivity, a coherence that can prove to be more future-proof, being grounded in the human nature.

REFERENCES

[1] E. Folmer. and J. Bosch "A pattern framework for software quality assessment and tradeoff analysis." International Journal of Software Engineering and Knowledge Engineering, Vol.17, no. 04, pp.515-538, 2007.

[2] G. Shlezinger, I. Reinhartz-Berger, and D. Dori. "Modeling design patterns for semi-automatic reuse in system design. Cross-Disciplinary Models and Applications of Database Management: Advancing Approaches." Advancing Approaches, pp.29, 2011.

[3] S. Henninger. and V. Corrêa. "Software pattern communities: Current practices and challenges." In Proceedings of the 14th Conference on Pattern Languages of Programs, ACM,, 2007.

[4] D. J. Ram and M.S. Rajasree. "Enabling Design Evolution in Software through Pattern Oriented Approach, in Object-Oriented Information Systems" In Proceedings of 9th INternational Conference, OOIS 2003, Geneva, Switzerland, PP. 179- 190, September 2003.

[5] C. Larman. Applying UML and patterns: an introduction to object-oriented analysis and design and iterative development. 2005: Pearson Education India.

[6] L. Ackerman and C. Gonzalez. "The value of pattern implementations." DR DOBBS JOURNAL, Vol. 23, no. 6, pp. 28-34, 2007.

[7] J. Vlissides, et al. "Design patterns: Elements of reusable object-oriented software." Reading: Addison-Wesley, Vol. 49, no. 120, pp. 11, 1995..

[8] P. Tarret al. «N degrees of separation: multi-dimensional separation of concerns." In Proceedings of the 21st international conference on Software engineering. 1999. ACM.

[9] V. Kulkarni and S. Reddy "Separation of concerns in model-driven development." IEEE software, Vol. 20, no. 5. Pp. 64- 69, 2003.

[10] M. Aksit, B. Tekinerdogan, and L. Bergmans. Achieving adaptability through separation and composition of concerns. 1997.

[11] T. Mens and M. Wermelinger "Separation of concerns for software evolution." Journal of software maintenance and evolution: research and practice, vol. 14, no. 5, pp. 311-315, 2002.

[12] Z. Moudam and N. Chenfour "Design Pattern Support System: Help Making Decision in the Choice of Appropriate Pattern." Procedia Technology, Vol. 4, pp. 355-359, 2012.

[13] R. Subburaj, G. Jekese, and C. Hwata "Impact of Object Oriented Design Patterns on Software Development." International Journal of Scientific & Engineering Research, vol. 6, no. 2, pp. 961-967, 2015.

[14] D. Manolescu et al. "The growing divide in the patterns world." Software, IEEE, vol. 24, no. 4. Pp. 61-67, 2007.

[15] F. Khomh and Y. G. Guéhéneuc. "Do design patterns impact software quality positively?" In Software Maintenance and Reengineering, 2008. CSMR 2008. 12th European Conference on. 2008. IEEE.

[16] L. Rising. "The Benefit of Patterns." IEEE software, vol. 27, no. 5, pp. 15-17, 2010.

[17] B. Wydaeghe et al. «Building an OMT-editor using design patterns: An experience report." In Technology of Object-Oriented Languages, 1998. TOOLS 26. Proceedings. 1998. IEEE.

[18] A. E. Clarke. and S.L. Star "The social worlds framework: A theory/methods package." The Handbook of Science & Technology Studies, vol. 3, pp. 113-137, 2008.

[19] A. L. Strauss. Scientists and the evolution of policy arenas: The case of AIDS., in stone symposium of the society for the study of symbolic interaction. 1991: San Fransico, CA.

[20] T. Shibutani. "Reference Groups as Perspectives." American Journal of Sociology, vol. 60, no. 6, pp. 562-569, 1955.

[21] B. Elkjær. "Organizational learning the 'third way'."Management learning, vol. 35, no. 4, pp. 419-434, 2004.

[22] B. Elkjærand M. Huysman "Social worlds theory and the power of tension." IN: D., Barry & H., Hansen (Eds.), The SAGE handbook of new approaches in management and organization, pp. 170-177, 2008.

[23] M. Huysman and B. Elkjær. "Organizations as arenas of social worlds: Towards an alternative perspective on organizational learning?" In Organizational Learning and Knowledge Capabilities Conference. 2006.

[24] A. E. Clarke.. Social organization and social process: Essays in honor of Anselm Strauss, 1991.

[25] A. H. Van de Ven Engaged scholarship : a guide for organizational and social research. 2007, Oxford ; New York: Oxford University Press. xii, 330 p.

[26] A. H. Van de Ven Engaged scholarship a guide for organizational and social research. 2007, Oxford University Press: Oxford ; New York. p. 1 online resource.

[27] A. Alnusair T. Zhao, and G. Yan "Rule-based detection of design patterns in program code." International Journal on Software Tools for Technology Transfer, vol. 16, pp. 315-334, 2014.

[28] T. A. Judge and J.E. Bono. "Relationship of core self-evaluations traits—self-esteem, generalized self-efficacy, locus of control, and emotional stability—with job satisfaction and job performance: A meta-analysis." Journal of Applied Psychology, vol. 86, pp. 80-92, 2001.

[29] J. L. Pierce and D.G. Gardner. "Self-Esteem Within the Work and Organizational Context: A Review of the Organization-Based Self-Esteem Literature." Journal of Management, vol. 30, no. 5, pp. 591-622, 2004.

[30] D. Alur et al. Core J2EE Patterns (Core Design Series): Best Practices and Design Strategies. 2003: Sun Microsystems, Inc.

[31] M. P. Cline. "The pros and cons of adopting and applying design patterns in the real world." Communications of the ACM, vol. 39, no. 10, pp. 47-49, 1996.

[32] A. M. Kanstrup and E. Christiansen. Model power: still an issue?, in Proceedings of the 4th decennial conference on Critical computing: between sense and sensibility, pp. 165-168, 2005, ACM: Aarhus, Denmark.

[33] A. Hantho, L. Jensen, and K. Malterud. "Mutual understanding: a communication model for general practice. "Scandinavian Journal of Primary Health Care, vol. 20, no. 4, pp. 244-251, 2002.

[34] T. Margaret. "Establishing Mutual Understanding in Systems Design: An Empirical Study." Journal of Management Information Systems, vol. 10, no. 4, pp. 159-182, 1994.

[35] B. Marne et al. "A Design Pattern Library for Mutual Understanding and Cooperation in Serious Game Design, in Intelligent Tutoring Systems". 11th International Conference, ITS 2012, Chania, Crete, Greece, June 14-18, 2012. Proceedings, S.A. Cerri, et al., Editors., pp. 135-140, 2012, Springer Berlin Heidelberg: Berlin, Heidelberg.

[36] F. Buschmann, K. Henney, and D. Schimdt. Pattern Oriented Software Architecture, vol. 5, 2007: John Wiley & Sons.

[37] S. J. Bleistein et al. Linking requirements goal modeling techniques to strategic e-business patterns and best practice. in 8th Australian Workshop on Requirements Engineering (AWRE'03). 2003. Citeseer.

[38] V. Holmstedt and S. A. Mengiste. «Effect of Code Maintenance on Confidence in introductory object oriented programming Courses." IN: IRIS2016. 2016: Sweden. Unpublished

[39] P. Hegedűs et al.. Myth or reality? analyzing the effect of design patterns on software maintainability, in Computer Applications for Software Engineering, Disaster Recovery, and Business Continuity, pp. 138-145, 2012, Springer.

[40] L. Tahvildari and K. Kontogiannis. «On the role of design patterns in quality-driven re-engineering. in Software Maintenance and Reengineering." IN: Proceedingsof Sixth European Conference on. 2002. IEEE.

[41] Standish Group 2015 Chaos Report, available at: https://www.infoq.com/articles/standish-chaos-2015 [accessed March 2017]

[42] http://www.qsrinternational.com/what-is-nvivo [accessed March 2017]

A Model-Driven Approach for Evaluating Traceability Information

Hendrik Bünder

itemis AG,
Bonn, Germany
Email: buender@itemis.de

Christoph Rieger, Herbert Kuchen

ERCIS, University of Münster,
Münster, Germany
Email: {c.rieger,kuchen}@uni-muenster.de

***Abstract*—A traceability information model (TIM), in terms of requirement traceability, describes the relation of all artifacts that specify, implement, test, or document a software system. Creating and maintaining these models takes a lot of effort, but the inherent information on project progress and quality is seldom utilized. This paper introduces a domain-specific language (DSL) based approach to leverage this information by specifying and evaluating company- or project-specific analyses. The capabilities of the Traceability Analysis Language (TAL) are shown by defining coverage, impact and consistency analysis for a model according to the Automotive Software Process Improvement and Capability Determination (A-SPICE) standard. Every analysis is defined as a rule expression that compares a customizable metric's value (aggregated from the TIM) against an individual threshold. The focus of the Traceability Analysis Language is to make the definition and execution of information aggregation and evaluation from a TIM configurable and thereby allow users to define their own analyses based on their regulatory, project-specific, or individual needs. The paper elaborates analysis use cases within the automotive industry and reports on first experiences from using it.**

Keywords*–*Traceability; Domain-Specific Language; Software Metrics; Model-driven Software Development; Xtext.

I. Introduction

Traceability is the ability to describe and follow an artifact and all its linked artifacts through its whole life in forward and backward direction [1]. Although many companies create traceability information models for their software development activities either because they are obligated by regulations [2] or because it is prescribed by process maturity models, there is a lack of support for the analysis of such models [3].

On the one hand, recent research describes how to define and query traceability information models [4][5]. This is an essential prerequisite for retrieving specific trace information from a Traceability Information Model (TIM). However, far too little attention has been paid to taking advantage of further processing the gathered trace information. In particular, information retrieved from a TIM can be aggregated in order to support software development and project management activities with a real-time overview of the state of development.

On the other hand, research has been done on defining relevant metrics for TIMs [6], but the data collection process is non-configurable. As a result, potential analyses are limited to predefined questions and cannot provide comprehensive answers to ad hoc or recurring information needs. For example, projects using an iterative software development approach might be interested in the achievement of objectives within each development phase, whereas other projects might focus on a comprehensive documentation along the process of creating and modifying software artifacts.

The approach presented in this paper fills the gap between both areas by introducing the Traceability Analysis Language. By defining coverage, impact and consistency analyses for a model based on the Automotive Software Process Improvement and Capability Determination (A-SPICE) standard use cases for the Traceability Analysis Language (TAL) features are exemplified. Analyses are specified as rule expressions that compare individual metrics to specified thresholds. The underlying metrics values are computed by evaluating metrics expressions that offer functionalities to aggregate results of a query statement. The TAL comes with an interpreter implementation for each part of the language, so that rule, metric, and query expressions cannot only be defined, but can also be executed against a traceability information model. More specifically, the analysis language is based on a traceability meta model defining the abstract artifact types that are relevant within the development process. All TAL expressions therefore target the structural characteristics of the TIM.

The contributions of this paper are threefold: first, we provide a domain-specific Traceability Analysis Language to define rules, metrics, and queries in a fully configurable and integrated way. Second, we demonstrate the feasibility of our work with a prototypical interpreter implementation for real-time evaluation of those trace analyses. In addition, we illustrate the TAL's capabilities in the context of the A-SPICE standard and report on first experiences from real-world projects in the automotive sector.

Having discussed related work in Section II, Section III presents the capabilities of the TAL by exemplifying impact, coverage, and consistency analyses, as well as the respective rule, metrics, and query features for retrieving information from the TIM in an automotive context. In Section IV, the language, our prototypical implementation, and first usage experiences are discussed before the paper concludes in Section V.

II. Related Work

Requirements traceability is essential for the verification of the progress and completeness of a software implementation [7]. While, e.g., in the aviation or medical industry traceability is prescribed by law [2], there are also process maturity models requesting a certain level of traceability [8].

Traceable artifacts such as *Software Requirement*, *Software Unit*, or *Test Specification*, and the links between those such as *details*, *implements*, and *tests* constitute the TIM [9]. Retrieving traceability information and establishing a TIM is beyond the scope of this paper and approaches for standardization such as [10] have already been researched.

In contrast to the high effort that is made to create and maintain a TIM, only a fraction of practitioners takes advantage of the inherent information [2]. However, Rempel and Mäder (2015) have shown that the number of related requirements or the average distance between related requirements have a positive correlation with the number of defects associated with this requirement. Traceability models not only ease maintenance tasks and the evolution of software systems [11] but can also support analyses in diverse fields of software engineering such as development practices, product quality, or productivity [12]. In addition, other model-driven domains, such as variability management in software product lines, benefit from traceability information [13].

Due to the lack of sophisticated tool support, these opportunities are often missed [3]. On the one hand, query languages for TIMs have been researched extensively, including Traceability Query Language (TQL) [4], Visual Trace Modeling Language (VTML) [5], and Traceability Representation Language (TRL) [14]. On the other hand, traceability tools mostly offer a predefined set of evaluations, often with simple tree or matrix views, e.g., [15]. Hence, especially company- or project-specific information regarding software quality and project progress cannot be retrieved and remains unused.

Our approach integrates both fields of research using a textual DSL [16] that is focused on describing customized rule, metric and query expressions. In contrast to the Traceability Metamodelling Language [17] defining a domain-specific configuration of traceable artifacts, our work builds on a model regarding the specification of type-safe expressions and for deriving the scope of available elements from concrete TIM instances.

III. An Integrated Traceability Analysis Language

A. Scenarios for Traceability Analyses

The capabilities of the TAL will be demonstrated by defining analyses from the categories of coverage, impact and consistency analysis as introduced by the A-SPICE standard [18]. In addition to these rather static analyses, there are also traceability analyses focusing on data mining techniques as introduced by [12]. Even though some of these could be defined using the introduced domain-specific language, they remain out of scope of this paper.

The first scenario focuses on measuring the impact of the alteration of one or more artifacts on the whole system [19]. Recent research has shown that artifacts with a high number of trace links are more likely to cause bugs when they are changed [6]. Moreover, the impact analysis can be a good basis for the estimation of the costs of changing a certain part of the software. This estimation then not only includes the costs of implementing the change itself, but also the effort needed to adjust and test the dependent components [20].

The second scenario appears to be the most common, since many TIM analyses are concerned with verifying that a certain path and subsequently a particular coverage is given, e.g., "*are all requirements covered by a test case*" or "*have all test cases a link to a positive test result*" [3]. In addition to verifying that

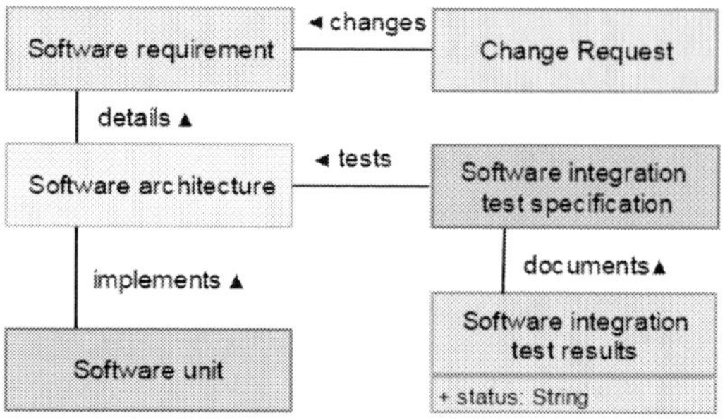

Figure 1. Traceability Information Configuration Model.

certain paths are available within a TIM, coverage metrics are mostly concerned with the identification of missing paths [9].

The third use case describes the consistency between traceable artifacts. Besides ensuring that all requirements are implemented, consistency analyses should also ensure that there are no unrequested changes to the implementation [21]. Consistency is generally required between all artifacts within a TIM in accordance to the Traceability Information Configuration Model (TICM), so that all required trace links for the traced artifacts are available [18].

Figure 1 shows a simplified TICM based on the A-SPICE standard [18] that defines the traceable artifact types *Change Request, Software Requirement, Software Architecture, Software Unit, Software Integration Test Specification,* and *Software Integration Test Result.* Also, the link types *changes, details, implements, tests,* and *documents* are specified by the configuration model. The arrowheads in Figure 1 represent the primary trace link direction, however, trace links can be traversed in both directions [22]. The traceable artifact *Software Integration Test Result* also defines a customizable attribute called "status" that holds the actual result.

Considering the triad of economic, technical, and social problem space, the flexibility to adapt to existing work practices increases the productivity of a traceability solution [23]. Therefore, configuration models provide the abstract description of traced artifact types in a company context. A TIM captures the concrete artifact representations and their relationships according to such a TICM and constitutes the basis for the analyses (cf. Section III-B).

Figure 2 shows a traceability information model based on the sample TICM described above. The TIM contains multiple instances of the classes defined in the TICM that can be understood as proxies of the original artifacts. Those artifacts may be of different format, e.g., Word, Excel or Class files. Within the traceability software, adapters can be configured to parse an artifact's content and create a traceable proxy object in accordance to the TICM. In addition, the underlying traceability software product offers the possibility to enhance the proxy objects with customizable attributes. The *Software Integration Test Result* from Figure 1, for example, holds the actual result of the test case in the customizable attribute "status".

1) Impact Analysis: The impact analysis shown in Figure 3 checks the number of related requirements (NRR) [6] starting from every *Change Request* by using the aggregated results of a metric expression which is based on a query. The analysis begins after the *rule* keyword that is followed by an arbitrary name. The right hand side of the equation specifies the severity

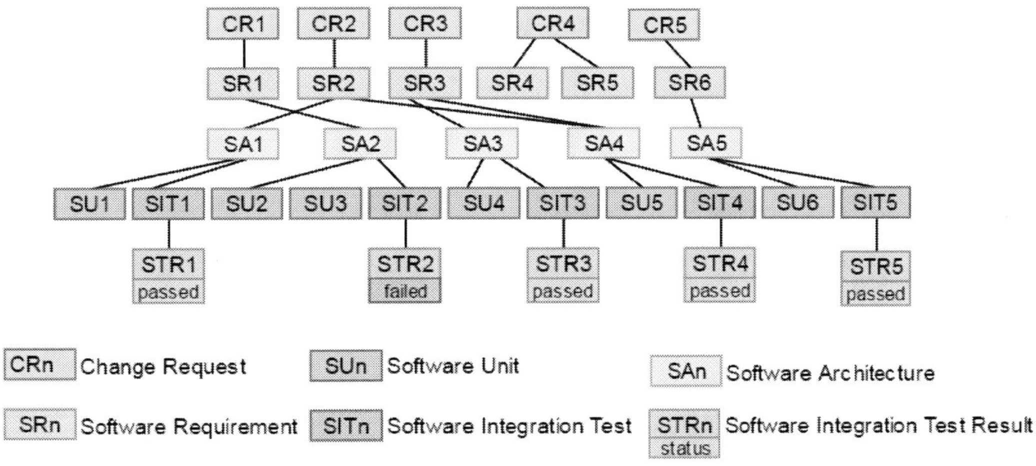

Figure 2. Sample Traceability Information Model.

of breaking the rule stated in the parentheses. In this case, a rule breach will lead to a warning message with the text in quotation marks. The most important part of the analysis is the comparison part that specifies the threshold which in this case, is a number of related requirements greater than 2. If the metrics' value is greater, the warning message will be returned as a result of the analysis.

```
result relatedReqs =
  tracesFrom Software Requirement to Software Requirement
  collect(start.name ->srcRequirement,
          end.name   -> trgtRequirement)
metric NRR = count(relatedReqs.srcRequirement)
rule NRRWarning = warnIf(NRR>2, "A high number of related
     software requirements could provoke errors.")
```

Figure 3. Metric: Number of related requirements (NRR).

The second component of the TAL expression is the metric expression that in this case, counts the related requirements. Each metric is introduced by the keyword *metric*, again followed by an arbitrary name which is used to reference a metric either from another metric or from a rule as shown in Figure 3. The expression uses the *count* function to compute the number of related requirements. The *count* function takes a column reference to count all rows that have the same value in the given column. In the metric expression shown above, all traces from one *Software Requirement* to a *Software Requirement* have the name of the source *Software Requirement* in their first column, so that the *count* function will count all traces per *Software Requirement*. As shown in Table I, the result of the metric evaluation is a tabular data structure with always two columns. The first holds the source artifact and the second column holds the evaluated metric value. For the given example, the first column holds the name of each *Software Requirement* and the second column contains the evaluated number of directly and indirectly referenced *Software Requirements*.

Finally, the metric is based on a query expression that is used to retrieve information from the underlying TIM. The *tracesFrom... to...* function returns all paths between source and target artifact passed into the function as parameters. In comparison to expressing this statement in other query languages such as Structured Query Language (SQL), no knowledge about the potential paths between the source and target artifacts in the TIM is needed.

TABLE I. NRR METRIC: TABULAR RESULT STRUCTURE.

Software Requirement	*NRR*
SR1	1
SR2	2
SR3	2
SR4	2
SR5	1

Figure 3 shows that the columns of the tabular result structure are defined in the brackets after the keyword *collect*. In the first column the name of the *Software Requirement* of each path is given and in the second column the name of each target *Software Requirement* is given. Both columns can contain the same artifacts multiple times, but the combination of each target with each source artifact is only contained once.

2) Coverage Analysis: Figure 4 shows a coverage analysis that is concerned with the number of related test case results per software requirement. In contrast to the analysis shown in Figure 3, it introduces two new concepts. First, the analysis is not dependent on a metric expression, but directly bound to a query result. Since metric and query expression results are returned in the same tabular structure, rules can be applied to both. Second, the analysis shown in Figure 4 demonstrates the concept of a staggered analysis, i.e., one column or metric is referenced once from a warning and error rule, respectively. The rule interpreter will recognize this construct and will return the analysis result with the highest severity, e.g., when the error rule applies, the warning rule message is omitted. The rules shown above ensure that the test of each *Software Requirement*

```
result tracesSwReqToTestResult =
  tracesFrom Software Requirement
  to         Software Integration Test Result
  collect(start.name-> name, count(1)-> tcrs)
  where(end.status = "passed")
  groupBy(name)
rule lowTC = warnIf(tracesSwReqToTestResult.tcrs < 2,
"Low number of test results!")
rule noTC = errorIf(tracesSwReqToTestResult.tcrs < 1,
  "No test results found!")
```

Figure 4. Software Requirement Test Result Coverage Analysis.

is documented by at least one test result. However, to fulfill the rule completely, each *Software Requirement* should be covered by two *Software Integration Tests* and subsequently two *Software Integration Test Results*.

TABLE II. COVERAGE ANALYSIS: TABULAR RESULT STRUCTURE.

Software Requirement	*Analysis Result*
SR1	No test results found!
SR2	Ok
SR3	Ok
SR4	No test results found!
SR5	No test results found!
SR6	Low number of test results!

Table II shows the result of the staggered analysis. The test coverage analysis returns an "Ok" message for two of the six *Software Requirements*, while one is marked with a warning message and the remaining three caused an error message.

The query expressions result is limited to *Software Integration Test Results* with status "passed" by evaluating the customizable attribute "status" using a *where* clause. Since the query language offers some functions to do basic aggregation, it is possible to bypass metric expressions in this case. In Figure 4 the aggregation is done by the *groupBy* and the *count* function. The second column specifies an aggregation function that counts all entries in a given column per row based on the column name passed as parameter. In general, the result of this function will be 1 per row since there is only one value per row and column but in combination with the "groupBy" function the number of aggregated values per cell is computed. The resulting tabular structure contains one row per *Software Requirement* with the respective name and the cumulated number of traces to different Software Integration Test Results as columns.

3) Consistency Analysis: The following will show two consistency analysis samples to verify that all *Software Requirements* are linked to at least one *Software Unit* and vice versa. Figure 5 shows a consistency analysis composed of a rule and

```
result consistetSrcTrgt =
  tracesFrom Software Requirement to Software Unit
  collect(start.name ->name, count(1)-> targets)
  groupBy(name)
rule notCoveredError = errorIf(swUnits<1, "The software
    requirement is not implemented.")
```

Figure 5. Consistency Analysis.

a query expression. The rule *notCoveredError* returns an error message if the number of traces between *Software Requirements* and *Software Units* is smaller than one which means that the particular *Software Requirements* is not implemented.

TABLE III. CONSISTENCY ANALYSIS: SOFTWARE REQUIREMENT IMPLEMENTATION.

Name	*Analysis Result*
SR1	Ok
SR2	Ok
SR3	Ok
SR4	The Software Requirement is not implemented!
SR5	The Software Requirement is not implemented!
SR6	Ok

Table III shows the result of the analysis as defined in Figure 5. For "SR4" and "SR5" there is no trace to a *Software Unit* so that the analysis marks these two with an error message. To verify that all implemented *Software Units* are requested by a *Software Requirement*, the query can easily be altered by switching the parameters of the "tracesFrom... to..." function and by changing the error message. Table IV shows the result of the altered analysis revealing that "SU3" despite all others has not been requested.

TABLE IV. CONSISTENCY ANALYSIS: SOFTWARE UNIT REQUESTED.

Name	*Analysis Result*
SU1	Ok
SU2	Ok
SU3	The Software Requirement has not been requested!
SU4	Ok
SU5	Ok
SU6	Ok

These examples show that the language offers extensive support for retrieving and aggregating information in TIMs. The following sections will demonstrate how the TAL integrates with the traceability solution it is build upon, and how the different parts of the language are defined.

B. *Composition of the Traceability Analysis Language*

1) Modeling Layers: Figure 6 shows the integration between the different model layers referred to in this paper, starting from the *Eclipse Ecore Model* as shared meta meta model [24]. The Xtext framework which is used to define the analysis language generates an instance of this model [25] to represent the *Analysis Language Meta Model* (ALMM). Individual queries, metrics, and rules are specified within a concrete instance, the *Analysis Language Model* (ALM), using the created domain-specific language. An interpreter was implemented using Xtend, a Java extension developed as part of the Xtext framework and specially designed to navigate and interact with the analysis language's Eclipse Ecore models [26].

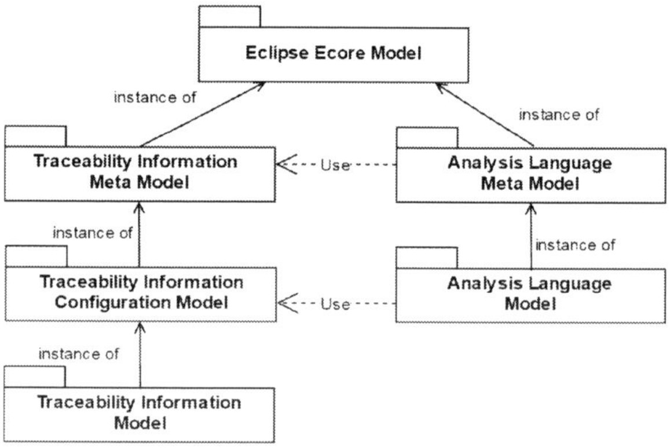

Figure 6. Conceptual Integration of Model Layers.

Likewise, the *Traceability Information Model* used in this paper contains the actual traceability information, for example the concrete software requirement *SR1*. It is again an instance of a formal abstract description, the so called TICM. The TICM describes traceable artifact types, e.g., *Software Requirement* or *Software Architecture*, and the available link types, e.g., *details*. This model itself is based on a proprietary *Traceability Information Meta Model* (TIMM) defining the basic traceability constructs such as an artifact type and link type. To structure the DSL, the TAL itself is hierarchically subdivided into three components, namely rule, metric, and query expressions.

2) Rule Grammar: Since a query result or a metric value alone delivers few insights into the quality or the progress of a project, rule expressions are the main part of the TAL. Only by comparing the metric value to a pre-defined threshold or another metrics' value information is exposed. The grammar contains rules for standard comparison operations which are *equal, not equal, greater than, smaller than, greater or equals,* and *smaller or equals.* A rule expression can either return a warning or an error result after executing the comparison including an individual message. Since query and metrics result descriptions implement the same tabular result interface, rules can be applied to both. Accordingly, the result of an evaluated rule expression is also stored using the same tabular interface.

```
WarnIf = ID '=' 'warnIf(' RuleBody ')';
RuleBody = (MetricDefinition | ResultDeclaration '.' Column)
     Operator RuleAtomic ',' MESSAGE;
```

Figure 7. Rule Grammar.

The *RuleBody* rule shown in Figure 7 is the central part of the rule grammar. On the left side of the *Operator* a metric expression or a column from a query expression result can be referenced. The next part of the rule is the comparison *Operator* followed by a *RuleAtomic* value to compare the expression to. The *RuleAtomic* value is either a constant number or a reference to another metrics expression.

3) Metrics Grammar: Complimentary to recent research that focuses on specific traceability metrics and their meaningfulness [6], the approach described in this paper allows for the definition of individual metrics. An extended Backus-Naur form (EBNF)-like Xtext grammar defines the available features including arithmetic operations, operator precedence using parentheses, and the integration of query expressions. The metrics grammar of the TAL itself has two main components. One is the *ResultDeclaration* that encapsulates the result of a previously specified query. The other is an arbitrary number of metrics definitions that may aggregate query results or other metrics recursively.

```
MetricDefinition = 'metric' ID '=' MetricExpression;

MetricExpression = Term  { ('+' | '-') Term};
Term = Factor { ('*' | '/') Factor};
Factor = SumFunction | CountFunction | LengthFunction |
     DOUBLE | ColumnSelection | MetricDefinition | '('
     MetricExpression ')' ;
```

Figure 8. Grammar rules for metrics expressions.

Figure 8 shows a part of the metric grammar defining the support for the basic four arithmetic operations as well as the correct use of parentheses. Since the corresponding parser generated by Another Tool for Language Recognition (ANTLR) works top-down, the grammar must not be left recursive [27]. First, the rule *Factor* allows for the usage of constant double values. Second, metric expressions can contain pre-defined functions such as sum, length, or count to be applied to the results of a query. Due to a lack of space, their grammar rules are not elaborated further. Third, columns from the result of a query can be referenced so that metric expressions per query expression result row can be computed. Finally, metric expressions can refer to other metric expressions to further aggregate already accumulated values. Thereby, interpreting metric expressions can be modularized to reuse intermediate metrics and to ensure maintainability.

The metrics grammar as part of the TAL defines arithmetic operations that aggregate the results of an interpreted query expression. The combination of a configurable query expressions with configurable metric definitions allows users to define their individual metrics.

4) Query Grammar: The analyses defined using metric and rule expressions depend on the result of a query that retrieves the raw data from the underlying TIM. Although there are many existing query languages available, a proprietary implementation is currently used because of three reasons.

First, the query language should reuse the types from TICM to enable live validation of analyses even before they are executed. The Xtext-based implementation offers easy mechanisms to satisfy this requirement, while others such as SQL are evaluated only at runtime. Second, some of the existing query languages such as SQL or Language Integrated Query (LINQ) are too verbose (cf. Figure 9) or do not offer predefined functions to query graphs. Finally, other languages such as SEMMLE QL [28] or RASCAL [29] are focused on source code analyses and do not interact well with Eclipse Modeling Framework (EMF) models.

The formal description of the syntax of a query is quite lengthy and out of scope of this paper, where we focus on the metrics and rules language. From the example in Section III, the reader gets an idea, how a query looks like. The query expressions offer a powerful and well-integrated mechanism to retrieve information from a given TIM. Especially, the integration with the traceability information configuration model enables the reuse of already known terms such as the trace artifact type names. Furthermore, complex graph traversals are completely hidden from the user who only specifies the traceable source and target artifact based on the TICM. For example, the concise query of Figure 4 already requires a complex statement when expressed in SQL syntax (cf. Figure 9).

```
SELECT r.name, count(u.id) AS tcrs
FROM SwRequirement r
INNER JOIN SwRequirement_SwArchitecture ra ON r.id=ra.r_id
INNER JOIN SwArchitecture a ON ra.a_id=a.id
INNER JOIN SwArchitecture_SwIntegrationTest ai
  ON a.id=ai.a_id
INNER JOIN SwIntegrationTest i ON ai.i_id=i.id
INNER JOIN SwIntegrationTest_SwIntegrationTestResult it
  ON i.id=it.i_id
INNER JOIN SwIntegrationTestResult t ON it.t_id=t.id
WHERE t.status='passed'
GROUP BY r.name;
```

Figure 9. SQL equivalent to query of Figure 4.

IV. Discussion

A. Eclipse Integration and Performance

To demonstrate the feasibility of the designed TAL and perform flexible evaluations of traceability information models, a prototype was developed. The analysis language is based on the aforementioned Xtext framework and integrated in the integrated development environment Eclipse using its plug-in mechanism [30]. The introduced interpreter evaluates rule, metric, and query expressions whenever the respective expression is modified and saved in the editor.

Currently, both components are tentatively integrated in a software solution that envisages a commercial application. Therefore, the analysis language is configured to utilize a proprietary TIMM from which traceability information configuration models and concrete TIMs are defined. At runtime, the expression editor triggers the interpreter to request the current TIM from the underlying software solution and subsequently perform the given analysis. Within our implementation, traceable artifacts from custom traceability information configuration models as shown in Figure 1 can be used for query, metrics, and rule definitions. Due to an efficient implementation used by the *tracesFrom... to...* function, analysis are re-executed immediately when an analysis is saved or can be triggered from a menu entry. The efficiency of the depth-first algorithm implementation was verified by interpreting expressions using TIMs ranging from 1,000 to 50,000 artificially created traceable artifacts. The underlying TICM was build according to the traceable artifact definitions of the A-SPICE standard [18].

TABLE V. DURATION OF TAL EVALUATION.

Artifacts	*Start Artifacts*	*Duration (in s)*
1,000	300	0.012
8,000	1,500	0.1
50,000	8,500	2.2

Table V shows the duration for interpreting the analysis expression from Figure 4 against TIMs of different sizes. The first column shows the overall number of traceable artifacts and links in the TIM. The second column gives the number of start artifacts for the depth-first algorithm implementation, i.e., the number of *Software Requirements* for the exemplary analysis expression. The third column contains the execution time on an Intel Core i7-4700MQ processor at 2.4 GHz and 16 GB RAM. As shown, executing expressions can be done efficiently even for large size models, sufficient for real-world applications to regular reporting and ad hoc analysis purposes.

B. Applying the Analysis Language

Defining and evaluating analysis statements with the prototypical implementation has shown that the approach is feasible to collect metrics for different kinds of traceability projects. The most basic metric expression reads like *the proportion of artifacts of type A that have no trace to artifacts of type B*. Some generic scenarios focused on impact, coverage, and consistency analyses have been exemplified in Section III-A. However, there are more specific metrics that are applicable and reasonable for a particular industry sector, a specific project organization, or a certain development process.

Industry-specific metrics, e.g., in the banking sector, could focus on the impact of a certain change request regarding coordination and test effort estimation. Project-specific management rules may for instance highlight components causing a high number of reported defects to indicate where to perform quality measures, e.g., code reviews. Moreover, the current progress of a software development project can be exposed by defining a staggered analysis relating design phase artifacts (e.g., *Software Requirements* that are not linked to a *Software Architecture*) and implementation artifacts (e.g., *Software Architectures* without trace to a *Software Unit*) in relation to the overall number of *Software Requirements*. Analysis expressions could also be specific to the software development process. In agile projects for example the velocity of an iteration could be combined with the number of bugs related to the delivered functionality. Thereby, it could be determined whether the number of bugs correlates with the scope of delivered functionality. These use cases emphasize the flexibility of the analysis language — in combination with an adaptable configuration model — for applying traceability analyses to a variety of domains, not necessarily bound to programming or software development in general. For example, a TIM for an academic paper may define traceable artifacts such as *authors*, *chapters*, and *references*. An analysis on such a paper could find all papers that cite a certain author or the average number of citations per chapter. It is therefore possible to execute analyses on other domains with graph-based structures that can benefit from traceability information.

Besides theoretical usage scenarios for the TAL, first experiences in real-world projects were gained with an automotive company. The Traceability Analysis Language was used in five projects with TIMs ranging from 30,000 to 80,000 traceable artifacts defined in accordance to the Automotive SPICE standard. For all five projects, a predefined analysis was created to compute the test coverage of each system requirement. A system requirement is considered fully tested when all linked system and software requirements have a test case with a positive test result linked (cf. Section III-A2). The execution time of the analysis in the real world projects confirmed the results from the artificial sample explained in Table V. The predefined analysis has replaced a complex SQL statement that included seven joins to follow the links trough the traceability information model. Because the *tracesFrom... to...* function encapsulates the graph traversal, the TAL analysis is also more resilient to changes of the traceability configuration model.

C. Limitations

The approach presented in this paper is bound to limitations regarding both technical and organizational aspects. Regarding the impact of the developed DSL on software quality management practices, first investigations have taken place, however, more are needed to draw sustainable conclusions.

Using the TAL in industry projects has shown the need for additional analysis capabilities. One main requirement is to evaluate how much of an expected trace path is available in a certain TIM. If there is no complete path from a *System Requirement* to a *Software Integration Test Result*, it would be beneficial to show partial matches, for instance if there is no *Software Integration Test Result* or if there is no *Software Integration Test Specification* at all. Extending the result of an analysis in accordance to this requirement would enhance the information about the progress of a project.

From a language user perspective, the big advantage of being free to configure any query, metric or rule expression is also a challenge. A language user has to be aware of the traceable artifacts and links in the TIM and how this trace information could be connected to extract reasonable measures. Moreover, the context-dependent choice of suitable metrics in terms of type, number, and thresholds is subject to further research. These limitations do not impede the value of our work, though. In fact, in combination with the discussed application scenarios they provide the foundation for our future work.

V. CONCLUSION

This work describes a textual domain-specific language to analyze existing traceability information models. The TAL is divided into query, metric, and rule parts that are all implemented with the state-of-the-art framework Xtext. The introduced approach goes beyond existing tool support for querying traceability information models. By closing the gap between information retrieval, metric definition, and result evaluation, the analysis capabilities are solid ground for project- or company-specific metrics. Since the proposed analysis language reuses the artifact type names from the traceability information configuration model, the expressions are defined using well known terms. In addition to reusing such terms, the editor proposes possible language statements at the current cursor position while writing analysis expressions. Utilizing this feature could lower the initial effort for defining analysis expressions and could result in faster evolving traceability information models.

On the one hand, the introduced approach is based on an Eclipse Ecore model and is thereby completely independent of the specific type of traced artifacts. On the other hand, it is well integrated into an existing TICM and IDE using Xtext and the Eclipse platform. All parts of the TAL are fully configurable regarding analysis expression, limit thresholds, and query statements in an integrated approach to close the gap between *querying* and *analyzing* traceability information models. Subsequently, measures for traceability information models can be specific to a certain industry sector, a company, a project or even a role within a project. The scenarios described in section III-A propose areas in which configurable analyses provide benefits for project managers, quality managers, and developers. Using the implemented interpreter for real-time execution of expressions, first project experiences within the automotive industry have shown that the TAL analyses are evaluated efficiently and are more resilient than other approaches, e.g., SQL-based analyses.

Future work could focus on further assessing the applicability in real world projects and defining a structured process to identify reasonable metrics for a specific setting. Such a process might not only support sophisticated traceability analyses but could also propose industry-proven metrics and thresholds. Some advanced features such as metrics comparisons over time using TIM snapshots to further enhance the analysis are yet to be implemented. In addition to evaluating the metrics against static values, future work might also focus on utilizing statistical methods from the data mining field. Classification algorithms or association rules for example could be used to find patterns in traceability information models and thus gain additional insights from large-scale TIMs.

REFERENCES

[1] O. C. Z. Gotel and C. W. Finkelstein, "An analysis of the requirements traceability problem," in Proceedings of IEEE International Conference on Requirements Engineering, 1994, pp. 94–101.

[2] J. Cleland-Huang, O. Gotel, J. Huffman Hayes, P. Mäder, and A. Zisman, "Software traceability: Trends and future directions," in Proceedings of the on Future of Software Engineering. ACM, 2014, pp. 55–69.

[3] E. Bouillon, P. Mäder, and I. Philippow, "A survey on usage scenarios for requirements traceability in practice," in Requirements Engineering: Foundation for Software Quality. Springer, 2013, pp. 158–173.

[4] J. I. Maletic and M. L. Collard, "Tql: A query language to support traceability," in ICSE Workshop on Traceability in Emerging Forms of Software Engineering, 2009, pp. 16–20.

[5] P. Mäder and J. Cleland-Huang, "A visual language for modeling and executing traceability queries," Software and Systems Modeling, vol. 12, no. 3, 2013, pp. 537–553.

[6] P. Rempel and P. Mäder, "Estimating the implementation risk of requirements in agile software development projects with traceability metrics," in Requirements Engineering: Foundation for Software Quality. Springer, 2015, pp. 81–97.

[7] M. Völter, DSL engineering: Designing, implementing and using domain-specific languages. CreateSpace Independent Publishing Platform, 2013.

[8] J. Cleland-Huang, M. Heimdahl, J. Huffman Hayes, R. Lutz, and P. Maeder, "Trace queries for safety requirements in high assurance systems," LNCS, vol. 7195, 2012, pp. 179–193.

[9] P. Mader, O. Gotel, and I. Philippow, "Getting back to basics: Promoting the use of a traceability information model in practice," 7th Intl. Workshop on Traceability in Emerging Forms of Software Engineering, 2013, pp. 21–25.

[10] A. Graf, N. Sasidharan, and Ö. Gürsoy, "Requirements, traceability and dsls in eclipse with the requirements interchange format (reqif)," in Second International Conference on Complex Systems Design & Management. Springer, 2012, pp. 187–199.

[11] P. Mäder and A. Egyed, "Do developers benefit from requirements traceability when evolving and maintaining a software system?" Empirical Softw. Eng., vol. 20, no. 2, 2015, pp. 413–441.

[12] A. Begel and T. Zimmermann, "Analyze this! 145 questions for data scientists in software engineering," in 36th International Conference on Software Engineering. ACM, 2014, pp. 12–23.

[13] N. Anquetil et al., "A model-driven traceability framework for software product lines," Software & Systems Modeling, vol. 9, no. 4, 2010, pp. 427–451.

[14] A. Marques, F. Ramalho, and W. L. Andrade, "Trl: A traceability representation language," in Proceedings of the 30th Annual ACM Symposium on Applied Computing. ACM, 2015, pp. 1358–1363.

[15] H. Schwarz, Universal traceability. Logos Verlag Berlin, 2012.

[16] M. Mernik, J. Heering, and A. M. Sloane, "When and how to develop domain-specific languages," ACM Comput. Surv., vol. 37, no. 4, 2005, pp. 316–344.

[17] N. Drivalos, D. S. Kolovos, R. F. Paige, and K. J. Fernandes, "Engineering a dsl for software traceability," in Software Language Engineering. Springer, 2009, vol. 5452, pp. 151–167.

[18] Automotive Special Interest Group, "Automotive spice process reference model," 2015, URL: http://automotivespice.com/fileadmin/software-download/Automotive_SPICE_PAM_30.pdf [retrieved: 1.3.2017].

[19] R. S. Arnold and S. A. Bohner, "Impact analysis-towards a framework for comparison," in ICSM, vol. 93, 1993, pp. 292–301.

[20] C. Ingram and S. Riddle, "Cost-benefits of traceability," in Software and Systems Traceability, J. Cleland-Huang, O. Gotel, and A. Zisman, Eds. Springer London, 2012, pp. 23–42.

[21] N. Kececi, J. Garbajosa, and P. Bourque, "Modeling functional requirements to support traceability analysis," in 2006 IEEE International Symposium on Industrial Electronics, vol. 4, 2006, pp. 3305–3310.

[22] J. Cleland-Huang, O. Gotel, and A. Zisman, Eds., Software and Systems Traceability. Springer London, 2012.

[23] H. U. Asuncion, F. François, and R. N. Taylor, "An end-to-end industrial software traceability tool," in 6th Joint Meeting of the European Software Engineering Conference and the ACM SIGSOFT Symposium on The Foundations of Software Engineering. ACM, 2007, pp. 115–124.

[24] R. C. Gronback, Eclipse Modeling Project: A Domain-Specific Language (DSL) Toolkit, 1st ed. Addison-Wesley Professional, 2009.

[25] The Eclipse Foundation, "Xtext documentation," 2017, URL: https://eclipse.org/Xtext/documentation/ [retrieved: 1.3.2017].

[26] ——, "Xtend modernized java," 2017, URL: http://eclipse.org/xtend/ [retrieved: 1.3.2017].

[27] L. Bettini, Implementing domain-specific languages with Xtext and Xtend. Packt Pub, 2013.

[28] M. Verbaere, E. Hajiyev, and O. d. Moor, "Improve software quality with SemmleCode: An eclipse plugin for semantic code search," in 22nd ACM SIGPLAN Conference on Object-oriented Programming Systems and Applications Companion. ACM, 2007, pp. 880–881.

[29] P. Klint, T. van der Storm, and J. Vinju, "Rascal: A domain specific language for source code analysis and manipulation," in 9th IEEE International Working Conference on Source Code Analysis and Manipulation. IEEE Computer Society, 2009, pp. 168–177.

[30] The Eclipse Foundation, "PDE/user guide," 2017, URL: http://wiki.eclipse.org/PDE/User_Guide [retrieved: 1.3.2017].

On the Effect of Minimum Support and Maximum Gap for Code Clone Detection — An Approach Using Apriori-based Algorithm —

Yoshihisa Udagawa
Computer Science Department, Faculty of Engineering,
Tokyo Polytechnic University
Atsugi-city, Kanagawa, Japan
e-mail: udagawa@cs.t-kougei.ac.jp

***Abstract*— Software clones are introduced to source code by copying and slightly modifying code fragments for reuse. Thus, detection of code clones requires a partial match of code fragments. The essential idea of the proposed approach is a combination of a partial string match using the longest-common-subsequence (LCS) and an *apriori*-based mining for finding frequent sequences. The novelty of our approach includes the maximal frequent sequences to find the most compact representation of sequential patterns. After outlining the proposed methods, the paper reports on the results of a case study using *Java SDK 1.8.0_101 awt* graphics package with highlighting the effect analysis on thresholds of the proposed algorithm, i.e., a minimum support and a maximum gap. The results demonstrate the proposed algorithm can detect all possible code clones in the sense that code clones are similar code segments that occur at least twice in source code under consideration.**

Keywords—Code clone; Maximal frequent sequence; Longest common subsequence(LCS) algorithm; Java source code.

I. INTRODUCTION

Two fragments of source code are called software clones if they are identical or similar to each other. Software clones are very common in large software because they can significantly reduce programming effort and shorten programming time. However, many researchers in clone code detection point out that software clones introduce difficulties in software maintenance and cause bug propagation. For example, if there are many copy-pasted code fragments in software source code and a bug is found in one code clone, the bug has to be detected within a piece of software thoroughly and fixed consistently.

Different types of software clones exist depending on the degree of similarity between two code fragments [1][2]. Type 1 is an exact copy without modification, with the exception of layout and comments. Type 2 is a slightly different copy typically due to renaming of variables or constants. Type 3 is a copy with further modifications typically due to adding, removing, or changing code units of at least one code unit.

Research on Type 3 clones has been conducted in recent decades because there are substantially more significant clones of Type 3 than there are of Types 1 or 2 in software for industrial applications. Our approach also focuses on finding Type 3 clones. To find such type of clone, the following problems must be addressed.

(1) How to handle gaps in a context of similarity.
There are many algorithms that are tailored to handle gaps in similarity measure such as sequence alignment, dynamic pattern matching, tree-based matching and graph-based matching techniques [2].

(2) How to find frequently occurring patterns.
The detection of frequently occurring patterns in a set of sequence data has been conducted intensively, as reported in sequential pattern mining literature [3]-[8]. There are several studies [9]-[12] using the *apriori*-based algorithm to discover software clones in source code.

Code clones are defined as a set of syntactically and/or semantically similar fragments of source code [1][2]. Since source code is represented by a sequence of statements, finding clone code is a problem of finding similar sequences that occur at least twice. *Apriori*-based sequential pattern mining algorithms are worth studying because they are designed to detect a set of frequently occurring sequences. The algorithms take a positive integer threshold set by a user called "minimum support" or "minSup" for short. The minSup controls the level of frequency [3][8].

In [12], Udagawa shows that repeated structures in a method adversely affect the performance especially when a minSup is two or three. This paper pushes forward the study using a large scale software, i.e., *Java SDK 1.8.0_101 awt*, and analyzes to what extent a minSup affects the number of retrieved sequences and time performance. For this purpose, a proposed *apriori*-based sequential mining algorithm is properly revised to deal with the repeated structures in a method.

The contributions of this paper are as follows:

(I) the design and implementation of a code transformation parser that extracts code matching statements, including control statements and typed method calls;

(II) the design and implementation of a sequential data mining algorithm that maintains performance at a practical level until a threshold minSup reaches down to two;

(III) the evaluation of the proposed algorithm using *Java SDK 1.8.0_101 awt* with respect to minSup of two to ten and gap size of zero to three. In addition to time performance, the number of retrieved sequences is analyzed for each length of sequences showing that the number of repeated structures in a method accounts for a large part on numbers especially in the case when minSup is two.

The remainder of the paper is organized as follows. After presenting some basic definitions and terminologies on frequent sequence mining technique in Section II, we overview the proposed approach in Section III. Section IV describes the proposed algorithm for discovering clone candidates using an *apriori*-based maximal frequent sequence mining technique. Section V presents the experimental results using *Java SDK 1.8.0_101 awt* package. Section VI presents some of the most related work. Section VII concludes the paper with our plans for future work.

II. Basic Definitions

Defnition 1 (sequence and sequence database). Let $I = \{ i_1, i_2, \ldots, i_h\}$ be a set of items (symbols). A sequence s_x is an ordered list of items $s_x = x_{j1} \rightarrow x_{j2} \rightarrow \ldots \rightarrow x_{jn}$ such that $x_{jk} \subseteq I$ $(1 \leq jk \leq h)$. A sequence database SDB is a list of sequences $SDB = <s_1, s_2, \ldots, s_p>$ having sequence identifiers (SIDs) 1, 2,…,p.

Denition 2 (sequence containment). A sequence $s_a = a_1 \rightarrow a_2 \rightarrow \ldots \rightarrow a_n$ is said to be contained in a sequence $s_b = b_1 \rightarrow b_2 \rightarrow \ldots \rightarrow b_m$ $(n \leq m)$ iff there exists the strictly increasing sequence of integers q taken from [1, n], $1 \leq q[1] < q[2] < \ldots < q[n] \leq m$ such that $a_1 = b_{q[1]}$, $a_2 = b_{q[2]}, \ldots, a_n = b_{q[n]}$ (denoted as $s_a \sqsubseteq s_b$).

Definition 3 (gapped sequence containment). Let maxGap be a threshold set by the user. A sequence $s_a = a_1 \rightarrow a_2 \rightarrow \ldots \rightarrow a_n$ is said to be contained in a sequence $s_b = b_1 \rightarrow b_2 \rightarrow \ldots \rightarrow b_m$ with respect to maxGap iff we have $a_1 = b_{q[1]}$, $a_2 = b_{q[2]}, \ldots, a_n = b_{q[n]}$ and $q[j] - q[j-1] - 1 \leq maxGap$ for all $2 \leq j \leq n$.

Denition 4 (prefx and postfix with respect to maxGap). A sequence $s_a = a_1 \rightarrow a_2 \rightarrow \ldots \rightarrow a_n$ is called a prefix of a sequence $s_b = b_1 \rightarrow b_2 \rightarrow \ldots \rightarrow b_m$ iff s_a is a gapped sequence containment of maxGap. A subsequence $s'_b = b_{n+1} \rightarrow \ldots \rightarrow b_m$ is called postfix of s_b with respect to prefix s_a donoted as $s_b = s_a \rightarrow s'_b$.

Denition 5 (support with respect to maxGap). Given a maxGap, the support of a sequence s_b in a sequence database SDB with respect to maxGap is defined as the number of sequences $s \in SDB$ such that $s_b \sqsubseteq s$ with respect to maxGap and is denoted by $sup_{maxGap}(s_b)$.

Denition 6 (multi occurrence mode and single occurrence mode). Given a maxGap and a sequence $s_b = b_1 \rightarrow b_2 \rightarrow \ldots \rightarrow b_m$ with a prefix s_a, the sequence s_b has the support of $sup_{maxGap}(s_b)$ that is greater than zero.

When the prefix s_a is contained in a postfix of s_b, i.e., $s'_b = b_{n+1} \rightarrow \ldots \rightarrow b_m$, the support is calculated as $sup_{maxGap}(s_b) + 1$.

This calculation is recursively applied for each postfix of s_b to count the support number. The support number recursively calculated is named the support number in *multi occurrence mode* in this paper. This mode is critical when dealing with long sequences such as nucleotide DNA sequences [4] [5] and periodically repeated patterns over time [6]. On the other hand, the support number without the calculation of the postfix of s_b is named the support number in *single occurrence mode*. The algorithm proposed in the paper supports both of the modes.

Denition 7 (frequent sequences with maxGap). Let maxGap and minSup be a threshold set by the user. A sequence s_b is called a frequent sequences with respect to maxGap iff $sup_{maxGap}(s_b) \leq minSup$. The problem of sequence mining on a sequence database SDB is to discover all frequent sequences for given integers maxGap and minSup.

Definition 8 (closed frequent sequence). A closed frequent sequence is defined to be a frequent sequence for which there exists no super sequence that has the same support count as the original sequence [5][8].

Definition 9 (maximal frequent sequence). A maximal frequent sequence is defined to be a frequent sequence for which none of its immediate super sequences are frequent [7][8].

The closed frequent sequence is widely used when a system is designed to generate an association rule [3][8] that is inferred from a support number of a frequent sequence. On the other hand, the maximal frequent sequence is valuable, because it provides the most compact representation of frequent sequences [7][13].

III. Overview of Proposed Approach

Fig. 1 depicts an overview of the proposed approach [12]. According to the terminology in the survey [1], our approach can be summarized in three steps, i.e., transformation, match detection and formatting, and aggregation.

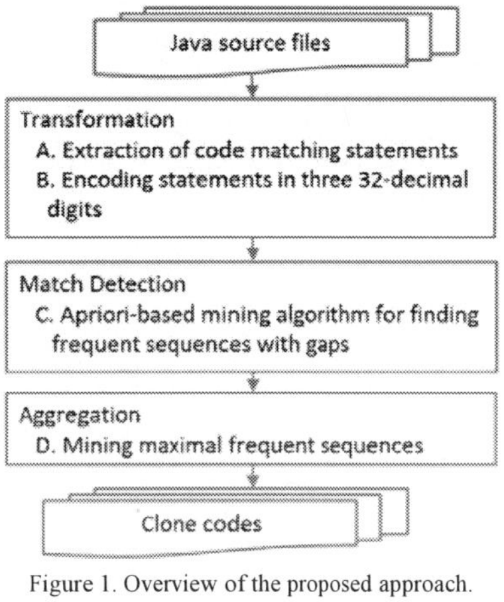

Figure 1. Overview of the proposed approach.

A. Extraction of code matching statements

Under the assumption that method calls and control statements characterize a program, the proposed parser extracts them in a Java program. Generally, the instance method is preceded by a variable whose type refers to a class object to which the method belongs. The proposed parser traces a type declaration of a variable and translates a variable identifier to its data type or class identifier as follows. The translation allows us to deal with Type 2 clone.

<variable>.<method identifier>

is translated into

<data type>.<method identifier> or

<class identifier>.<method identifier>.

The parser extracts control statements with various levels of nesting. A block is represented by the "{" and "}" symbols. Thus, the number of "{" symbols indicates the number of nesting levels. The following Java keywords for 15 control statements are processed by the proposed parser.

if, else if, else, switch, while, do, for, break, continue, return, throw, synchronized, try, catch, finally

We selected the *Java SDK 1.8.0_101 awt* package as our target of the study. The number of total lines is 166,016, which means the *awt* package is a kind of large scale software in industry.

Fig. 2 shows an example of the extracted structure of the *getFlavorsForNatives(String[] natives)* method in the *SystemFlavorMap.java* file of the *java.awt.datatransfer* package. The three numbers preceded by the # symbol are the number of comments, and blank and code lines, respectively.

In this study, we deal only with Java. However, a clever modification of the parser allows us to apply the proposed approach to other languages such as C/C++ and Visual Basic.

```
SystemFlavorMap::getFlavorsForNatives(String[] natives)
  #    5    8   12
{
    if{
        getNativesForFlavor()
        List.toArray()
    }
    HashMap()
    for{
        getFlavorsForNative()
        HashMap.put()
    }
    return
}
```

Figure 2. Example of the extracted structure.

B. Encoding statements in three 32-decimal digits

The conventional longest-common-subsequence (LCS) algorithm takes two given strings as input and returns values depending on the number of matching characters of the strings. Due to fact that the length of statements in program code differs, the conventional LCS algorithm does not work effectively. In other words, for short statements, such as *if* and *try* statements, the LCS algorithm returns small LCS values for matching. For long statements, such as *synchronized* statements or a long method identifier, the LCS algorithm returns large LCS values.

We have developed an encoder that converts a statement to three 32-decimal digits (to cope with 32,768 identifiers), which results in a fair base for a similarity metric in clone detection. Fig. 3 shows the encoded statements that correspond to the code shown in Fig. 2. Fig. 4 shows a part of the mapping table between three 32-decimal digits and a code matching statement extracted from the original source files.

```
SystemFlavorMap::getFlavorsForNatives (String[] natives)
→001→004→0VH→0VQ→003→044→04E→0VI→0VR
→003→009→003
```

Figure 3. Encoded statements corresponding to Fig. 2.

001, {	04E, for{
002, this()	...
003, }	0VH, getNativesForFlavor()
004, if{	0VI, getFlavorsForNative()
...	...
044, HashMap()	0VQ, List.toArray()
...	0VR, HashMap.put()

Figure 4. Mapping table between three 32-decimal digits and a code matching statement used to encode statements in Fig. 3.

C. Apriori-based mining algorithm for finding frequent sequences with gaps

We have developed a mining algorithm to find frequent sequences based on the *apriori* principle [3][8], i.e, *if an itemset is frequent, then all of its subsets must be frequent.*

Frequent sequence mining is essentially different from itemset mining because a subsequence can repeat not only in different sequences but also within each sequence. For example, given two sequences C→<u>C→A</u> and B→<u>C→A</u>→B →A→<u>C→A</u>, there are three occurrences of the subsequence <u>C→A</u>. The repetitions within a sequence [4]-[6] are critical when dealing with long sequences such as protein sequences, stock exchange rates, customer purchase histories.

Note that the proposed algorithm is implemented to run in two modes, i.e., *multi occurrence mode* to find all subsequences included in a given sequence, and *single occurrence mode* to find a subsequence in a given sequence even if there exists several subsequences.

As described in Section V, the multi occurrence mode detects so many code matching that it has an adverse effect on performance especially when a minSup is two and a maxGap is one to three.

The LCS algorithm is also tailored to match three 32-decimal digits as a unit. That algorithm can match two given sequences even if there is a "gap." Given two sequences of matching strings S1 and S2, let |lcs| be the length of their longest common subsequence, and let |common (S1, S2)| be the common length of S1 and S2 from a back trace algorithm. The "gap size" gs is defined as gs = |common (S1, S2)| – |lcs|.

D. *Mining maximal frequent sequences*

Frequent sequence mining tends to result in a very large number of sequential patterns, making it difficult for users to analyze the results. A closed and maximal frequent sequences are two representations for alleviating this drawback. The closed frequent sequence needs to be used in case a system under consideration is designed to deal with an association rule [3][8] that plays an important role for knowledge discovery. The maximal frequent sequence is such a sequence that are frequent in a sequence database and that is not contained in any other longer frequent sequence. It is a subset of the closed frequent sequence. It is representative in the sense that all sequential patterns can be derived from it [7]. Because we are just interested in finding a set of frequent sequences that are representative of code clone, we developed an algorithm to discover the maximal frequent sequences.

IV. PROPOSED FREQUENT SEQUENCE MINING

We have developed two algorithms for detecting software clones with gaps. The first is for mining frequent sequences, and the second is for extracting the maximal frequent sequences from a set of frequent sequences.

A. *Proposed Frequent Sequence Mining Algorithm*

The proposed approach is based on frequent sequence mining. A subsequence is considered frequent when it occurs no less than a user-specified minimum support threshold (i.e., minSup) in a sequence database. Note that a subsequence is not necessarily contiguous in an original sequence.

We assume that a sequence is "a list of items," whereas several algorithms for sequential pattern mining [4]-[7] deal with a sequence that consists of "a list of sets of items." Our assumption is rational because we focus on detecting code clones that consist of "a list of statements." In addition, the assumption simplifies the implementation of the proposed algorithm, which makes it possible to achieve high performance as described in Section V.

The proposed frequent sequence mining algorithm comprises two methods, i.e., GProbe (Fig. 5) and Retrieve_Cand (Fig. 6). It follows the key idea behind *apriori* principle; *if a sequence S in a sequence database appears N times, so does every subsequence R of S at least.* The algorithm takes two arguments, minSup and maxGap (the allowable maximal number of gaps).

```
1  GProbe(String[] args){
2     k= 1;
3     Initialization: Set the 15 control statements of Java to LinkedList<String> Sk
4     do {
5        Retrieve_Cand();   // Find a set of sequences of length k+1 that matches Sk.
6                           // Store the set of sequences in Ck.
7        k= k+1;
8        Sk.clear();        // Clear Sk in order to store frequent sequences of length k.
9        while( For all elements e in Ck ){
10          if ( Frequency of  e  >= minSup ){
11                Print e and sequence ids of e in the database to output file.
12                Add e and the sequence ids to Sk;
13                Scan the database to find a set of gap synonyms of e;
14                Add each gap synonym and the sequence ids to Sk;
15                }
16          }
17       }
18    } while (Sk.size() > 0);
19 }
```

Figure 5. Frequent sequence detection of the proposed algorithm.

```
1  Retrieve_Cand(){
2     Ck.clear();
3     for (each element s in Sk) {
4        for (each element t in the sequence database) {
5           for ( each position p that s matches in t){
6              Compute LongestCommonSubsequence between s and t at position p;
7              if (match count >= k && gap count  <=  maxGap ){
8                 Put s and frequency of s to Ck;
9                 Extract gap synonym g of s from t.
10                Put g and frequency of s to Ck;
11             }
12          }
13       }
14    }
15 }
```

Figure 6. Candidate sequences retrieval for the next repetition.

The variable k indicates the count of the repetition (line 2, Fig. 5). LinkedList < String > Sk is initialized to hold 15 control statements. The Retrieve_Cand method (line 5, Fig. 5) discovers a set of sequences of length k+1 from a sequence database that matches statement sequences in Sk. The while loop (lines 9–17) finds frequent sequences and sequence IDs in a sequence database. Lines 12–14 maintain the frequent sequences. Note that the proposed algorithm handles gapped sequences. Thus, both a frequent sequence and its "gap synonyms" are prepared for the next repetition. Here, "gap synonyms" means a set of sequences that match a given subsequence under a given gap constraint.

Briefly, the Retrieve_Cand() method in Fig. 6 works as follows. HashMap <String, Integer> Ck holds a sequence (String) and its frequency (Integer). First, Ck is cleared (line 2, Fig. 6). The three for loops examine all possible matches between an element in Sk and sequences in a sequence database. The longest common subsequence algorithm is tailored to compute the match count and gap count (line 6, Fig. 6). The *if* statement (line 7, Fig. 6) screens a sequence based on the match count and gap count. Lines 8–10 maintain the frequency of sequences and its "gap synonyms."

B. *Extracting Frequent Sequences*

In our approach, we assume a program structure is represented as a sequence of statements preceded by a class-method ID. Each statement is encoded to three 32-decimal digits so that the LCS algorithm works correctly, regardless of the length of the original program statement.

The proposed algorithm is illustrated for the given sample sequence database in Fig. 7. MTHD# is an abbreviated notation for a class-method ID.

```
MTHD1→005→003
MTHD2→005→00A→003→003
MTHD3→005→003→00F→006→005→003
MTHD4→005→006→003→005→00C
```

Figure 7. Example sequence database.

Fig. 8 shows the result of the frequent sequences in the multi occurrence mode for a gap of 0 and minSup of 50%, which is equivalent to a minSup count of 2. "005" is a frequent sequence with a minSup count of 6 because "005" occurs once in the first and second sequences and twice in the third and fourth sequences. The proposed algorithm maintains an ID-List, which indicates the positions where a frequent sequence appears in a sequence database. The ID-List for "005" is 1|2|3+3|4+4.

Similarly, 005→003→ is a frequent sequence with a minSup count of 3, i.e., the ID-List for 005→003→ is 1|3+3.

005→	N=6 (1|2|3+3|4+4)
005→003→	N=3 (1|3+3)

Figure 8. Result of the frequent sequences (gap, 0; minSup, 50%).

Fig. 9 shows the result of the frequent sequences for a gap of 1 and minSup of 50%. "005" is a frequent sequence with a minSup count of 6, which is the same in the case of a gap of 0.

Similarly, 005→003→ is a frequent sequence with a minSup count of 5. In addition to the consecutive sequence 005→003→, the proposed algorithm detects gapped sequences. In the case of 005→003→, the algorithm detects 005→00A→003→ in the second sequence and 005→006→003→ in the fourth sequence. Thus, the ID-List for 005→003→ is 1|2|3+3|4.

005→	N=6 (1|2|3+3|4+4)
005→003→	N=5 (1|2|3+3|4)

Figure 9. Result of the frequent sequences (gap, 1; minSup, 50%).

Fig. 10 shows the result of the frequent sequences for a gap of 2 and minSup of 50%. In addition to 005→ and 005→003→, 005→006→ is detected as a frequent sequence because 005→003→00F→006→ in the third sequence matches 005→006→ with a gap of 2, and 005→006→ in the fourth sequence with a gap of 0. Thus, the ID-List for 005→006→ is 3|4.

005→	N=6 (1|2|3+3|4+4)
005→003→	N=5 (1|2|3+3|4)
005→006→	N=2 (3|4)

Figure 10. Result of the frequent sequences (gap, 2; minSup, 50%).

C. *Extracting Maximal Frequent Sequences*

A frequent sequence is a maximal frequent sequence and no super sequence of it is a frequent sequence. In addition, it is representative because it can be used to recover all frequent sequences. Several algorithms for finding maximal frequent sequences and/or itemsets employ sophisticated search and pruning techniques to reduce the number of sequence and/or itemset candidates during the mining process.

However, we wish to measure the effects of a maximal frequent sequence; therefore, the proposed algorithm first extracts a set of frequent sequences and then detects a set of maximal frequent sequences.

Screening maximal frequent sequences from frequent sequences with a gap of zero is fairly simple. Given a set of frequent sequences Fs, the set of maximal frequent sequences MaxFs is defined by the following formula:

$$MaxFs = \{x \in Fs \mid \forall y \in Fs\ (x \not\subset y) \wedge (|x| + 1 = |y|)\}.$$

$x \not\subset y$ says that a sequence x is not included in a sequence y. Since a gap equals zero, the length of the immediate super sequence is $|x| + 1$.

The proposed algorithm is described using the sample sequence database in Fig. 11.

```
001→
003→
004→
005→
001→005→
004→003→
004→003→005→
004→001→004→003→
```

Figure 11. Example frequent sequences.

Fig. 12 shows a set of maximal frequent sequences. The frequent sequence 001→ is not a maximal frequent sequence because there is a frequent sequence 001→005→ that includes a sequence 001 and whose length is two. For the same reason, 003→, 004→, 005→ are not maximal frequent sequences. In this manner, we see that the sequence 004→003→ is not a maximal frequent sequence. However, 001→005→ is a maximal frequent sequence because there are no super-sequences that exactly include 001→005→. 004→003→005→ and 004→001→004→003→ are maximal frequent sequences.

```
001→005→
004→003→005→
004→001→004→003→
```

Figure 12. Result of maximal frequent sequences (gap, 0).

The definition of the maximal frequent sequence is simply extended to those dealing with gaps, as described in [12].

V. Experimental Results

This section shows statistical evaluation of experimental results using *Java SDK 1.8.0_101 awt* package. The number of total source code lines is 166,016. The extracted statement sequences comprise 5,108 lines which are roughly corresponding to the number of methods in the package. The number of extracted unique IDs is 3,175. We performed the experiments using the following environment:

CPU: Intel Core i7-6700 (3.40 GHz)
Main memory: 8 GB
OS: Windows 10 HOME 64 Bit
Programming Language: Java 1.8.0_101.

A. Numbers of Retrieved Frequent Sequences

Fig. 13 compares the number of retrieved frequent sequences with respect to maxGap (0 to 3) and minSup (2 to 10) with the number of retrieved frequent itemsets for the *apriori* algorithm [14]. The proposed algorithm for a maxGap of zero is comparable to the *apriori* algorithm for a minSups of six to ten. The *apriori* algorithm fails to generate frequent itemsets for a minSup of two, due to it never completes the process in three hours.

As expected, the number of retrieved frequent sequences increases as maxGap increases and minSup decreases. The proposed algorithm can find frequent sequences that occur at least twice in the sequence database, which is necessary for finding all possible code clones. One of the important findings of the experiment is that the effect of repetitions within a sequence becomes conspicuous when a minSup equals two. A detailed analysis of the retrieved frequent sequences is discussed in Subsection "*C. Sequence Length Analysis.*"

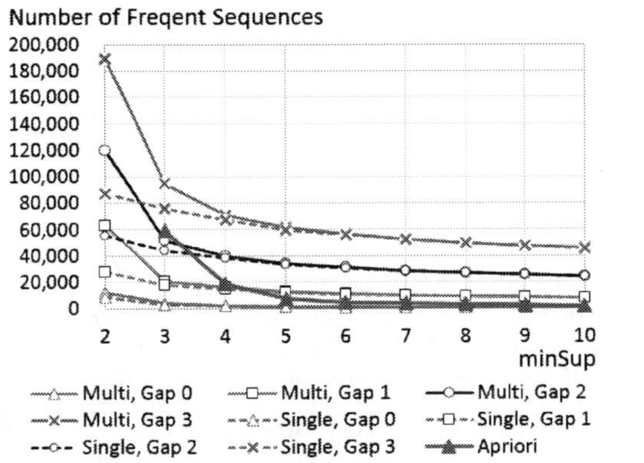

Figure 13. Numbers of retrieved frequent sequences (gap size, 0 and 1-3; minSup, 2-10) and frequent itemsets for *apriori* algorithm.

Fig. 14 shows the ratio of the number of maximal frequent sequences to the number of frequent sequences. In most of the cases, the ratio decreases as minSup values decrease. This can be explained by the fact that decreasing minSup values probably has a negative effect on the relevance of frequent sequences. Thus, redundant frequent sequences are likely mined as minSup values decrease, resulting in the low ratio of the number of maximal frequent sequences to the number of frequent sequences.

The ratios are generally smaller in the multi occurrence mode than in the single occurrence mode. It can be a fair explanation that the single occurrence mode suppresses extraction of frequent subsequences caused by repetitions within a sequence. The results show that the gap size affects the ratio up to approximately 5.55% for a maxGap of two.

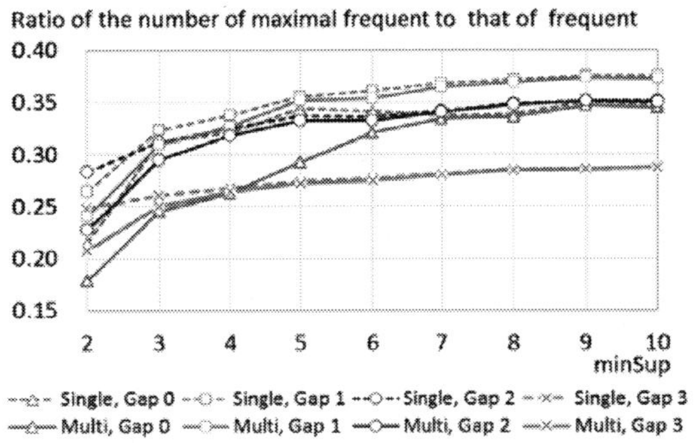

Figure 14. Ratio of the number of maximal frequent sequences to the number of frequent sequences (gap size, 0 and 1-3; minSup, 2-10).

B. Time Analysis

Fig. 15 shows the elapsed time in milliseconds for retrieving frequent sequences for a minSup of two to ten. The proposed algorithm for a maxGap of zero is comparable to the *apriori* algorithm for a minSup of five to ten as for performance.

The proposed algorithm can retrieve frequent sequences fairly efficiently. For example, it takes 816,534 milliseconds to identify 27,435 frequent sequences for a maxGap of one and a minSup of two in the single occurrence mode. Note that elapsed time increases as maxGap increases. This tendency is obvious for a minSup ranging from two through ten. As for a minSup of two in the multi occurrence mode, the elapsed time jumps up from 2.36 (for a maxGap of three) to 4.65 (for a maxGap of one) times of those for a minSup of three in the multi occurrence mode. A reason for performance degradation is analyzed in the next subsection.

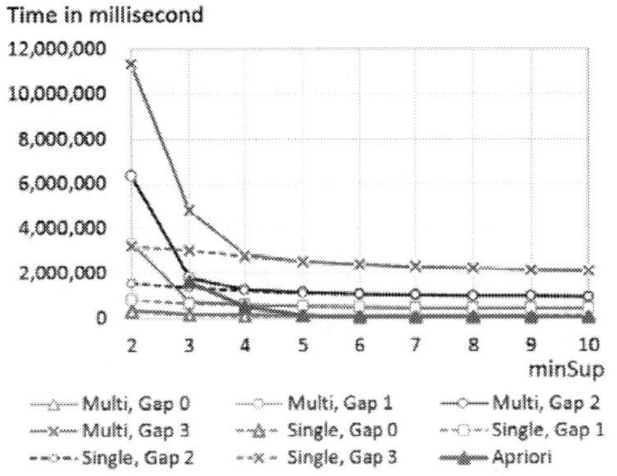

Figure 15. Elapsed time (milliseconds) for retrieving frequent sequences (gap size, 0-3; minSup, 2-10) and frequent itemsets for *apriori* algorithm.

C. Sequence Length Analysis

Fig. 16 shows the number of retrieved sequences for each length of sequences in the multi occurrence mode and a maxGap of three with a minSup ranging from two to five. The maximum length of the retrieved sequence is 244. Note that Fig. 16 omits the results on 31 to 244 of the length of sequence. The number of retrieved sequences reaches peaks around a sequence length of eight to ten for each minSup of two to five. This suggests that code clones of length eight to ten occur most frequently.

The sequence length of 244 is extracted from the *GetLayoutInfo()* method in *GridBagLayout.java* file of *java.awt* package, consisting of 569 source lines including comments and blank lines. The sequence is detected as a frequent sequence, because the sequence includes "*if{ * }*" statements 244 times caused by repetitions within the sequence of *GetLayoutInfo()* method. It is clear that the detection is not preferable for finding code clone detection.

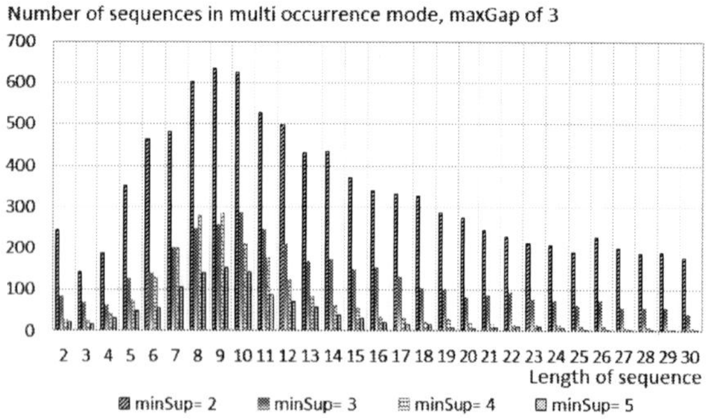

Figure 16. Number of retrieved sequences for each length in multi occurrence mode and maxGap of three.

Fig. 17 shows the number of retrieved sequences for each length of sequence in the single occurrence mode and a maxGap of three with a minSup ranging from two to five.

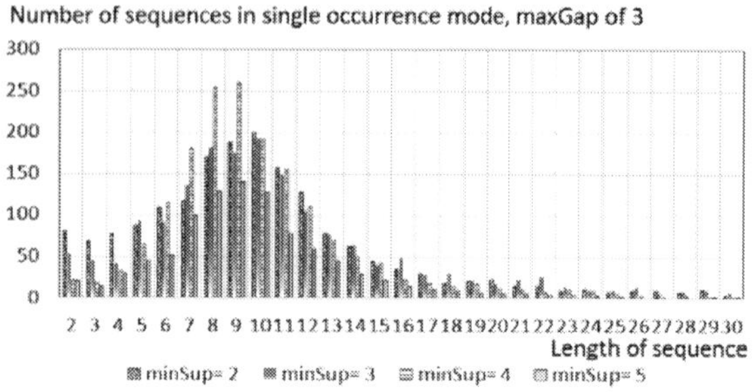

Figure 17. Number of retrieved sequences for each length in single occurrence mode and maxGap of three.

The maximum length of the retrieved sequence is 53 in the single occurrence mode. The sequence of length 53 is extracted from the *getDataElements()* method in *Banded SampleModel.java* file of *java.awt.image* package and the *getDataElements()* method in *ComponentSample Model.java* file. The two methods are the same except for minor syntactic structure, e.g., *if <single statement>* and *if {<single statement>}*, which suggests that they are code clone. Fig. 18 shows the encoded sequence of *getDataElements()* method in *BandedSampleModel.java* file.

```
BandedSampleModel::getDataElements(int x:int y:Object
obj:DataBuffer data) →
001→004→003→24A→24B→007→008→004→003→006→
003→04E→24C→003→00M→008→008→004→003→006→
003→04E→24D→003→00M→008→004→003→006→003→
04E→24E→003→00M→008→004→003→006→003→04E→
24F→003→00M→008→004→003→006→003→04E→24G→
003→00M→003→009→003
```

Figure 18. Encoded sequence of *getDataElements()* method in *BandedSampleModel.java* file.

VI. RELATED WORK

Zhu and Wu [4] propose an *apriori*-like algorithm to mine a set of gap constrained sequential patterns which can be found in a long sequences such as stock exchange rates, DNA and protein sequences. Ding et al. [5] discuss an algorithm to mine repetitive gapped subsequence and apply the proposed algorithm to program execution traces. Kiran et al. [6] propose a model to mine periodic-frequent patterns that occurs at regular intervals or gaps. Fournier-Viger et al. [7] discuss the importance of the maximal sequential pattern mining and propose an efficient algorithm to find the maximal patterns.

Wahler et al. [9] propose a method to detect clones of the Types 1 and 2 which are represented as an abstract syntax tree (AST) in the Extensible Markup Language (XML) by applying a frequent itemset mining technique. Their tool uses the *apriori* algorithm to identify features as frequent itemsets in large amounts of software program statements. They devise an efficient link structure and a hash table for achieving efficiency for practical applications.

Li et al. propose a tool named CP-Miner [10] that uses the closed frequent patterns mining technique to detect frequent subsequences including statements with gaps. CP-Miner shows that a frequent subsequence mining technique can avert redundant comparisons, which leads to improved time performance.

El-Matarawy et al. [11] propose a clone detection technique based on sequential pattern mining. Their method treats source code lines as transactions and statements as items. Their algorithm is applied to discover frequent itemsets in the source code that exceed a given frequency threshold, i.e., minSup. Finally, their method finds the maximum frequent sequential patterns [7][8] of code clone sequences. Their method is fairly similar to ours except for a code transformation parser and systematic handling of gaps of similar sequences based on an LCS algorithm.

Accurate detection of near-miss intentional clones (NICAD) [15] is a text-based code clone detection technique. NICAD uses a parser that extracts functions and performs pretty-printing to standardize code format and the longest-common-subsequence (LCS) algorithm [16] to compare potential clones with gaps. Unlike an *apriori*-based approach, NICAD compares each potential clone with all of the others. Regarding LCS, Iliopoulos and Rahman [17] introduce the idea of gap constraint in LCS to address the problem of extracting multiple sequence alignment in DNA sequences.

Murakami et al. [18] propose a token-based method. The method detects gapped software clones using a well-known local sequence-alignment algorithm, i.e., the Smith-Waterman algorithm [19]. They discuss a sophisticated backtracking algorithm tailored for code clone detection.

VII. CONCLUSIONS AND FUTURE WORK

In this paper, we have presented an attempt to identify Type 3 code clones. Our approach consists of four steps, i.e., extraction of code matching statements, encoding statements in 32-decimal digits, detecting frequent sequences with gaps, and mining the maximal frequent sequences. The paper mainly deals with the last two steps.

Through the experiments using *Java SDK 1.8.0_101 awt* package source code, the proposed algorithm works out successfully for finding clones with respect to a maxGap of zero through three and a minSup of two through ten.

Because a minSup of two poses heavy process loads for the proposed algorithm, we analyze the effect of the repeated subsequences in a method and conclude that the repeated subsequences have adverse effects on both performance and the quality of retrieved code clone especially lower minSup, i.e., minSup of two or three.

So long as code clone is syntactically defined as similar code segments that occur at least twice, the proposed algorithm achieves 100% recall and 100% precision due to the nature of the *aprior*-based data mining with a minSup of two [11]. However, we do not believe that the situation is so simple that syntactically defined recall and precision evaluate the quality of mined code clones. Actually, we find a large number of mined code sequences that mainly consist of control statements. Many of these sequences are not clone from programmer's point of view. We are still only halfway to detecting code clones for industry use especially regarding the quality of mined code clones.

Future work will include the development of functions for clustering and ranking mined code clones for the programmer's sake, and the improvement of the transformation for extracting code matching statements.

ACKNOWLEDGEMENT

The authors would like to thank the anonymous reviewers for their invaluable feedback. This research is supported by the JSPS KAKENHI under grant number 16K00161.

REFERENCES

[1] C. K. Roy and J. R. Cordy "A survey on software clone detection research," Queen's Technical Report:541 Queen's Uni-versity at Kingston, Ontario, Canada, Sep. 2007, pp.1-115.

[2] A. Sheneamer and J. Kalita. "A survey of software clone detection techniques," International Journal of Computer Applications, Vol.137, Issue 10, Mar. 2016, pp.1-21.

[3] R. Agrawal, T. Imielinski, and A. Swami "Mining association rules between sets of items in large databases," Proc. ACM SIGMOD International Conference on Management of Data, June 1993, pp.207-216.

[4] X. Zhu, and X. Wu "Mining complex patterns across sequences with gap requirements," Proc. 20th International Joint Conference on Artifical Intelligence(IJCAI'07), Jan. 2007, pp.2934-2940.

[5] B. Ding, D. Lo, J. Han,and S-C. Khoo "Efficient Mining of Closed Repetitive Gapped Subsequences from a Sequence Database," Proc. 25th IEEE International Conference on Data Engineering (ICDE 2009), March 2009, pp.1024-1035.

[6] R. U. Kiran, M. Kitsuregawa, and P. K. Reddy "Efficient discovery of periodic-frequent patterns in very large databases," Journal of Systems and Software, Vol.112, Issue C, Feb. 2016, pp.110-121.

[7] P. Fournier-Viger, C-W. Wu, A. Gomariz, and V. S-M. Tseng "VMSP: Efficient Vertical Mining of Maximal Sequential Patterns," Proc. 27th Canadian Conference on Artificial Intelligence (AI 2014), May 2014, pp.83-94.

[8] P-N. Tan, M. Steinbach, and V. Kumar "Introduction to Data Mining," Addison-Wesley, March 2006.

[9] V. Wahler, D. Seipel, J. Wolff, and G. Fischer "Clone detection in source code by frequent itemset techniques," Proc. IEEE International Workshop on Source Code Analysis and Manipulation, Oct. 2004, pp.128-135.

[10] Z. Li, S. Lu, S. Myagmar, and Y. Zhou "CP-Miner: A tool for finding copy-paste and related bugs in operating system code," Proc. 6th Symposium on Operating System Design and Implementation, Dec, 2004, pp.289-302.

[11] A. El-Matarawy, M. El-Ramly, and R. Bahgat "Code clone detection using sequential pattern mining," International Journal of Computer Applications, Vol.127, Issue 2, Oct. 2015, pp.10-18.

[12] Y. Udagawa, "Maximal Frequent Sequence Mining for Finding Software Clones," Proc. 18th International Conference on Information Integration and Web-based Applications & Services (iiWAS 2016), Nov. 2016, pp.28-35.

[13] R. Verma, "Compact Representation of Frequent Itemset," http://www.hypertextbookshop.com/dataminingbook/public_version/contents/chapters/chapter002/section004/blue/page001.html, 2009.

[14] M. Monperrus, N. Magnus, and S. Yibin "Java implementation of the Apriori algorithm for mining frequent itemsets," GitHub, Inc., https://gist.github.com/monperrus/7157717, 2010.

[15] C. K. Roy and J. R. Cordy "NICAD: Accurate detection of near-miss intentional clons using flexible pretty-printing and code normalization," Proc. 16th IEEE International Conference on Program Comprehension, June 2008, pp.172-181.

[16] J. Hunt, W. and Szymanski, T. G. "A fast algorithm for computing longest common subsequences," Comm. ACM, Vol.20, Issue.5, May 1977, pp.350-353.

[17] C. S. Iliopoulos and M. S. Rahman "Algorithms for computing variants of the longest common subsequence problem," Theoretical Computer Science Vol.395, Issues 2–3, May 2008, pp.255–267.

[18] H. Murakami, K. Hotta, Y. Higo, H. Igaki, and S.Kusumoto "Gapped code detection with lightweight source code analysis," Proc. IEEE 21st International Conference on Program Comprehension (ICPC), May 2013, pp.93-102.

[19] "Smith–Waterman algorithm," https://en.wikipedia.org/wiki/Smith%E2%80%93Waterman_algorithm, Aug. 2016.

Function Points and Service-Oriented Architectures

A reference model for component based architectures

Roberto Meli
Data Processing Organization Srl
Rome, Italy
email: roberto.meli@dpo.it

Abstract — **Software Service Oriented Architectures (SOA) are characterized by the distribution of data processing components on separate and cooperating technology platforms. Unfortunately, this model represents a technology perspective that is not useful to identify software objects to be measured starting from the user's (business) point of view, as required by international standards of functional measurement (ISO 14143). To solve this problem we have defined the concept of Measurable Software Application (MSA). In the proposed model, each MSA must lie in one and only one layer but may use or incorporate services belonging to different layers. In each layer, we can find generalized software components designed to give a specific and reusable support to the implementation of particular functional or non-functional requirements of the business (application) layer. The identification of generalized software components that belong to lower level layers with respect to the business one, is also crucial to quantify the rate of reuse that should be computed in each project measure for the correct calculation of economical reward, as defined in a customer-supplier contract.**

Keywords-function point analysis; SOA; component; middleware; measurement.

I. Introduction

The goal of this paper is to show a model of a software application specifically suited to allow Functional Size Measurement Methods (also known as Function Points) to be applied to this kind of architecture.

Software Service Oriented Architectures (SOA) are characterized by the distribution of data and processing logic components among separate and cooperating technology platforms [1]-[5].

The execution of a process is often implemented dynamically on the most appropriate element of the architecture at any given time. This organization allows to reuse generalized components (often called services), through standardization and specialization, in order to construct any new transaction. Models that describe these architectures use the concept of layers, which is a way to aggregate those components on the basis of homogeneity of logical representation and usage.

These model, however, are seen from a technological perspective, oriented to the software design and implementation rather than the to the final user point of view.

One of the main values of Function Point Analysis is to allow comparing the convenience of implementing the same user functional requirements (same FP size) with competitive architectures in such a way to choose the most productive one. If any different technical organization of the implemented user requirements had a different logical size this comparison would not be possible. On the other side we should have a practical way to allocate size and consequently effort and costs in the places where that effort and cost is originated. This is the goal that we had in mind in proposing the following approach.

Section II recalls some concepts related to a typical SOA architecture; Section III presents a model for functional measurement of component based architecture; Section IV illustrates how to consider embedded services provided by an application to another one; Section V presents a comparison with related works; Section VI explains the needs for further research and finally Section VII shows the conclusions.

II. A Typical SOA Model

In a distributed architecture, the business layer is associated to the user needs and the typical way of using a system requested by the final user. A Data Base Management System (DBMS) layer, instead, is associated to the requirements of data treatment and storage regardless to their semantic content for the end user; in other words, it is a layer that manipulates the information from a structural point of view rather than from the final user semantic point of view. To the DBMS point of view, the user "meaning" of a table and its data fields is not important. The structured relationships between tables and data fields, the integrity rules, the allowed operations, etc., are important independently by the business meaning of the entity represented by the table(s).

The most used layers to aggregate software components are (Figure 1):

- Presentation Layer: contains the user interface, typically the internet browser. From this layer it is only possible to call services/classes that are in the Business Layer.
- Business Layer: contains services/classes that perform the processing functions required. They can be called either by one or more classes in the Presentation Layer, or even from classes that are in the Business layer itself.
- Data Access Layer: contains services/classes that enable the management of DB data. They can be called only by the Business Layer services/classes.

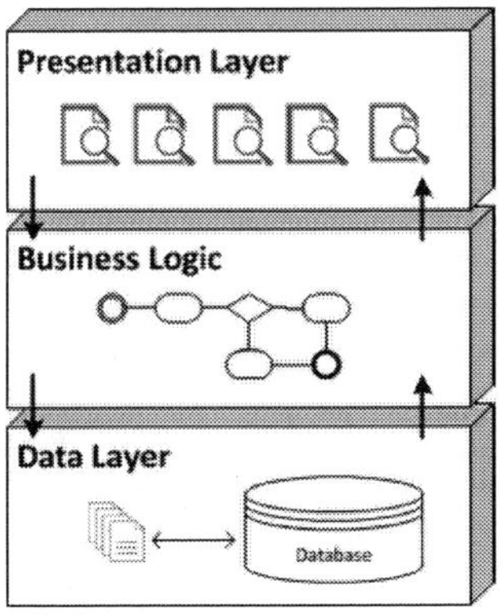

Figure 1. Three-Layers Architectural Scheme

In fact, this scheme highlights the distribution and relationship of client and server components on the specific physical nodes of an information system network of data processing.

But this kind of elements is not relevant and useful for the identification of the software objects to be measured from the user's (business) point of view. From the final user point of view, a typical elementary process (also known as Base Functional Component in the ISO standards for Functional Measurement [2]) normally begins with the business user that activates a functionality (i.e., a trigger to collect information for searching or writing data) handled by the Presentation Layer. This action activates specific features of the business logic (Business Layer) and, according to the business rules, it executes the steps needed to fulfil user requests, generally through accessing or writing permanent archives (Data Access Layer). The scenario ends crossing the layers again (in the opposite direction) to show the results to the requesting user (or to other destination users) through the Presentation Layer features. This set of steps, which are considered by the user meaningful and self-contained as a whole, crosses the layers previously identified several times.

This means that a partitioning of software application in such a way doesn't allow the proper identification of the right software items to be measured in the user functional perspective.

III. Model for Functional Measurement of Component Based Architecture

A more usable model for a functional measurement is shown in Figure 2.

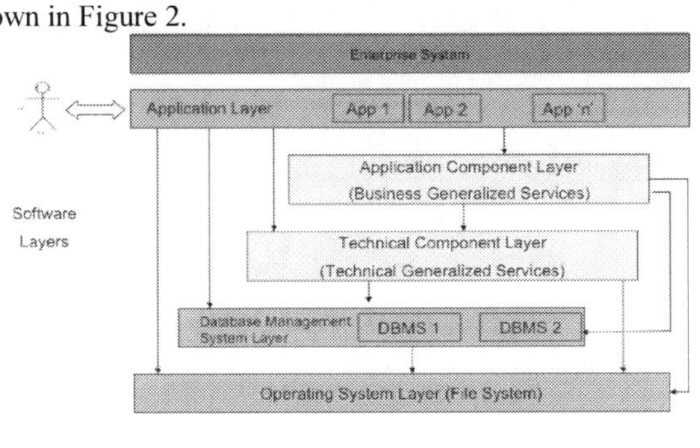

Figure 2. Multi-Layer Model for a Functional Measurement point of view

In the diagram, we see that an enterprise system can be considered as an interface for the activation of a set of applications that are available for the users in a multi-channel way and that rest, in turn, on various underlying software layers, each of them providing "services" to the above layer in a direct or indirect manner.

To clearly identify the entire domain of what to measure, from the user's point of view, we introduce the concept of Measurable Software Application (MSA).

A MSA is defined as "an aggregate of specific functional features conceived from a user point of view, homogeneous in terms of level of logical abstraction."

The term "Measurable" is necessary since very often, as we have already seen, the term Application alone is often already associated (in organization's catalogues) to groups of functionalities aggregated on a technological base instead of a logical one.

For example, in a web environment we may distinguish between a client application (browser), a data base server application, a Content Management System, a generalized "log on" feature and a library of components/web services. From the user's point of view, all these pieces are technically cooperating to support a Business Application at a logical level that is unitary in the user's view. This aggregation is called MSA.

A layer is linked, therefore, to a certain level of abstraction in the representation of data and related functions, this, in turn, determine a different concept of user associated with that particular layer.

Any MSA, by definition, should lie down on a specific and unique layer. An MSA may belong to one and only one layer so the measurement is consistent in terms of level of abstraction and it does not depend on the internal modular organization but only on the external functional user requirements.

In Figure 2, the arrows show the "call direction" of the components on the underlying layers. Between the typical Application layer and the Operating System one or two intermediate layers have been inserted: the layer of generalized business components and the one that includes generalized technical components.

The former are business functions recognizable by the user at the application level, but not sufficiently independent to be considered part of the upper level (otherwise such these business functions would be recognizable as further MSAs).

In fact they represent a kind of "recognizable pieces" of software that need to be "composed" and "aggregated" together in order to fulfil a unique user need (i.e., a component for the verification of a Security Social Number, to be inserted in several elementary processes of the Application component layer).

The latter are technical generalized functions that enables features for the management of applications (such as print programs, or a piece of software for the design of generic form, as well as a physical security service, a network service, access identification and management or client-server services too).

So, any MSA might incorporate and execute components that are distributed across multiple layers, each one containing generalized software (technical or business) components designed to give specific support to the implementation of reusable and specific functional or non-functional requirements.

Therefore, in this model, a middleware layer contains a set of functions defined by the "software architect", working to aid specific requirements of factorization and independence from hardware, operating systems and DBMS environments.

As the middleware functionalities are generalized, they can then be used by different MSA (Figure 3), even not initially considered in defining the technical architecture layers.

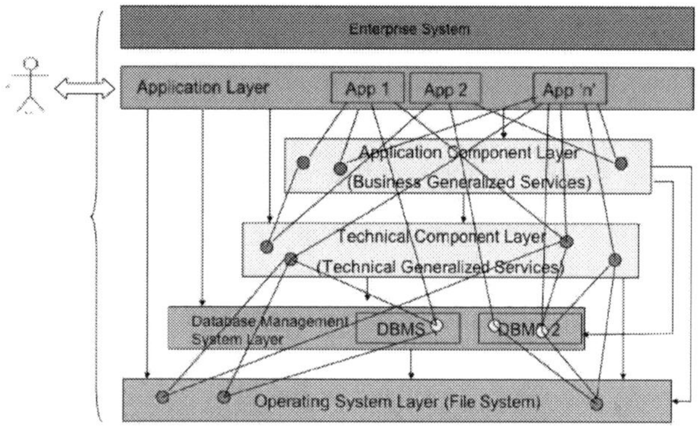

Figure 3. Link between architectural components

The IFPUG Function Point Analysis [7] requires the measurements of the software functionalities as recognized by the final user, while the functionality provided by the middleware are usually not perceived by the user him/herself, although he/she takes advantages of their presence in the systems. For example, a logon transaction for authentication of authorized users of a system can be considered as an EI (External Input) from the user's point of view since, from the software designer point of view, there may be many other elementary functions and/or intermediate software transactions, performed by the middleware and necessary for the completion of authentication service.

The functional requirements can be represented in the system specifications at different, and often not entirely consistent, conceptual and decomposition levels.

In this case a mapping activity can be necessary to correctly assign the functional user requirements (FUR) among the different software layers, to identify the software components to be measured independently each from the others.

Information exchange between different layers may be modeled and measured but different layer's measures can only be cumulated for managerial or contractual reasons. Given a certain MSA, its unique size is calculated on a single specific layer defined by its users.

In other words, the baseline FP measure of an MSA (useful, for example, to define specific service level agreements) must not be obtained as the sum of single measures performed on different layers.

It is possible to measure components at a lower level or macro functions at a higher level if we do not add their values in the asset evaluation for that specific MSA.

For example, a measurement on a Technical Generalized Services Layer can be performed to reward the development of middleware components that the supplier needs to design and build to fulfil non-functional user requirements or technological constrains that cannot be satisfied by standardized commercial-off-the-shelf solutions.

The identification of generalized software components that belong to lower level layers with respect to the business one is also crucial to quantify the rate of reuse that should be computed in each project measure for the right calculation of compensation, as defined in the contract.

The previous concepts are incorporated into the Simple Function Point specification [8], which is a more recent Functional Size Measurement Method with respect to the IFPUG one.

IV. How to consider embedded services provided by other MSA

Sometimes it can be necessary to perform a new software development or a software enhancement of an MSA including elementary processes that use services of other MSA that have to be developed, modified, cancelled or remain unchanged for this purpose.

Figure 4. shows the various functional elements introduced so far to help in the understanding of what and where counting in such cases. A software development or enhancement of an MSA (MSA01 in the picture), which involves the add, change or delete of common services of another MSA (MSA02 in the picture), will count:

- within the MSA01 domain, the user functionality required;
- within the MSA02 domain, the common services that MSA02 "published" to make them available for other MSA that are affected by add, change or delete operations in order to implement the functional user requirements of MSA02.

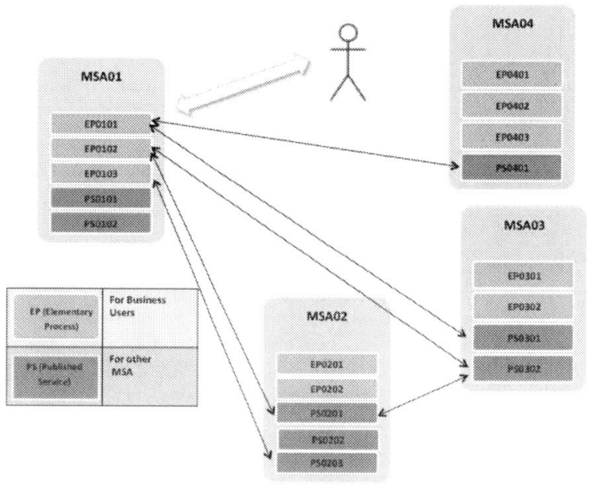

Figure 4. Relationships between MSA's components

The main cases that may occur are listed below. Suppose that an elementary process EP0103 (that is part of MSA01) uses the "published service" PS0203 (that is part of MSA02).

The most relevant scenarios are:

1) ADD of Elementary Process EP0103 (within MSA01) involves ADD of "Published Service" PS0203 (within MSA02)

2) ADD of Elementary Process EP0103 (within MSA01) involves CHG of "Published Service" PS0203 (within MSA02)

3) ADD of Elementary Process EP0103 (within MSA01) involves doing nothing for "Published Service" PS0203 (within MSA02)

4) CHG of Elementary Process EP0103 (within MSA01) involves ADD of "Published Service" PS0203 (within MSA02)

5) CHG of Elementary Process EP0103 (within MSA01) involves CHG of "Published Service" PS0203 (within MSA02)

6) CHG of Elementary Process EP0103 (within MSA01) involves DEL of "Published Service" PS0203 (within MSA02)

7) CHG of Elementary Process EP0103 (within MSA01) involves doing nothing for "Published Service" PS0203 (within MSA02)

8) DEL of Elementary Process EP0103 (within MSA01) involves CHG of "Published Service" PS0203 (within MSA02)

9) DEL of Elementary Process EP0103 (within MSA01) involves DEL of "Published Service" PS0203 (within MSA02)

10) DEL of Elementary Process EP0103 (within MSA01) involves doing nothing for "Published Service" PS0203 (within MSA02)

11) Doing nothing for Elementary Process EP0103 (within MSA01) involves CHG of "Published Service" PS0203 (within MSA02)

As an example, let's concentrate on the first case:

1) ADD of Elementary Process EP0103 (within MSA01) involves ADD of "Published Service" PS0203 (within MSA02)

In this case the elementary process EP0103 in MSA01 is created simultaneously with the creation of a common service (PS0203) in MSA02. From the perspective of MSA01, the measurement of the elementary process EP0103 is reduced because of the advantage (in terms of effort savings) earned using components "published" by the service PS0203.

This lowering is not applicable in case of baseline measurement that is a measurement for asset evaluation purposes.

From the perspective of MSA02, the service PS0203 was not pre-existing, so it is completely counted and charged as ADD, and classified as a middleware elementary process.

As in this case it is possible that some new functionalities can be built starting from pre-existing software component, allowing to obtain a significant reuse. In such cases it's possible to adopt a "lowering by reuse", applying a reducing factor (50% for example) to the data and/or transactional functions that are reusing such components.

The reuse of logical entities within a new software development means the use of logical archives already implemented in other MSAs. In this case it's no necessary to design and maintain a new data structure in the database, cause it can be reused an existing one.

This is a constraint that must be followed mainly to assure project and data integrity, and that has a consequent impact on the right calculation of FP functional size.

For transactional functions the reuse may be related to the integration of common services and application components defined and made available by corporate software frameworks.

A common service can be a set of architectural classes, support and/or shared services that have to be specially used to standardize the software behaviour and to obtain the same technical solution for some common application issues.

Any "lowering by reuse" should not be carried out in case of baseline measurement (that is a measurement for asset evaluation purposes) but only to determine the right size of new software development and enhancements.

Using this approach it is possible to allocate an adequate amount of size to the appropriate development teams that are responsible to maintain different MSA. The total size recognized for the development or enhancement task is so still consistent with an external user point of view but, at the same time, it is useful for management of different teams or even suppliers and contracts.

In an analogous way, it is possible to deal with the other 10 cases listed before.

To be clear with IFPUG experts, we are not proposing a change in IFPUG counting rules but a smart usage of the delivered size measure which becomes "worked or workable" size measure useful for managerial goals. If we look at the released functions, the standard IFPUG measure (without reuse impact) gives a size value to the end user consumable solution. The new measure (Corrected or Contractual Functional Size) is closer to the "worked size" which may be very different to the "usable size". Existing productivity rates (like ISBSG data) may be used on the Corrected Functional Size more consistently because are non "polluted" by the reuse factor.

V. COMPARISON WITH RELATED WORKS

Measuring Function Points of a SOA software application has been frequently approached using a traditional way [9][10][11].

The most used approach consists in setting the boundaries of the "objects" to be measured between the "calling" software and the "called" services, separating them and measuring the interactions among them as if they were "peer to peer" applications. This may be useful to assign to a single (used) service a sizing weight on its own but it is confusing when we consider the "calling" software that, in addition to its usual "end user interactions", has to add functionalities to deal with the usage of lower "incorporated" components in order to release "end user" transactions. This may easily lead to an over-measurement of functional size which is in contrast with the idea that software developed in a SOA environment should be "smaller" than software developed in a traditional way because of reusable component. If we have a library of reusable components we need to develop less functionalities "by scratch" and we would like to express this "saving" quantifying the software size that is reused and the size which remains to be developed completely. In the model presented in this paper, we approach the measuring of a SOA based application as a situation of component reuse: the delivered external size of the application (the released functionalities) is calculated as usual and it is not dependent on its internal architecture. In addition to this size we may calculate e second size - called "worked" or "contractual" size - which can be more useful for estimation goals. Single services may still be measured separately in the traditional way if we like to manage them by metrics.

VI. Need for Further Research

In order to confirm the validity of the proposed approach for software governance goals an empirical research is needed to provide evidence that effort and costs may be correlated to the functional size so configured.

VII. Conclusions

The approach presented here, to measure software applications organized by the use of SOA architectures, is consistent with the ISO/IEC 14143 requirements but, at the same time, it might be useful to manage distributed efforts in software development and enhancement processes and contract management.

References

[1] The Open Group, SOA Source Book (First Edition), Van Haren Publishing, Apr 2009

[2] A. Schmietendorf and R. Dumke, "Guidelines for the Service-Development within Service-oriented Architectures", SMEF2007, 2007

[3] P.C. Clemens, "Software Architecture Documentation in Practice", SEI Symposium, Pittsburgh, 2000

[4] OASIS SOA Reference Model Technical Committee, "Reference Model for Service Oriented Architecture 1.0 OASIS Standard", 12 October 2006, Organisation for the Advancement of Structured Information Standards, https://www.oasis-open.org/standards#soa-rmv1.0, [retrieved: Mar, 2017].

[5] T. Erl, "Service-Oriented Architecture – Concepts, Technology, and Design", Prentice Hall/PearsonPTR, 2006.

[6] ISO/IEC 14143-1:2007, Information Technology – Software Measurement – Functional Size Measurement – Part 1: Definition of Concepts, February 2007

[7] International Function Point Users Group, "Function Point Counting Practices Manual - Release 4.3.1", January 2010.

[8] SiFPA, "Simple Function Point Functional Size Measurement Method - Reference Manual SiFP-01.00-RM-EN-01.01", http://www.sifpa.org/en/index.htm, [retrieved: Mar, 2017].

[9] L. Santillo, `Seizing and sizing SOA applications with COSMIC function points', Proc. Fourth Software Measurement European Forum, (SMEF 2007), May 2007, Roma, Italy.

[10] J. Lindskoog,: Applying function points within a SOA environment, IFPUG Proceedings ISMA4, http://www.ifpug.org/Conference%20Proceedings/ISMA4-2009/ISMA2009-20-Lindskoog-APPLYING-FUNCTION-POINTS-WITHIN-A-SOA-ENVIRONMENT.pdf, [retrieved: Mar, 2017]

[11] Y. M. P. Gomes, "Functional Size, Effort and Cost of the SOA Projects with Function Points", Service Technology Magazine, Issue LXVIII• November 2012

Overview of a Domain-Driven Design Approach to Build Microservice-Based Applications

Roland H. Steinegger, Pascal Giessler, Benjamin Hippchen and Sebastian Abeck

Research Group Cooperation & Management (C&M)
Karlsruhe Institute of Technology (KIT)
Zirkel 2, 76131 Karlsruhe, Germany
Email: (steinegger | pascal.giessler | abeck)@kit.edu, benjamin.hippchen@student.kit.edu

***Abstract*—The current trend of building web applications using microservice architectures is based on the domain-driven design (DDD) concept, as described by Evans. Among practitioners, DDD is a widely accepted approach to building applications. Applying and extending the concepts and tasks of DDD is challenging because it lacks a software development process description and classification within existing software development process approaches. For these reasons, we provide a brief overview of a DDD-based software development process for building resource-oriented microservices that takes into consideration the requirements of the desired application. Following the widely accepted engineering approach suggested by Brügge et al., the emphasis is on the analysis, design, implementation and testing phases. Furthermore, we classify DDD and microservice-based application into regular software development activities and software architecture concepts. After the process is described, it is applied to a case study in order to demonstrate its potential applications and limitations.**

Keywords–Domain-driven design, API, resource-orientation, domain model, software development process, microservices, backend-for-frontend

I. Introduction

Over the past few years, microservice architectures have evolved into a popular method for building multiplatform applications. A well-known example is Netflix, who offers applications for a number of platforms, including mobile devices, smart TVs and gaming consoles [1]. Service-oriented architectures are the foundation of microservice architectures, as microservices have special properties [2]. A microservice is autonomous and provides a limited set of (business) functions. In service-oriented architectures, designing services and selecting boundaries is a key problem.

The traditional approach, as discussed by Erl [3], suggests a technical and functional separation of services. In contrast, according to Evans [4], domain-driven design (DDD) provides the key concepts required to compartmentalize microservices [1]. The DDD approach provides a means of representing the real world in the architecture, e.g., by using bounded contexts representing organizational units [5], and also identifies and focuses on the core domain; both of these characteristics lead to improved software architecture quality [6]. In microservice architectures, these bounded contexts are used to arrange and identify microservices [1]. Using DDD is a key success factor in building microservice-based applications [1].

When applying DDD to the development of microservice-based applications, several problems may arise, depending on the level of experience of the development team. Domain-driven design offers principles, patterns, activities and examples of how to build a domain model, which is its core artifact. However, it neither provides a detailed and systematic development process for applying these principles and patterns nor does it classify them into the field of software engineering. Classifying the activities, introduced by DDD, into the activities of a software development process could improve the applicability. Futher, the classification of the patterns and principles into software architecture concepts, such as architecture perspectives and architecture requirements, supports software architects in desiging microservice architectures.

In addition, there are no clear proceeding regarding how to derive the necessary web application programming interfaces (web APIs) that act as a service contract between microservices and the application. The importance of a service contract is described by Erl [3]. From the business perspective, the web APIs also have strategic value; therefore, they must be designed in manner that emphasizes quality [7].

Furthermore, applications and, in particular, user interfaces, are often not considered or only considered superficially during the process of designing service-oriented architectures [1] [3]. However, the application can play a major role when building the underlying microservices. Domain-driven design emphasizes that the application is necessary to determine the underlying domain logic of microservices; the user interface is important to consider when designing specific web APIs for the UI when using the backends for frontends (BFF) pattern [1]. When designing microservices within the software-as-a-service (SaaS) context, there is no graphical user interface; instead, there is a technical one. The target group shifts from end users to external companies or independent developers who can benefit from the capabilities of the service offered. For this reason, a web API has to be designed in such a manner that it can map as many possible use cases for a particular domain as possible. The resulting set of use cases represents the requirements that must be handled by the web API and the microservices.

We experienced these challenges when establishing a software development process based on DDD to build SmartCampus, a service-oriented web application. During the process we could not find literature that addressed these problems. Thus, we classify DDD activities within the field of software engineering, arrange the components of a microservice-based application according to the layers of DDD and describe the activities necessary in building microservice-based applications. We apply these activities in an agile software development process used to build parts of the SmartCampus application and discuss both the results and limitations.

This article is structured as follows: In Section II, DDD and microservice architecture, including a general introduction to software architecture and development and other related concepts, are introduced. Section III classifies DDD and microservices and introduces the software development activities required in building microservice-based applications according to the requirements of DDD. In the next section, a case study demonstrates the application of these activities within a software development process, including artifacts. The limitations discovered while applying the activities are described in Section V. A conclusion regarding the activities and possible future areas of inquiry is presented in Section VI.

II. Foundation and Related Work

This section provides an overview of model-driven engineering (an approach that is similar to DDD), DDD itself, traditional software engineering activities (which are used to classify DDD activites), software architecture in general (as the foundation being the foundation for classifying microservice architecture) and microservice architecture.

A. Model-Driven Engineering

Douglas C. Schmidt [8] describes Model-Driven Engineering (MDE) as an approach that is used to effectively express domains in models. The Object Management Group (OMG) introduced their framework model-driven architecture (MDA) [9] to support the implementation of MDE. MDA identifies three steps necessary in moving from the abstract design to the implementation of an application. Three models are created by carrying out these steps: 1) computation independent model (CIM) provides domain concepts without taking technological aspects into consideration, 2) platform independent model (PIM) enriches the CIM with computational aspects; and 3) platform specific model (PSM) enriches the PIM with the aspects of implementation that are specific to a particular technological platform.

B. Software Engineering Activities and Domain-Driven Design

Brügge et al. [10] describe a widely accepted software engineering approach in the context of object-orientation. We use their concepts to classify the activities we identified to build microservice-based applications using DDD. This object-oriented approach works well when small teams build applications that range over few domains implemented. [10] offers an overview of the activities that take place during software development: requirements elicitation, analysis, systems design, object design, implementation, and testing. (These activites are discussed further in the article's introduction of the development activities.)

Domain-driven design is an approach that is used in application development where the domain model is the central artifact. Eric Evans introduced this approach in the book Domain-Driven Design and identified the essential principles, activities and patterns required when using DDD [4].

A domain model that conforms to Evans' DDD approach contains everything that necessary to understand the domain [4]. This approach goes beyond the traditional understanding of a domain model, which is connected to a formalized model using the unified modeling language (UML) [11]. To distinguish between the two concepts, following Fairbanks [12], we use the term information model which corresponds to a computation independent model (CIM). It is a part of the domain model and consists of concepts, relationships and constraints. In order to support downstream implementation, Evans adds implementation specific details to the model. The resulting domain model corresponds to a PIM. In Evans' approach to DDD, the central principle is to align the intended application with the domain model. The domain model shapes the ubiquitous language that is used among the team members and functions as a tool used to achieve this goal.

C. Microservice Architectures

Vogel et al. provide a comprehensive framework for the area of software architecture [13], which is used to classify microservices and DDD. Their architecture framework has six dimensions: 1) architectures and architecture disciplines, 2) architecture perspectives, 3) architecture requirements, 4) architecture means, 5) organizations and individuals and 6) architecture methods. The essential terms used in describing an architecture are: systems, which consist of software and hardware building blocks; a software building block can be a functional, technical or platform building block. Building blocks can also consist of other building blocks and may require them. The authors also introduce the concept of architecture views; their definition is influenced by the IEEE [14]. Architecture views are part of the documentation that describes the architecture. Architecture views are motivated by stakeholders' concerns. These concerns specify the viewpoint on the architecture and, thus, specify the views.

Newman provides a comprehensive overview of microservices and related topics from and industry perspective [1]. He defines a microservice as a "small, autonomous service" that does one thing well; and adds that the term "small" is difficult to define. In contrast to services in a service-oriented architecture according to Erl [3], the single purpose principle results in microservices having similar sizes within an architecture [2]. Two mapping studies regarding microservices and microservice architecture reveal that a gap in the literature regarding these topics exists [15] [16]. (Further relevant information is discussed during the section of this article that classifies microservice architectures.)

III. Process

This section classifies the activities involved in of DDD and concepts related to microservice architectures; furthermore, the software development activities involved in building microservice-based applications using DDD are introduced. The activities discussed can be applied to various software process models. However, DDD requires one to continuously question and adapt one's understanding of the domain. Thus, agile software development processes are most suitable.

A. Classification

We identify specifications, that are missing when just applying DDD to build a microservice-based application, by classifying DDD and microservice architecture using the software architecture concepts of Vogel et al. [13]. We divide the classification process into two parts: first, we discuss the architecture perspective and second the architecture requirements.

Concerning the architecture perspective, software architecture can be divided into macro- and micro-architecture; it can further be divided into organization, system and building block level. The organization and system levels form the macro-architecture whereas the building block level can be assigned either to the macro or micro-architecture depending on what is required for the concrete architecture. [13]

Despite their names, microservice architecture and the domain model describe the macro-architecture. A microservice is a functional or technical software building block that require a platform to run on. Neither DDD nor microservices limit the underlying platform. When using DDD, microservices are structured according to the organizational units using bounded contexts from the domain model [1] [17]. The domain objects within a bounded context specify the core architecture of a microservice.

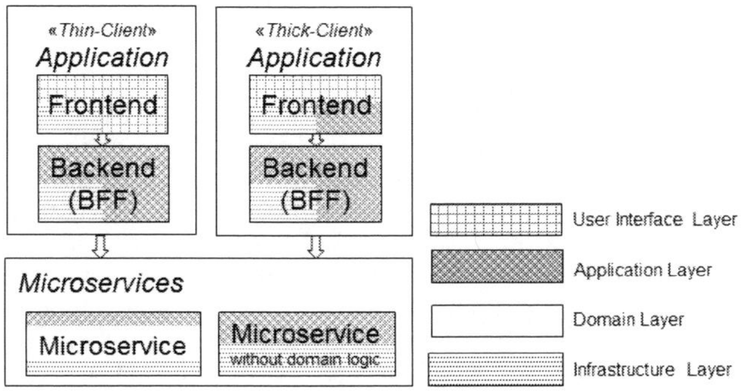

Figure 1. Software building blocks and their layers in a microservice-based application

Domain-driven design requires a layered architecture to separate the domain from other concerns [4]. Evans suggests a four layered architecture, consisting of the user interface, application, domain and infrastructure layers. Figure 1 shows the distribution of these layers among the software building blocks of microservice-based applications. On the highest abstraction level, microservice-based applications can be divided into applications and microservices. The application consists of a frontend, which is either thin or thick (meaning that it is with or without application logic), and its backend, which provides the application logic. The backend uses the microservices to access the domain layer or general infrastructure functionality. Each microservice has an application layer on top. The application layer translates requests into either the domain or infrastructure layers.Infrastructure logic *may* be part of each software building block. In our approach, we applied the layer distribution following Miller's approach [18].

In a layered architecture, higher layers can communicate with lower layers. Figure 2 depicts the layered architecture's communication process applied to the above-mentioned software building blocks [18]. The frontend should not directly call the microservices; we emphasize this by using dashed arrows.

Concerning architecture requirements, the decision to build microservice-based applications is taken at the organizational level (see the classification of service-oriented applications in [13]). Along with a microservice architecture, the organization

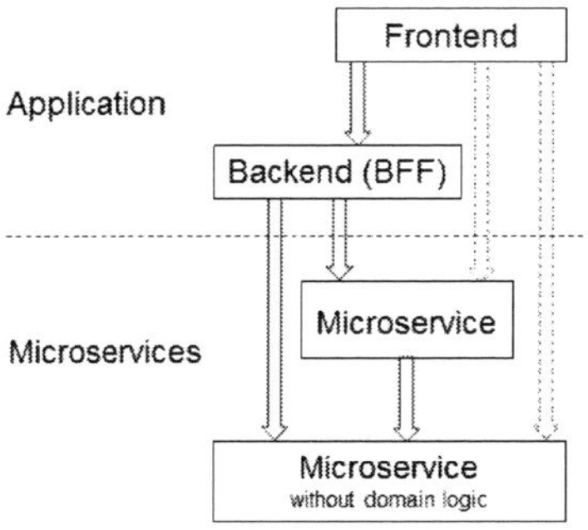

Figure 2. Communication between components

should choose a protocol that allows all of the microservices within the organization to communicate; e.g., using representational state transfer (REST) over hypertext transfer protocol (HTTP) with a set of guidelines or an event bus. The platform running the microservices (e.g., docker), the database technologies, the implementation of identity and access management etc. *might* also be organizational requirements; when building a microservice architecture the software architects have to decide, whether or not these concerns should be homogenous. We could not identify any requirements concerning the system or building block levels that are based on DDD or the microservice approach.

Some specification is still missing. The domain model specifies the functional view on the domain but does not consider technical aspects [4]. Thus, in addition to the domain model, there is a need for artifacts that describe the microservice architecture, including technical microservices and platform architecture. Furthermore, assuming that the domain model describes the architecture of the domain layer, the user interface, application, and infrastructure layer are not specified. Translating this into the context of the software building blocks, the frontend and backend may require specification. The decision to add further artifacts could be based on the risks involved in the application, as discussed by Fairbanks [12]. In our activities, we decided to add a user interface (UI)/user experience (UX) design, which specifies both the user interface and the user's interaction. Thus, this artifact specifies the frontend and backend.

B. Activity Overview

Next, we introduce the activities involved in building microservice-based applications. These activities facilitate the development of applications within similar domains. We align our activities with the traditional software development activities described by Brügge et al. [10]. Therefore, the activities end after testing, and we do not discuss deployment and/or maintenance. Figure 3 depicts the three activities and their interrelations: *requirements elicitation and analysis*, *design* and *implementation and testing*.

During the *requirements elicitation and analysis*, two sub-activities take place: first, the information model, as part of the domain model, is created by "crunching knowledge" with domain experts; second, a prototype is designed and is discussed with both the user and customer. As both activities are closely related (when discussing prototypes, the knowledge of the domain gets deeper, and when discovering the information

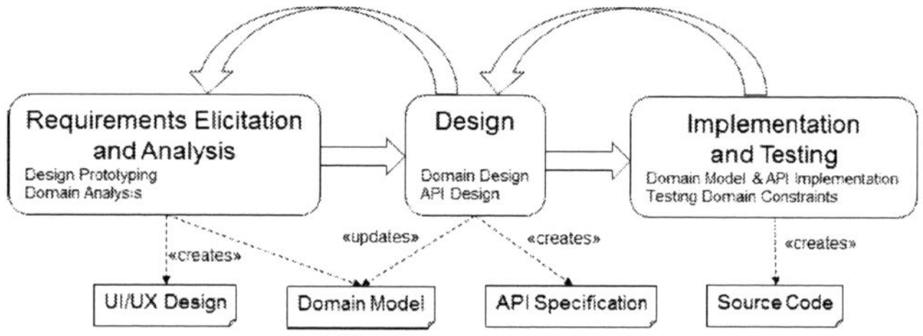

Figure 3. Overview of the activities used in building microservice-based applications

model, terms or workflows might change), we combined them into a single activity.

The *design* is comprised of the sub-activities involved in designing the domain and the APIs of the microservices. Based on the UI/UX design and further discussions with the user, the information model is refined, e.g., design decisions are made, and design patterns are applied. Domain design is comparable to the system design activity discussed by Brügge et al. [10]. The system is divided into subsystems that, according to Conway's Law [5], can be realized by individual teams using bounded contexts. Domain design results in a domain model that must be bound to the implementation artifacts. As the microservices offer access to the domain model and translate from the application layer to the domain layer, both the UI/UX design (representing the user interface layer and the application layer) as well as the domain model (representing the domain layer of DDD) is used to design the web APIs of the microservices. If using a BFF, its web API is designed, too. This activity can be assigned to the object design activity discussed by Brügge et al. [10].

After this preliminary work, the microservices are *implemented and tested*. The web APIs describe the microservices' entry points. These entry points and their application logic are implemented and tested, as the microservices' domain model. The constraints defined in the domain model, such as multiplicities or directed associations, are sources for domain tests.

Evans states that developing a "deep model" with which to facilitate software development requires "exploration and experimentation" [4]. Thus, software developers have to be open-minded to gain insights into the domain across the whole software development activities. This knowledge probably leads to changes in artifacts created during the previous activities. Therefore, iterations and jumping back to previous phases is possible in each phase. To be more clear, it is common to switch between phases and activities. Of course, experienced developers may do fewer mistakes and discover insights earlier, but hidden knowledge and misunderstandings are common. In the next sections, the phases are explained in more detail.

C. Requirements Elicitation and Analysis

The first activity is about understanding the needs of the user. Two non-chronological ordered activities take place in this phase: exploration of the domain and designing a prototype. These activities highly influence each other, e.g., the terms from the domain model are used in the prototype while new insights might change them. We see a strong binding between the origination process of the domain model and design prototyping, due to the missing specifications that are not captured during domain modeling. Every domain concept displayed on the design prototype has to be modeled in the domain model and vice versa. Small iterations within the analysis are needed in order to validate that both artifacts are consistent.

1) Domain Analysis: Exploring the Domain with DDD: Without a complete understanding, building satisfying applications is getting hard. In our presented approach, we focus on Evans book "Domain-Driven Design: Tackling Complexity in the Heart of Software" (DDD) to understand the needs and, thus, the domain through modeling [4]. Creating a comprehensive domain model in this phase needs experienced domain modelers to gain knowledge. After this step, we have a domain model that is equal to an information model (see Section II-B). Unified Modeling Language (UML) class diagram syntax is used to describe concepts and their relationships, constraints, etc. [19] [12].

According to DDD, collaboration with customers is essential to explore and particularly model the domain. So the first and recurring step of DDD is Knowledge Crunching [4]. Simultaneously to discussions with customers, the development team carries out the modeling activity and creates the domain model step by step. By following the pattern *Hands-On Modelers*, every team member involved in the software development process should also be part of the domain modeling to increase creativity [4]. In addition, a *Ubiquitous Language* will be established, which is the cross-team language. The origination process of the domain model is highly influenced by exploration and experimentation [4]. It is far better if a not completely satisfying model is going to implementation, than to refine the domain model over and over again without risking the implementation [4]. Creating the domain model under influence of DDD, makes it an iterative activity and fitting to principles from agile development processes, such as short time to market.

Complex domains automatically lead to a complex domain model. This complexity makes it hard for readers to understand the domain model. Due to that fact, it is necessary to split the model into multiple diagrams [18], which enables the modeler to model different aspects of the domain. Dynamic behavior, such as workflows, are relevant concepts of the domain. We adapt the view approach from software architecture [13] and introduced a concept named *domain views* to model different behaviors. We have created various types of domain views, such as an interactional view. They are motivated by a stakeholder with an special concern, too. During knowledge crunching, this predefinition makes it easy to choose the right person to discuss with.

The result of exploring the domain is a domain model, which contains relevant concepts of the domain, also called the domain knowledge [4]. DDD emphasizes this as focusing on the core domain that is relevant for the downstream implementation of the application [4].

2) Design Prototyping: By knowledge crunching, we get a complete understanding of the considered domain. The application requirements are use case specific and indicators for domain logic that has to be modeled in the domain model accordingly. Each identified use case based on the discussion with the stakeholders will be represented as part of a so-called design prototype. A prototype is an efficient way for trying out new design concepts and determine their efficiency [20]. The design prototype is a specialization and focuses on the UI and the UX of the application. Since the customer primarily interacts with the UI, it is also an ideal artifact for further discussions with customers along the domain model. Further benefits by using a prototype can be found in [20]. Similar to knowledge crunching, design prototyping is an iterative activity. Each iteration consists of a brain storming regarding design ideas with respect to given boundary conditions, realization of the previously chosen design ideas, presentation and review of the resulting design prototype. The feedback from the customer as part of the review will be collected and analyzed to derive the necessary design changes for the next iteration. The design prototyping is finished when the prototype represents all of the customer needs.

D. Design Phase

Two activities take place during the design phase: Domain and API Design. These activities require the domain model and the UI/UX design created during the previous phase. After the design phase, the domain model as well as the API specification are ready to be implemented.

1) Domain Design: From Computational to Platform Independent Model (PIM): An important idea of DDD is the binding of the domain to the implementation [4]. The domain model is the core artifact to achieve this goal in the domain layer. During the analysis phase a computational independent model, the information model as part of the domain model, is created. Now, first, this model is separated into bounded contexts and, second, these bounded contexts are extended and refined, e.g., by applying design patterns to fulfill application requirements. These activities are based on examples of Evans and Vaughn [4] [17].

The organizational structure is used to decompose the information model into bounded contexts. The task requires experience and several iterations due to its importance [17], [21]. The decomposition is tightly coupled to the division of the development teams, each working on a bounded context [1]. Thus, intermediate results are discussed with the domain experts and other team members. The result is a context map, showing the relations of the bounded contexts.

The next steps are mainly carried out by the development team that is responsible for each bounded context. The goal of the next activity is to refine and extend the domain model according to the requirements of the applications. The UI/UX design is the main source for the application requirements.

Probably, the domain objects in the information model are already marked with stereotypes indicating their type, i.e., aggregate root, value object, entity or domain event. Even some services might be identified during the analysis phase. Domain objects missing a stereotype should be treated first; a stereotype should be added. Next, the design patterns repository, factory and domain service are added according to the requirements. For example, if there is functionality needing to display a domain object in the UI, a repository is added, or if there is a complex aggregate root, a factory might be added [4]. During the whole design process, the domain experts and other sources of information are involved (continuous knowledge crunching). After applying the design patterns, the domain model is ready to get implemented.

2) API Design: Deriving the Web API from PIM: Microservices expose their implemented business functionality via web APIs [1]. A web API can be seen as a specialization of an traditional API, which is why, we extend the definition by Gebhart et. al a bit further: "a contract prescribing how to interact with the underlying system [over the Web]," [22, p. 139]. From business perspective, a web API can be seen as a highly valuable business asset [7], [23] that can also serve as a solution for digital transformation [22].

A web API can be used for composing microservices to map a complex business workflow onto the area of microservices or offering business functionality for third-party developers [22]. To facilitate the reuse and discovery of existing functionality in form of microservices, the exposed web APIs have to be designed with care. According to Newman [1], Jacobsen [23] and Mulloy [24], web APIs should adhere to the following informal quality criteria: 1) Easy to understand, learn and use from a service consumer point of view, 2) Abstracted from a specific technology, 3) Consistent in look and feel and 4) Robust in terms of its evolution.

To overcome these challenges, we have to form a systematic approach on how to derive the web API from the underlying domain model. First, we have made the decision to build web APIs in a resource-oriented manner that can be positioned on the second level of the Richardson Maturity Model [25]. We do not pursue the hypermedia approach by Fielding [26] to reduce the complexity when building microservice-based applications. Second, we have identified resources and sub resources from the underlying PIM by looking at the relationship between the domain objects. Third, we have derived the required HTTP methods as well as their request and response representations from the interactional view as one of the mentioned domain views (see Section III-C1). Besides this, we have also developed a set of guidelines to support architects and developers by fulfilling the previously described informal criteria web APIs. These guidelines were derived from existing best practices by designing resource oriented web APIs [27]. The result of this design work is finally structured according to OpenAPI specification, which has the goal to "define a standard, language-agnostic interface to REST APIs which allows both humans and computers to discover and understand the capabilities of the service without access to source code, documentation, or through network traffic inspection.," [28].

3) API Design: Deriving the Web API for BFF from Design Prototyp: A BFF is a common pattern to avoid so-called chatty APIs [1]. Chatty APIs often result in a huge amount of requests for the service consumer to get the needed information [24, p. 30f]. This is mainly due the fact that the needed domain information or logic is spread over multiple microservices and primarily designed for reusability rather than a specific use case in form of a concrete application. Besides, BFFs allow a development team to focus on the UI and UX specific requirements of an application by not restricting them on the exposed web APIs of the microservices. Additional and necessary application logic, such as data transformation, caching or orchestration can be implemented on the BFF level or application layer according to DDD [4]. That is why, the BFF can be seen as part of the UI [1].

In our approach, the UI and UX specific requirements are represented through a design prototype as a result of a conducted analysis phase (see Section III-C2). Similar to Section III-D2, we have decided to go with a resource-oriented style for the BFF web API and applied the same web API guidelines. Other solutions such as a method-oriented approach is also possible. For deriving the web API, we are looking at each view regarding the represented information as well as the interaction elements that cause data manipulations. This allows us to build resources, their representations as well as their needed operations. The resulting web API is highly coupled with the UI and now needs to be connected with the underlying domain represented by microservices. Since the domain model, as well as the design prototype are designed by using the *Ubiquitous Language*, the required microservices can be identified with minimal effort and orchestrated on the application layer to fulfill the requirements specified by the derived BFF web API.

E. Implementation and Testing

The domain model and web API specification enable the development team to implement the application. In this section, the implementation and testing of the microservices is introduced. We do not discuss the implementation of the UI/UX design, as we focus on DDD and building microservices. But, the implementation and testing of the BFF, being the connection between front end and microservices, is discussed.

First, we focus on implementing and testing the microservices. Each bounded context is implemented as an microservice using the specified API. A development project, e.g., a maven project including source code, is created and pushed into the version control repository. We recommend to offer the API specification as part of the microservice. It is added to the repository and delivered through its web interface. This way, changes to the API can be pushed to the repository together with their implementation. DDD highly recommends to use continuous integration [4], thus, the continuous integration pipeline is configured, too.

Venon [17] describes how to implement REST resources separating the application from the domain layer. The web API describes entry points to the microservice; it can be implemented straight forward. The logic at the entry points should be application specific in order to separate application specific parts from domain specific, e.g., the usage of REST. Thus, a microservice should have an application layer on top. Typically, this layer is implemented as an anti corruption layer; a design pattern to achieve a clean separation of application and domain terms [17]. Additionally, by preventing the use of domain objects as input parameters, the coupling of domain objects and web API is reduced. Thus, some minor changes in the domain model do not influence the implementation of the interface [17].

The domain layer is implemented according to the domain model. Thus, the domain objects in the bounded context are mapped to classes, when using an object-oriented programming language. Constraints, such as multiplicities, and domain logic is implemented in the domain object. If a domain object from another microservice is used, a reference to the object is saved, e.g., by using the identifier [17], [29]. Implemented domain objects are intelligent objects that ensure the constraints in the domain. The application layer should never have access to domain objects, that do not comply with the constraints. Development approaches, such as test-driven development [30] or even behavior-driven development [31] are a good choice in order to achieve this goal. These constraints might be distributed among the domain model, thus, constraints might be overseen. Separating tester and developer of functionality, pair-programming as well as reviews can help to overcome this problem.

Beside of the application and domain layer, the infrastructure layer is part of the microservice. This layer contains functionality to access databases, log events, enforce authorization, cache results, discover services etc.; everything supporting the application and domain layer. Apparent is the support for domain repositories. If a microservice has a repository, the infrastructure layer must offer access to a database.

Last, we discuss the implementation of the UI's backend. The backend is an application of the BFF pattern. Therefore, a main goal is to offer a facade hiding the microservice architecture. The implementation can be kept simple. Its web API is implemented according to the specification. In our case, the specification is oriented on the microservice web API specification, thus, the request can be directly forwarded to the microservice. Depending on the specification, the frontend supports further functionality, e.g., authentication and access control may be implemented in the UI's backend.

IV. CASE STUDY: THESIS ADMINISTRATION

In our case study, we were attempting a modernization of the thesis administration within the KIT department of informatics at Karlsruhe Institute of Technology. Our goal was to create an application based on microservices and to provide it to the university through the service-oriented platform SmartCampus [32] that we develop in our research group. For project execution, we chose Scrum as our software development process.

A. Crunching the Information Model

In relation to the presented approach, we started eliciting the domain knowledge with knowledge crunching. When we found the domain experts - members of the Main Examination Committee -, we started to discuss the domain. Quickly we noticed that the thesis is one of the main concepts of the domain. Thus, we explored the thesis by interviewing domain experts at first. Besides the concepts and relationships of the thesis, we also noticed constraints, which we included in the information model. Figure 4 shows a piece of our crunched information model. We put the *Thesis* in the middle of the model to reflect the central position within the core domain.

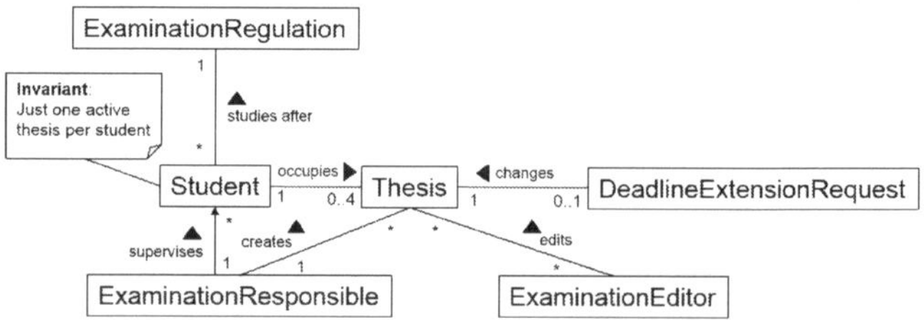

Figure 4. Piece of the information model showing concepts of the thesis domain object

Deeper discussions about the thesis told us somewhat about states that a thesis can occupy. At this point, we took into account the approach of domain views. We modeled a finite automaton to determine our understanding and discuss it with the domain expert, as shown in Figure 5. The diagram supports the understanding without using UML typical elements.

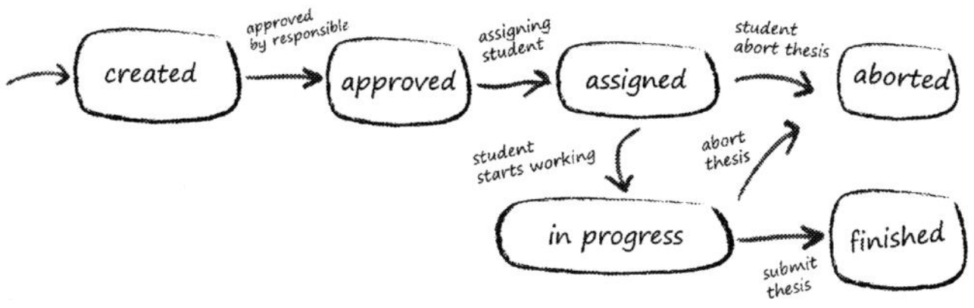

Figure 5. Finite automaton sketches the possible thesis states

After discussions with the domain experts, we had our desired information model and were able to transform it into a PIM.

B. Creating the Design Prototype

Besides crunching the information model, we started the design prototyping and sketched each identified use case. In Figure 6 we illustrate an information page of a specific thesis. This prototype was used to validate the elicited domain knowledge.

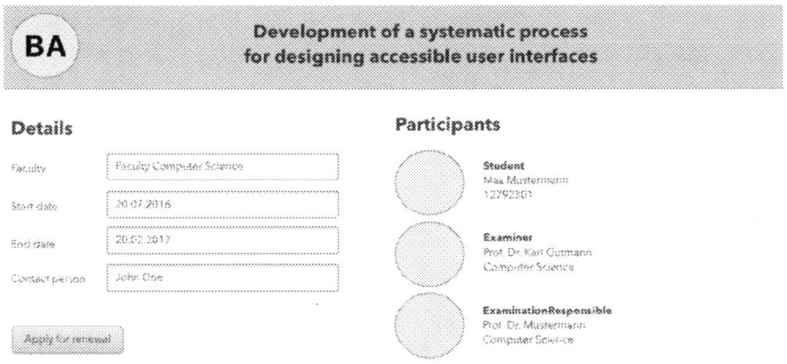

Figure 6. Design mockup (in early phase) for visualizing details about a thesis

C. Enriching the Information Model

After eliciting the domain knowledge and creating a design prototype, we were able to enrich our information model with implementation details. Mainly we focused on using the DDD patterns such as Bounded Context, Entities, Value Objects or Repositories [4]. At first, we structured the domain into bounded context according to Conway's Law [5] and, thus, divide the thesis administration domain into microservices. Then we could create the context map by the composition of the bounded contexts (see Figure 7).

Afterward, we started to identified entities, value objects and made a decision about persistence within our intended application through repositories. We oriented ourselves to the requirements of the application when applying the patterns. For example, we decided that the domain object "Student" in Figure 8 did not need a repository because it does not need to be globally accessible.

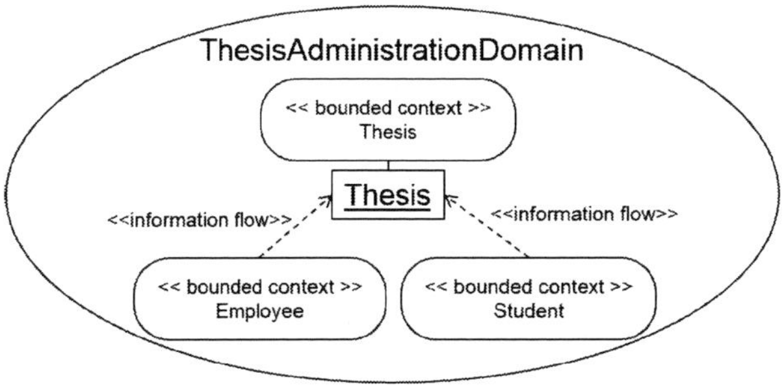

Figure 7. Context map composing bounded contexts of the thesis administration domain

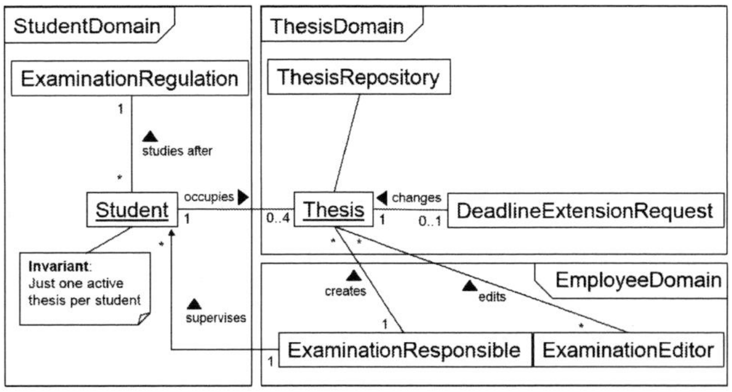

Figure 8. Thesis specific piece of the domain model including DDD patterns

D. Design and Implementation of the API Specification

The API specification was designed according to the domain model and UI/UX design. Figure 9 shows how to access a single thesis resource and its attributes. The attributes are mainly influenced by the information modeled in the design prototype.

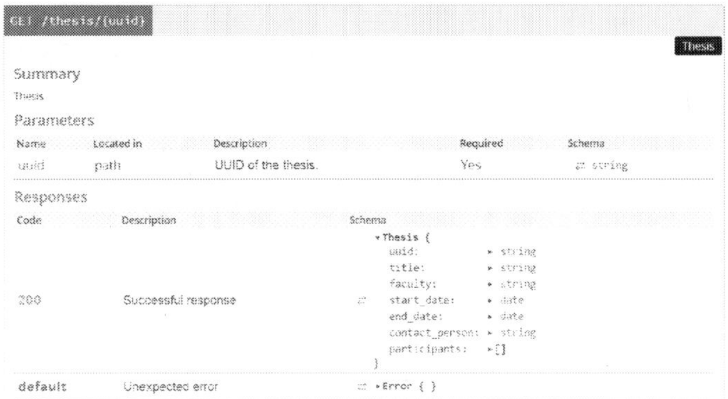

Figure 9. OpenAPI specification of getting single thesis displayed with SwaggerUI

During the implementation phase, the domain objects in the bounded context were mapped to the source code. We used Java and the Spring Framework, which supported to focus on the domain layer. Spring is implemented having the concepts of DDD in mind. We separated the application and domain layers into different packages. We did not need an infrastructure layer, because Spring Data directly supports repositories through specialization. The database can be configured using configuration files. The entry point to the application is a Spring Controller. Several annotations helped to map HTTP requests to methods. Even more annotations enable the use of dependency injection, so that we could depend on repository interfaces while spring injected their implementation. The development team added sequence diagrams to model the interaction of the controllers. This is also due to a lack of experience.

E. Synergy between Approach and Scrum

It turned out that our presented approach complements itself well with Scrum. During each activity we did, we always had the Scrum artefacts in mind and tried to create them directly. Also the iterative approach from Scrum fit well to our executed activities. This corresponds to the principle of exploration and experimentation presented by Eric Evans in DDD [4].

Through the combination of information model and design prototypes, we could easily fill the Product Backlog. Also we were able to extract the user stories and their task within to create the Sprint Backlog from the PIM and API Specification. After each Sprint, we could adjust the PIM, transfer the changes into the Product Backlog and start a new Sprint.

V. LIMITATIONS

The activities we introduced provide an overview of the activities that take place when applying DDD in building microservice-based applications. These activities represent a first step towards a complete process that includes all of the required artifacts. Our research indicated that several topics require further investigation and more detailed descriptions; for example, it is quite difficult to systematize the design of the domain model according to DDD. Best practices could be identified and added to the process description to support the performance of this activity.

During the case study, we received useful feedback from the software development team. In Section III-A on classification, we discussed concerns regarding the specification that are not covered by the artifacts. We used the UI/UX design in addition to DDD and the microservice approach to provide the missing specification in the user interface and application layers; however, the development team still had problems implementing the functionality in the application layer. To address these problems, they added additional sequence diagrams that specified the usage of the domain layer within a microservice. It is likely, that there are more specification artifacts that must be identified, as, using the Spring framework, which supports developers in several ways, much of the application and infrastructure layer source code is supplied, which makes specification unnecessary.

While discussing the implementation process and testing activities, we noted that the implementation of a domain model created according to DDD is (slightly) bound to object-oriented programming languages. This is due to the fact that the concepts and diagrams introduced in [4] have object-oriented programming in mind. The use of a functional programming language might require a different set of patterns and diagrams; as such, the process identified in this article is also somewhat bound to implementation using an object-oriented language.

VI. CONCLUSION AND FUTURE WORK

DDD offers key concepts and activities to build applications based on a microservice architecture, whereby the activities are missing links to existing software engineering knowledge. We classified both into software architecture concepts and software development activities. Further, we introduced an overview of software development activities and artifacts for building microservice-based applications, which extend DDD. In a case study, we showed the application of the activities in an agile software development process to build a thesis management applications as part of the SmartCampus and gave examples of the resulting artifacts. The overview of activities and their classification is a first step towards a complete process for developing such web applications and, thus, we described its limitations and missing artifacts.

DDD is about focusing on the domain including its concepts, their relationships and business logic. Microservice architecture is about arranging and dividing distributed software building blocks. We showed missing requirement specifications and missing artifacts with our classification and the case study. We will further refine the activities towards a software development process to identify a sufficient set of artifacts.

A major advantage of DDD and microservices is the reuse of existing functionality. Identity and access management is a domain (almost) each application needs, thus, we will investigate in building a knowledge repository and enriching the activities and artifacts so that models and functionality in this domain can be reused among applications. In addition to this research topic, we will continue to focus on how we can systematically derive web APIs for microservices with quality aspects in mind such as evolvability. The web API also plays a significant role in discovering and reusing microservices in the context of a microservice landscape.

ACKNOWLEDGMENT

We are very thankful to Pascal Burkhardt for his contributions, both through discussions and the input he provided regarding his projects, as well as to Philip Hoyer for providing his opinions during our discussions. Furthermore, we would like to thank the following members of the development team and domain experts for participating in the case study: Florian BReuer, Lukas Bach, Anne Sielemann, Johanna Thiemich, Rainer Schlund, Niko Benkler, Adis Heric, Pablo Castro, Mark Pollmann, Iona Gheta, Johannes Theuerkorn and David Schneiter.

REFERENCES

[1] S. Newman, Building Microservices, 1st ed. O'Reilly Media, Inc., 2015.

[2] M. Richards, Microservices vs. service-oriented architecture. O'Reilly Media, Inc., 2015.

[3] T. Erl, SOA Principles of Service Design (The Prentice Hall Service-Oriented Computing Series from Thomas Erl). Upper Saddle River, NJ, USA: Prentice Hall PTR, 2007.

[4] E. Evans, Domain-driven design: tackling complexity in the heart of software. Addison-Wesley Professional, 2003.

[5] M. E. Conway, "How do committees invent," Datamation, vol. 14, no. 4, 1968, pp. 28–31.

[6] E. Landre, H. Wesenberg, and H. Rønneberg, "Architectural improvement by use of strategic level domain-driven design," in Companion to the 21st ACM SIGPLAN Symposium on Object-oriented Programming Systems, Languages, and Applications, ser. OOPSLA '06. ACM, 2006, pp. 809–814, URL: http://doi.acm.org/10.1145/1176617.1176728 [retrieved: 2017-03-03].

[7] B. Iyer and M. Subramaniam, "The Strategic Value of APIs," January 2015, URL: https://hbr.org/2015/01/the-strategic-value-of-apis [retrieved: 2017-03-03].

[8] D. C. Schmidt, "Model-driven engineering," COMPUTER-IEEE COMPUTER SOCIETY-, vol. 39, no. 2, 2006, p. 25.

[9] A. G. Kleppe, J. Warmer, W. Bast, and M. Explained, "The model driven architecture: practice and promise," 2003.

[10] B. Bruegge and A. H. Dutoit, Object-Oriented Software Engineering Using UML, Patterns and Java-(Required). Prentice Hall, 2004.

[11] I. Jacobson, G. Booch, and J. Rumbaugh, The unified software development process. Addison-wesley Reading, 1999, vol. 1.

[12] G. Fairbanks, Just enough software architecture: a risk-driven approach. Marshall & Brainerd, 2010.

[13] O. Vogel, I. Arnold, A. Chughtai, and T. Kehrer, Software Architecture: A Comprehensive Framework and Guide for Practitioners. Springer Berlin Heidelberg, 2011, URL: http://dx.doi.org/10.1007/978-3-642-19736-9 [retrieved: 2017-03-03].

[14] I. A. W. Group et al., "Ieee recommended practice for architectural description," IEEE Std, vol. 1471, 1998.

[15] N. Alshuqayran, N. Ali, and R. Evans, "A systematic mapping study in microservice architecture," in Service-Oriented Computing and Applications (SOCA), 2016 IEEE 9th International Conference on. IEEE, 2016, pp. 44–51.

[16] C. Pahl and P. Jamshidi, "Microservices: A systematic mapping study," in Proceedings of the 6th International Conference on Cloud Computing and Services Science, 2016, pp. 137–146.

[17] V. Vernon, Implementing domain-driven design. Addison-Wesley, 2013.

[18] S. Millett, Patterns, Principles and Practices of Domain-Driven Design. John Wiley & Sons, 2015.

[19] Y. T. Lee, "Information modeling: From design to implementation," in Proceedings of the second world manufacturing congress. Citeseer, 1999, pp. 315–321.

[20] J. Arnowitz, M. Arent, and N. Berger, Effective Prototyping for Software Makers. San Francisco, CA, USA: Morgan Kaufmann Publishers Inc., 2006.

[21] E. Evans, "Tackling complexity in the heart of software," January 2016, domain-Driven Design Europe 2016, URL: https://hbr.org/2015/01/the-strategic-value-of-apis [retrieved: 2017-03-03].

[22] M. Gebhart, P. Giessler, and S. Abeck, "Challenges of the digital transformation in software engineering," ICSEA 2016 : The Eleventh International Conference on Software Engineering Advances, 2016, pp. 136–141.

[23] D. Jacobson, G. Brail, and D. Woods, APIs: A Strategy Guide. O'Reilly Media, Inc., 2011.

[24] B. Mulloy, "Web API Design - Crafting Interfaces that Developers Love," March 2012, URL: http://pages.apigee.com/rs/apigee/images/api-design-ebook-2012-03.pdf [retrieved: 2017-03-03].

[25] J. Webber, S. Parastatidis, and I. Robinson, REST in Practice: Hypermedia and Systems Architecture, 1st ed. O'Reilly Media, Inc., 2010.

[26] R. T. Fielding, "Architectural styles and the design of network-based software architectures," Ph.D. dissertation, University of California, Irvine, 2000.

[27] P. Giessler, M. Gebhart, D. Sarancin, R. Steinegger, and S. Abeck, "Best Practices for the Design of RESTful web Services," International Conferences of Software Advances (ICSEA), 2015, URL: http://www.thinkmind.org/download.php?articleid=icsea_2015_15_10_10016 [retrieved: 2017-03-03].

[28] OpenAPI, "The OpenAPI Specification (fka The Swagger Specification)," 2017, URL: https://github.com/OAI/OpenAPI-Specification [retrieved: 2017-03-03].

[29] O. Gierke, "DDD & REST - Domain Driven APIs for the Web," November 2016, SpringOne Platform, URL: https://www.infoq.com/presentations/ddd-rest [retrieved: 2017-03-03].

[30] K. Beck, Test-driven development: by example. Addison-Wesley Professional, 2003.

[31] D. North, "Behavior modification: The evolution of behavior-driven development," Better Software, vol. 8, no. 3, 2006.

[32] R. Steinegger, J. Schäfer, M. Vogler, and S. Abeck, "Attack surface reduction for web services based on authorization patterns," The Eighth International Conference on Emerging Security Information, Systems and Technologies (SECURWARE 2014), 2014, pp. 194–201.

Consistent Cost Estimation for the Automotive Safety Model based Software Development Life cycle

Demetrio Cortese
FPT Embedded Software Development
CNH Industrial
Turin, Italy
Email: Demetrio.Cortese@cnhind.com

Abstract—The Safety Model based Software Development Life-cycle, focused on high-level executable models of the automotive systems to be fielded, has a high maturity level. It allows compression of the development cycles through a wide range of exploration and analysis including high fidelity of simulation, automatic test case generation and even test session at low cost early in the development phase. Many Software Development Teams in the automotive industry are already using model-based development for their safety critical software. The current software development effort estimation through sophisticated models and methods (COCOMO COnstructive COst MOdel, COCCOMOII, functional point, etc.), obtained at the early stages of development life cycle, is often inaccurate because of the long duration between the initialing phase of the project and delivery phase. Also, not many details of the functions are available at that time. All these models require as inputs accurate estimates of specific attributes, such as line of code (LOC), number of complex interfaces, etc. that are difficult to predict during the initial stage of software development. Effective software project estimation is one of the most challenging and important activities in software development. Proper project planning and control is not possible without a sound and reliable estimate. The basis of our approach for estimation of the development cost of a new model based development project is to describe it in terms of complexity and then to use this description to find other similar model–based functions that have already been completed.

Keywords-Model Based; Executable specification; Cost estimation; Embedded Software; Autocode generation; Software Engineering; Functional Safety.

I. INTRODUCTION

The assessment of the main risks in software development discloses that a major threat of delays is caused by poor effort/cost estimation of a project. As a consequence, more projects will face budget and/or schedule overruns. This risk can affect all phases of the software development life cycle, i.e., Analysis, Design, Coding and Testing. Hence, mitigating this risk may reduce the overall risk impact of the project in a consistent way.

Existing estimation techniques, such as function point and use case estimation, are done after the analyses phase and the cost/effort is measured in terms of lines of codes for each functionality to be incorporated into the software. Therefore, it is very clear that only a specific part of the total software development effort is estimated and this estimation is delayed until after all the analyses and designs are completed. Current software cost estimation methods first try to determine the size of the software to be built. Based upon this size, the expected effort is estimated and it is utilized to calculate the duration (i.e., time required) and cost (monetary/human resources) of the project.

We have adapted a different approach and suggested that effort estimation shall be carried out for each phase of the development process. Applying a phase-based approach offers a project manager the possibility to estimate the cost at different moments in the life cycle. A milestone offers the possibility to assess each phase and to measure and analyze possible differences between the actual and the estimated, step by step. Each milestone should, therefore, be considered the time for deciding whether the estimation can be adjusted. This mechanism leads to continuous and dynamic assessment of the relation between activities and relevant costs estimation. The philosophy, therefore, is to identify the project functionalities and define the software development process in all phases. It is clear that the end of a phase is characterized by a milestone.

Our approach is a quick and consistent method, based on:

1. Reference Model based Software Life cycle in all phases, as described in Section II,
2. Definition of an implementation scale of the existing model based functionalities (five levels), as described in Section III, subsection A;
3. Definition of a complexity scale of the existing model based functionalities (five levels), as described in Section III, subsection B;
4. Complexity Functionality by asking System Experts for estimate on each functionality of the new project, as described in Section III, subsection B;
5. Calculation of uncertainty, as reported in Section IV;
6. Affinity process through comparison and tuning for the new functionalities having as reference the historical data from point 1 and 2, as given in Section V;
7. Corrector factors (Team Skill, process customization) to be adjusted according to their risk, considered in Section V;

In this paper, the application of the above effort estimation model for a Software development project for a new Engine ECU (Electronic Control Unit) will be also presented.

II. MODEL BASED APPROACH APPLICATION

In the automotive domain, the model-based approach is a consistent way to master the management and complexity in the developing software systems. In last 10 years, the CNH industrial Embedded Software Development Team targets the Model-Based Application Software Development of the Functional Safety Systems for all CNH Industrial application by implementing a Methodology that ensures the safety critically relevant process satisfies important OEM (Original Equipment Manufacturer) requirements [8][9]:

- High quality
- Reduction in time to delivery
- Reduction in development cost

This strategy, through the CNH Industrial Infrastructure framework, allows innovation in existing processes and yield benefits in the medium term:

- A reduction of the Design Life-Cycle Process
- Anticipating issues at early design phases of development, leading to reduction in systems project risks
- Increasing effectiveness and timeliness of the system verification life-cycle, with reduction of systems time-to-delivery.

ISO (International Organization for Standardization standards) [4][5][6], such as ISO 26262 (Truck & Bus), ISO 13849 (Construction equipment) and ISO 25119 (Agricultural) do not specify formally any development process or validation tools but provide only recommendations. A clear description of the CNH Industrial process tailoring has been done in [1].

Here, we repeat the basic concept stating that, while the requirements of the Functional Safety standard cannot be tailored, the activities performed to meet the Standard can and should be tailored. That is, while the requirements must be met, the implementation and approach to meeting these requirements may and should vary to reflect the system to which they are applied. It is each software development's responsibility to produce evidence that they follow development processes addressing the safety-relevant requirements, and traceability from requirements to implementation. Additionally, traceability from requirements to test cases that checks the correctness of requirements against the developed software, is required. Besides, it is always important to verify that their development tools do not introduce errors in the final software product. In general, there two kinds of safety requirements: process oriented and technical. Both need to be addressed and properly documented within a project of software development. In the following, we identify process oriented requirements (what needs to be done to ensure software safety). Technical requirements are those that specify what the SW function must include. In order to manage the safety requirements, the software development process should:

- Identify, manage and monitor the safety requirements of the software product life-cycle, including generation of requirements, design, coding, test and operation of the software.
- Ensure that software acquisitions, whether off the-shelf or outsourcing, have been evaluated and assessed.
- Ensure that software verification activities include software safety verifications
- After the Final Software delivery, ensure that all changes and reconfigurations of the software are analyzed for their impacts to system safety.

In the last years, a consistent Model-Based Application software development Life–cycle (as shown in Figure 1,), compliant with ISO 26262 "Functional Safety", has been identified [2] in CNH Industrial.

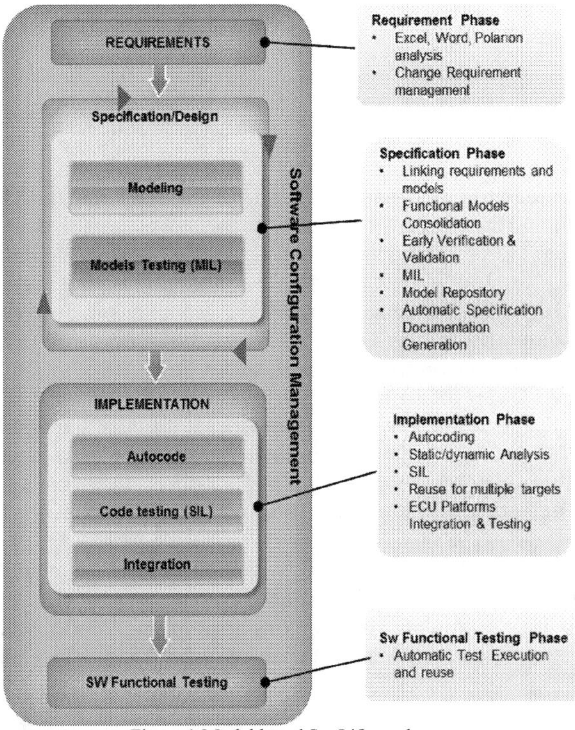

Figure 1 Model based Sw Life-cycle

Our approach responds to the demand of a collaborative environment that increases productivity and drastically cuts the development time. It will be obtained by capturing and disseminating the expertise of different and distributed teams. This comprehensive environment helps the Engineers in all life cycle stages from high-level data and architecture models through to fully tested and running Software Modules, harmonizing life cycle phases for the OEM application. One of the most powerful aspects of our approach is that it establishes a common language designed to engage all stakeholders in a process that leads to optimal applications outcomes, rather than outcomes that are locally optimized to the needs of any particular area.

Figure 1 describes our Model based Software development life cycle, where phases and tasks have been identified.

III. Project Complexity definition

Before we begin a piece of software development estimation, there needs to be an understanding of the scope of the project in terms of process and functionalities of the project. In case of the Model based development with a high maturity level, it can be extremely challenging to estimate the project effort through two pillars: complexity of the development process and complexity of the functionality content.

A. Software development process complexity

Today, engine functionalities often are large and complex, and the usual approach in our department consists of building the large functionality from smaller Software components. A Software component is a unit of complexity that required a reasonable effort, in general, and far less difficult than the whole functionality. We identified five different SW components: very simply, simply, medium, complex and very complex. The above classification is based on the timing specified by the Model based Software development process, as consolidated in the Embedded Software development department in FPT (FIAT PowerTrain) Industrial.

Successfully integrating components result in the whole SW functionality. Integrating the components into a larger software system consists of putting them together in a sufficiently careful manner, such that the components fit together. The use of models consisting of different submodels within software development has numerous advantages. Different persons may work on different submodels simultaneously driving forward the development of the system. Different types of submodels allow the separation of different aspects of the system, such as structural aspects or dynamic behavior of system components. On this basis, we are viewing each component in terms of complexity of software development life cycle phases. Each phase ends with a milestone and defined outcomes. Using a model based approach, as defined in previous section, we can estimate the effort needed to perform each phase. Our approach offers the SW manager the possibility to estimate different component/models at different moments in the life cycle for different complexities of the models (very simple, simple, medium, complex and very complex). Next, the milestones and the outcomes for each phase offer the possibility to measure and analyze possible differences between the actual and estimate step by step, such that the objectives, the estimate or the planning can be adjusted. By defining its own SW lifecycles, an organization can collect and use its own local historical data obtained from completed MBD (Model Based Development) projects. For example, we are using the Model based SW development process since 2005 and, therefore, we have consistent data to consolidate the estimation of effort, as shown in TABLE I.

This table represents the effort for each defined phase of the MBD Software development process for different complexity of the models. It uses 5 functional complexity indicators to show the development effort in 6 consolidated phases (with relevant tasks) of the CNH Industrial Model based Software development life-cycle. For Intellectual Property Rights (IPR) reason, the table is empty.

This mechanism leads to continuous and dynamic assessment of the relationship between process phase and costs. In case of automatism, we will be able to introduce it during the SW development process, as for example, more automatic HIL test procedures.

TABLE I. SOFTWARE DEVELOPMENT COMPLEXITY

Embedded Software Development (ESD)								
Work Estimation Details			***Very Simple***	***Simple***	***Medium***	***Complex***	***Very Complex***	***Remarks***
SW Development Phases	***Activity/Task***	***Owner***	***Effort Hrs***	***Effort Hrs***	***Effort Hrs***	***Effort Hrs***	***Effort Hrs***	
Requirements								
	Functionality Requirements Management	SW Project Leader						through Polarion customization
	Functionality Interfaces Requirement Specification	SW Project Leader						Interfaces definition
	Functionality Requirements Specification	System Engineer						traditional paper based specification
	Functionality Requirements Traceability	MBD Engineer						Requirements, Model, Code, Documentation, testing)
Specification								
	Requirement Specification Analysis	MBD Engineer						through traditional review of documents
	Functionality Modelling	MBD Engineer						through Simulink customization
	Modelling checking	MBD Engineer						through Model Advisor customization

Embedded Software Development (ESD)								
Work Estimation Details			***Very Simple***	***Simple***	***Medium***	***Complex***	***Very Complex***	***Remarks***
SW Development Phases	***Activity/Task***	***Owner***	***Effort Hrs***	***Effort Hrs***	***Effort Hrs***	***Effort Hrs***	***Effort Hrs***	
	MIL Testing (including the report generation)	MBD Engineer						including the MIL (Model In the loop) Test report; through Internal and automized tools
	Sw Functionality Documentation	MBD Engineer						through internal and automized tools
Implementation								
	AutoCoding	MBD Engineer						through Embedder coder Customization
	Code Review	MBD Engineer						through polyspace customization
	Code Integration in the ECU platform (with successful Compilation)	MBD Engineer						including configuration files, compilation
	Unit Testing	MBD Engineer						including the unit test report
Functional Testing								
	Test Environment Setup	System Engineer						HIL (Hardware In the Loop) Automatic setup including automation in test preparation, execution and reporting
	Integration Testing	System Engineer						
	Performance Testing	System Engineer						
Delivery								
	Software Configuration Management	SW Project Leader and MBD Engineer						Through configuration management tool
	Release/Build Updates	SW Project Leader						based on the Basic Software platform provided by the supplier
Support								
	Post delivery Support (eventual incremental version)	MBD Engineer						we plan a sw bug to consolidate the functionality
Work Estimate Totals			**y**	**1,8y**	**3.6y**	**4,8y**	**6,4y**	

B. *Functionality Complexity*

An engine ECU Software is a collection of software functionalities, describing features that can then be broken down into smaller and smaller components. Our idea is to assign a complexity rating to all functional components. The estimates, provided by an expert who has a background in the requirements definition, can be modified to suit the experience/expertise and performance of the team or people who might actually perform the work. This technique captures the experience and the knowledge of the experts. During the lifecycle, re-estimates should be done at major milestones of the project, or at specific time intervals. This decision will depend on the situation. SW Changes may be made during the project and therefore the cost estimates either increase or decrease. At the end of the project, a final assessment of the results of the entire cost estimation process should be done. This allows a company to refine the estimation process in the future because of the data results that were obtained, and also allows the developers to review the development process. It is also true that there are only very few cases where the software requirements stay fixed. Hence, how do we deal with software requirement changes, ambiguities or inconsistencies? During the estimation process, an experienced expert will detect the ambiguities and inconsistency in the requirements. As part of the estimation process, the expert will try to solve all these ambiguities by modifying the requirements. If the ambiguities or inconsistent requirements stay unsolved, then it will correspondingly affect the estimation accuracy.

The approach is flexible and allows us to account for the effort for all components. Once we have defined the functionality breakdown and set complexity estimates, we will be able to have the relevant effort estimation based on the concept introduced in the previous paragraph (Software development process complexity). As described in TABLE II, this is obviously a very simple spread sheet, and the calculations made are not in any way close to being hyper-accurate. It provides a handy mechanism to document and trace effort against functionalities, and a framework for distributing effort to project tasks (like requirement, implementation, testing etc.) across the total effort.

TABLE II. SW FUNCTIONALITY COMPLEXITY

Sw Layer	First level	Second level	Name	Tasks Number	Functional Complexity Breakdown					Development Time Estimation (Hours)					Total Effort Estimation
					1	*2*	*3*	*4*	*5*	*1*	*2*	*3*	*4*	*5*	*Hours*
ASW	Engine Function	Air System	AirMod	6		3	5			0	3x1,8y	5x 3,6y		0	
ASW	Vehicle Function	Active Surger Dumper	ASDCtl	2		1	1			0	1,8y	3,6y	0	0	
ASW	Engine Function	Air System	BstCtl	3		1	2			0	1,8y	2x 3,6y	0	0	
ASW	Engine Function	Air System	ChrCtl	5		3	2			0	3x1,8y	2x 3,6y	0	0	
ASW	Engine Function	Air System	ChrSet	4			1	1	2	0		3,6y	4,8y	2x6,4y	
ASW	Engine Function	Coordinator Engine	CoEng	5		2	3			0	2x1,8y	3x 3,6y	0	0	
ASW	Communicat ion	Vehicle	ComVe h	87	25	50	12			25x	50x1,8y	12x 3,6y	0	0	
ASW	Vehicle Function	Cruise Control	DrAs	9		4	5			0	4x1,8y	5x 3,6y	0	0	
....	......	....	......												
......	....	....	....	.	.	.	.	.							

TABLE II illustrates three important indicators for each functionality of the Application Software:

- Functional Complexity Breakdown: For each software functionality, we followed the same approach. We interviewed an adequate number of experts (Engine and Vehicle System Engineers). We defined each functionality as the composition of sub functionalities (tasks) with different complexity, starting from the experts experience with the most recent one and going back as far as they could.
- Development Time estimation: For each software functionality, the Software Manager will identify the estimation effort based on TABLE I.
- Total effort estimation: for each functionality, we show the effort in terms of Hours, days and months.

where
1= Very Simple, 2= Simple, 3=Medium, 4=Complex and 5=Very complex

IV. PROJECT DEFINITION ACCURACY

Accurate project estimation is one of the most challenging aspects of a project. The estimation becomes increasingly difficult as the project's complexity and uncertainty increases. Effort estimation accuracy depends on the available information. Usually, there is less information at the start the project (presales) and more information while working on the project, for example, after the requirement consolidation. In order to increase the accuracy level, the PERT (Program Evaluation and Review Technique) three-point estimates is used. It provides a range of project estimates and calculates the weighted average of that range. In order to use the PERT project estimation technique, we provide 3 data points, the "**best case**", "**most likely case**" and the "**worst case**".

The optimistic scenario (best case) is usually the shortest duration and/or the least costly estimate based on the notion that all will go well on the project. The pessimistic scenario (worst case) is the longest duration and/or the most costly estimate, based on the notion that problems may be encountered during the project. The most likely scenario falls somewhere in between the pessimistic and optimistic estimates, based on the notion that the project will progress under normal conditions.

In general, the experts will be asked to first provide their worst case estimate and then the best case estimate. Once these 2 points are agreed upon, it is easier for them to determine the most likely case, knowing their upper and lower limits.

Based on the above data, we obtain the PERT estimate:

$$E = (o + 4m + p) / 6. \qquad (1)$$

where E is Estimate; o = optimistic estimate; p = pessimistic estimate; m = most likely estimate.

Standard Deviation:

$$SD = (p - o) / 6 \qquad (2)$$

where SD is Standard Deviation; p = pessimistic estimate; o = optimistic estimate

E and SD values are then used to convert the project estimates to confidence levels as follows:

1. Confidence level in E value is approximately 75%
2. Confidence level in E value +/- SD is approximately 85%
3. Confidence level in E value +/- 2 × SD is approximately 95%
4. Confidence level in E value +/- 3 × SD is approximately 99.5%

TABLE III describes the approach.

TABLE III. SOFTWARE COST ACCURACY

Sw Layer	**First level**	**Second level**	**Name**	**Best case**	**Most Likely case**	**Worst Case**	**Standard Deviation**	**0.75 Confidence**	**0.85 Confidence**	**0.95 Confidence**	**0.995 Confidence**
				Effort Hrs	***Effort Hrs***	***Effort Hrs***		***Effort Hrs***	***Effort Hrs***	***Effort Hrs***	***Effort Hrs***
ASW	Engine Function	Air System	AirMod								
ASW	Vehicle Function	Active Surger Dumper	ASDCtl								
ASW	Engine Function	Air System	BstCtl								
ASW	Engine Function	Air System	ChrCtl								
ASW	Engine Function	Air System	ChrSet								
ASW	Engine Function	Coordinator Engine	CoEng								
ASW	Communication	Vehicle	ComVeh								
ASW	Vehicle Function	Cruise Control/Speed Limiter	DrAs								
....	………… …	………… ………..	…….	………	…						
……											

This technique works great for several reasons:

- Psychologically, it is easier to provide a number when you can provide a wide range
- Starting with the worst case often leads to less resistance
- Once worst case and best case are identified, it becomes easier to provide the most likely case
- Reduces the natural instinct to inflate estimates

V. SOFTWARE DEVELOPMENT PROCESS COST ESTIMATION

As introduced in the previous sections, the cost of development activities is primarily the development effort costs. This is the most difficult to estimate and control, and has the most significant effect on the overall project cost. Software cost estimation is a continuing activity which starts at the proposal stage and continues throughout the lifetime of a project. Projects normally have a budget, and continual cost estimation is necessary to ensure that spending is in line with the budget. Therefore, it is very important to estimate the software development effort as accurately as possible. A basic cost equation can be defined as:

Total_SW_Project = SW_Development_Labor + Other_Labor

In fact, we may have to consider other labor costs, such as:

- Software project management, performed by the project Manager, to plan and direct the software project
- Facility Administration, for example software configuration management and tools maintenance. The software development facility (SDF) is composed, generally, of hardware, software, and services utilized by the MBD Engineering Team to generate and test code, perform the engineering analysis, generate all of the required documents and manage the software development.
- SW Process Enhancement & Innovation.

The Innovation activity is a great way to improve the SW development process and the quality of the software product. Enhancement actions of software development helps organizations to establish a mature and disciplined engineering practice that produces secure, reliable software in less time and at lower costs. It gives us a potential better way of doing business. Normally, innovation is associated with higher costs but that's exactly the wrong way to looking at it. This is especially true if the company and finally the customer do not appreciate the change. It is more common for an automotive company, for example during a crisis period, to look at the innovation investment, as an item to be subject to an eventual optimization (reduction) cost process. In order to protect and to reduce the risk of reduction of innovation, it could be useful to allocate the above costs among all the SW development projects.

TABLE IV. SW LIFE CYCLE COST

Software Engineering Development Effort Element	**0.75 Confidence**	**0.85 Confidence**	**0.95 Confidence**	**0.995 Confidence**	**Comments**
	Effort Hrs	*Effort Hrs*	*Effort Hrs*	*Effort Hrs*	
Project management					3.2 % of Total Project Estimate
Facility Administration					1.5 % of development Estimate
SW Process Enhancement & Innovation					2 % of Development phase Estimate
SW Development Dependent phases					as from previous sheet;
SW Engineering Total Effort Estimation					

TABLE IV defines the cost for other Organizational support processes, as Project management, Facility Administration, Sw Process Enhancement & Innovation, depending of the direct SW development cost. The above costs are hardly specific of the Organization structure. The values, reported in the comments Column, are based on our experience. The Cost estimation is based on the assumption that the team will be composed of experienced (more 1+ year) MBD Software Engineers. In case of inexperienced MBD SW engineers, we need to consider the learning process cost.

VI. CONCLUSIONS

Today, many software development Managers have problems in providing accurate and reliable cost estimates, and, therefore sometimes do not undertake estimation at all. Besides, the existing cost estimation methods and tools are more complex and not customized for each specific software development process. Our approach aims at yielding more reliable estimates, based on the experience of all actors involved in the software development life cycle and it is based on the phases of the software life cycle. The estimation process improves continuously with the availability of more data and it continuously adjusts itself to the evolution of the software development phases. The first time cost estimation can be done is at the beginning of the project after the requirements have been outlined. Cost estimation may even be done more than once at the beginning of the project. For example, several companies may bid on a contract based on some preliminary or initial requirements, and then once a company wins the bid, a second round of estimation could be done with more refined and detailed requirements. Doing cost estimation during the entire life cycle allows for the refinement of the estimate because there is more data available. Periodic re-estimation is a way to gauge the progress of the project and whether deadlines will be able to be met.

Effective monitoring and control of the software costs is required for the verification and improvement of the accuracy of the estimates. Tools are available to help organize and manage the cost estimates and the data that is captured during the development process. People are less likely to gather data if the process is cumbersome or tedious, and so using tools that are efficient and easy to use will save time. It is not always the most expensive tool that will be the best tool to buy, but rather the tool that is most suited to the development environment. Therefore, the success of our proposal is not necessarily the accuracy of the initial estimates, but rather the rate at which the estimates converge to the actual cost. We are using the proposed approach for our Software development projects for All Vehicle ECUs (i.e., Engine Control unit, Vehicle computer Module). Therefore, we have a very valuable database reflecting our distribution cost in all phases of the software life cycle. These data are used to develop a software cost estimation model tailored to all CNH Industrial applications.

REFERENCES

[1] D. Cortese, "New Model-Based Paradigm: Developing Embedded Software to the Functional Safety Standards, as ISO 26262, ISO 25119 and ISO 13849 through an efficient automation of Sw Development Life-Cycle" SAE Technical Paper 2014-01-2394, doi: 10.4271/2014-01-2394

[2] D. Cortese, "ISO 26262 and ISO IEC 12207: The International Standards Tailoring Process to the whole Sw Automotive Development Life Cycle by Model-Based Approach" SAE Technical Paper 2011-01-0053, 2011, doi:10.4271/2011-01-0053

[3] D. Cortese, "Model-based Approach for the realization of a Collaborative repository of All Vehicle Functionalities" FISITA Technical Paper F2008-05-039, 2008

[4] Road Vehicles – Functional Safety - International Standard ISO 26262 : 2011

[5] Tractor and machinery for agriculture and forestry – Safety-related parts of control systems – International Standard ISO 25119: 2010

[6] Safety of machinery – Safety-related parts of control systems – International Standard ISO 13849: 2006

[7] CNH Industrial Web site: http://www.cnhindustrial.com/it-IT/Pages/homepage.aspx

[8] D. Cortese, Iveco Develops a Shift Range Inhibitor System for Mechanical 9- and 16-Speed Transmissions in Six Weeks, "https://www.mathworks.com/tagteam/71432_91989v00_IVECO_UserStory_final.pdf

[9] D. Cortese, "Developing Embedded Software to International Standards and On-board Vehicle Software Architectural Standardization" Course for PH.D. Program in Computer Science, 2013, http://dott-informatica.campusnet.unito.it/do/corsi.pl/Show?_id=1f5e

A Team Allocation Technique Ensuring Bug Assignment to Existing and New Developers Using Their Recency and Expertise

Afrina Khatun
Institute of Information Technology
University of Dhaka
Dhaka, Bangladesh
Email: bit0411@iit.du.ac.bd

Kazi Sakib
Institute of Information Technology
University of Dhaka
Dhaka, Bangladesh
Email: sakib@iit.du.ac.bd

Abstract*—Existing techniques allocate a bug fixing team using only previous fixed bug reports. Therefore, these techniques may lead to inactive team member allocation as well as fail to include new developers in the suggested list. A Team Allocation approach for ensuring bug assignment to both Existing and New developers (TAEN) is proposed, which uses expertise and recent activities of developers. TAEN first applies Latent Dirichlet Allocation on previous bug reports to determine the possible bug types. For new developers, TAEN identifies their preferred bug type, and adds them to the list of other developers, grouped under the identified bug types. Upon the arrival of a new bug report, TAEN determines its type and extracts the corresponding group of developers. A heterogeneous network is constructed using previous reports to find the collaborations among the extracted developers. Next, for each developer, a TAEN score is computed combining the expertise and recency of their collaborations. Finally, based on the incoming report's severity, a team of *N* members is allocated using the assigned TAEN score and current workloads. A case study conducted on Eclipse Java Development Tools (JDT), shows that TAEN outperforms K-nearest-neighbor Search And heterogeneous Proximity based approach (KSAP) by improving the team allocation recall from 52.88 up to 68.51, and showing the first correct developer on average at position 1.98 in the suggested list. Besides, a lower standard deviation of workloads, 30.05 rather than 46.33 indicates balanced workload distribution by TAEN.

Keywords*—*Bug Assignment; Team Allocation; Bug Report; Latent Dirichlet Allocation (LDA).

I. Introduction

With the increasing size of software systems, bug assignment has become a crucial task for software quality assurance. For example studies reveal that, near the release dates, about 200 bugs were reported daily for Eclipse [1]. As developers generally work in parallel, this turns bug resolution into a collaborative task as well. It is reported that Eclipse bug reports involve on average a team of 10 developers contributions. However, due to large number of bug reports, manually identifying developer collaboration is error-prone and time-consuming. Besides, industrial projects have reported the need for collaborative task assignments to utilize both existing and new developers [2]. It is common that new developers join the company or project during software development. Random bug report assignment to new developers always results in unnecessary bug reassignments, and increases the time needed for the bug to be fixed. In this context, an automatic approach can facilitate bug assignment by allocating teams utilizing both existing and new developers.

In order to assign newly arrived bugs to appropriate developers, available information sources such as bug reports, source code and commit logs are analysed. Recent commits generally exhibit developer's recent activities and previous bug report represent their expertise on fixing particular types of bugs. Team assignment is generally done by analysing previously fixed bug reports, which can help to recommend experienced developers. With the passage of time, developers may switch projects or company, therefore inactive members may be recommended. On the other hand, developers who joined recently, do not own any fixed bug reports or commits. So, the approaches which learn from these information sources, fail to assign tasks to new developers. Existing developers get overloaded with a queue of bug reports, whereas new developers are ignored in the allocation procedure. This leads not only to prolonged bug fixing time, but also to improper workload distribution.

Understanding the importance of bug assignment, various techniques have been proposed in the literature. BugFixer, a developer allocation method has been proposed by Hao et. al [3]. This method constructs a Developer-Component-Bug (DCB) network using past bug reports, and recommends developers over the network. This allocated list becomes less accurate with the joining of new developers. Baysal et al. have proposed a bug triaging technique using the user preference of fixing certain bugs [4]. The technique combines developer's expertise and preference score for ultimate suggestion. However, this technique also considers only historical activities. Afrina et. al [5] have proposed an Expertise and Recency based Bug Assignment (ERBA) approach that considers both fixed reports and commit history for recommendation. This technique is applicable for single developer recommendation, and it cannot allocate tasks to new developers. A team assignment approach using K-nearest-neighbor Search And heterogeneous Proximity (KSAP) has been proposed by Zhang et al. [6]. It creates a heterogeneous network from the past bug reports, and assigns a team based on their collaboration over the network. The main limitation of this technique is that it over-prioritizes previous activities.

A Team Allocation technique for ensuring bug assignment to both Existing and New developers (TAEN), using expertise and recency of developers has been proposed. TAEN allocates a team in five steps. The *Bug Solving Preference Elicitation* step takes bug reports, and applies Latent Dirichlet Allocation (LDA) model on these reports to determine the possible types of bug reports. For new developers, TAEN first elicits their bug solving preference by presenting them with main representative terms of each bug type, and groups them under the corresponding type. The *New Bug Report Processing* step extracts the *summary, description* and *severity* of incoming reports, and determines their bug types to identify the potential fixer group. Next, the *Developer Collaboration Extraction* step generates a heterogeneous network using attributes (four types of nodes and eight types of edges) extracted from previous bug reports, and finds collaborations among the identified fixer group members over the network. The *Expertise and Recency Combination* step then assigns a TAEN score to each developer by combining the number and recency of their extracted collaboration. Finally, based on the *severity* of the incoming report, the *Team Allocation* step suggests a team of *N* developers using the TAEN score and current workloads. After each reported bug is fixed, this step also updates developers contribution status.

A case study on an open source project, Eclipse Java Development Tools (JDT) has been conducted for assessment of TAEN. To evaluate compatibility, TAEN has been compared with an existing technique, KSAP [6]. A total of 2500 *fixed* and 676 *open* bug reports have been taken under consideration [7]. A test set of 250 *fixed* and 30 *open* bug reports have been applied on both techniques. The results showed that TAEN improved the recall of the allocated team from 52.88 up to 68.51. A decrease in the average position of the first correct developer from 3.1 to 1.98 indicates the increased effectiveness of TAEN. Besides, a lower standard deviation (30.05 instead of 46.33) of developer workloads shows more balanced task distribution by TAEN.

The remainder of the paper is organized as follows. Section II describes the existing efforts in the field of automated bug assignment. Section III presents the overall team allocation procedure of TAEN by discussing the detailed processing of each step. Section IV shows a case study on Eclipse JDT while applying TAEN. Lastly, Section V concludes the paper by summarizing its contribution and possible future directions.

II. Related Work

Due to the increased importance of automatic bug assignment, a number of techniques have been proposed. A survey on various bug triaging techniques has been presented by Sawant et. al [8]. The survey divided bug triaging techniques into text categorization, reassignment, cost aware and source based techniques etc. Studies focusing on industrial needs of bug assignment have also been proposed in literature [2], [9]. Significant related works are outlined in this section.

Text categorization based techniques build a model that trains from past bug reports to predict the correct rank of developers [1], [3], [4], [10], [11]. Baysal et al. have enhanced these techniques by adding user preference in the recommendation process [4]. The framework performs its task using three components. The *Expertise Recommendation* component creates a ranked developer list using previous expertise profiles. The *Preference Elicitation* component collects and stores a rating score regarding the preference level of fixing certain bugs through a feedback process. Lastly, knowing the preference and expertise of each developer, the *Task Allocation* component assigns bug reports. The applicability of this technique depends on user ratings, which can be inconsistent. Besides, for recommendation the technique does not take new developers into account. As a result, imbalanced workload distribution among developers may occur.

Reassignment based techniques have also been developed by researchers [12], [13], [14]. The main focus of these techniques is to reduce the number of passes a bug report goes through due to incorrect assignment. In such techniques, a graph is constructed using previous bug reports [13], [14]. As mentioned above, consideration of these past activities fail to accommodate the new developers in final recommendation. A fine grained incremental learning and multi feature tossing graph based technique has been proposed by Bhattacharya et. al [12]. It is an improvement over previous techniques because it considers multiple bug report features, such as product and component, when constructing the graph. Because it considers previous information, the technique results in search failure in case of new developers arrival.

CosTriage, a cost aware developer ranking algorithm has been developed by Park et. al [15]. The technique converts bug triaging into an optimization problem of accuracy and cost, which adopts Content Boosted Collaborative Filtering (CBCF) for ranking developers. As the input to the system is only previous bug history, the technique contains no clue regarding new developers to assign tasks.

Source based bug assignment techniques have also been proposed. Matter et. al have suggested DEVELECT, a vocabulary based expertise model for recommending developers [11]. The model parses the source code and version history to index a bag of words representing the vocabulary of source code contributors. For new bug reports, the model checks the report keywords against developer vocabularies using lexical similarities. The highest scored developers are taken as fixers. Another source based technique has been proposed in [16]. The technique first parses all the source code entities (such as name of class, attributes, methods and method parameters) and connects these entities with contributors to construct a corpus. In case of new bug reports, the keywords are searched in the index and given a weight based on frequent usage and time metadata. The main limitation of these techniques is, it suggests novice developers without considering their experience and preference. As these techniques require minimum one source commits, these also fail to include new developers in final suggestion.

Vaclav et al. have presented a study to compare the trend of bug assignment in the open source and industrial fields [2]. The study applies Chi-Square and t-test for evaluating the variability of those two fields dataset, and reports identical trends in terms of distribution. Most importantly, it concludes with some findings highlighting the need for balanced task assignment to individuals and team recommendation. Zhang et al. developed a team assignment technique called KSAP [6]. It initially constructs a heterogeneous network using existing bug reports. When a new bug report arrives, the technique applies cosine similarity between the document vectors of new and existing bug reports, and extracts the K nearest similar bug reports. Next, the commenters of these K similar bugs are taken as the candidate list. Finally, the technique computes a proximity score for each developer based on their collaboration on the network. The top scored Q number of developers are recommended as fixer team. Although this technique can meet the need of team recommendation, it fails to cover the requirement of balanced task distribution due to ignoring new developers in the assignment process.

Various techniques for automatic bug fixer suggestion have been proposed in the literature. Most of the techniques learn from previous fix or source history of software repositories. Consideration of only one of these information sources leads to inactive or inexperienced developer recommendation. Again, both of the sources lack information regarding the newly joined developers. As a result, all of these techniques fail to delegate tasks to newly joined developers resulting in unequal workload distribution.

III. METHODOLOGY

In order to allocate teams by ensuring task allocation to both existing and new developers, a technique called TAEN is proposed. Most of the existing techniques learn from previous fixed reports for recommending expert developers. Due to ignoring recent activities, these approaches may suggest inactive developers. Using only expertise information cannot satisfy the required information provided by the source contributions. Both information sources need to be considered to allocate expert and recent group of developers. Therefore, an expert and recent team allocator capable of allocating tasks to both existing and new developers is required. TAEN allocates a team in five steps which are described below.

A. Bug Solving Preference Elicitation of New Developers

As bug tracking and version control systems do not contain any record regarding the activities of new developers, existing approaches fail to recommend new developers. In this case, bugs are assigned randomly to these developers regardless of their abilities and preferences in solving the bugs, which always results in reassignment and prolonged fixing time. This step determines the bug solving preference of new developers in two phases - *Developer Group Creation* and *Preference Elicitation.*

1) Developer Group Creation: This phase groups developers based on the types of bugs they have worked on. In this context, first, the possible types of bugs needs to be determined. Therefore, this step takes bug reports as input in Extensible Markup Language (XML) format. A bug report generally contains a number of attributes such as *id, status, resolution, fixer, commenter, severity, summary, description, activity history* etc. For training and evaluation purpose, the bug reports which have *resolved* and *verified* as status, and *fixed* as resolution property are taken into consideration. Besides, in order to determine developers current workloads, the bug reports which have bug status either of *new*, *reopened* and *started* are collected.

Next, the *summary* and *description* property of each report are extracted and processed to represent its vocabulary. The processing steps are discussed in Subsection III-C. For identifying the type of bug reports, LDA modeling is used. Given a list of documents having mixtures of (latent) topics, LDA tends to determine the most relevant topic of the document. So, the bug reports are represented as documents, and fed into the LDA model to be divided into *n* types. At the end, the LDA model determines the most relevant type for each bug report. Each bug type is represented with the probabilities of each word to be in the type.

Once all the bug reports are labeled with one of the *n* types, the developers who have worked on similar types of bugs are grouped together. Hence, the algorithm in Figure 1 is proposed for creating developer groups. The *GroupDevelopers* procedure of Figure 1 takes the processed bug reports as input. This procedure keeps the grouped developers in a complex data structure called *bugTypes*, as shown in line 2. The outer map of *bugTypes* links each type to developers who have contributed to that specific type of bugs. The inner map connects each developers name to their contribution frequency on that type of bugs.

A *for* loop is defined at line 4 for iterating on the inputted bug reports. Each iteration of the loop first extracts the bug report's type determined by the LDA model. This task is done by calling a method, *GetBugType*, as shown in line 5. The method takes the *summary* and *description* of the report, and returns its *type*. The *GroupDevelopers* procedure also extracts and stores the contributor's name of each bug report in a *Set* of strings named *contributors*. Here, the contributors refers to the reporter and fixers of the bug report.

```
1: procedure GROUPDEVELOPERS(List < BugReport > BugReports)
2:     Map<String, Map<String, Integer> > bugTypes
3:     Map<String, Integer> developers, String type
4:     for each b ∈ BugReports do
5:         type ← GETBUGTYPE(b.summary, b.description)
6:         Set < String > contributors ← b.contributors
7:         developers ← bugTypes.get(type)
8:         if developers == null then
9:             developers ← new Map<String, Integer>()
10:            for each c ∈ contributors do
11:                developers.put(c, 1)
12:            bugTypes.put(type, developers)
13:        else
14:            for each c ∈ contributors do
15:                if devlopers.contains(c) then
16:                    developers.replace(c, developers[c]+1)
17:                else
18:                    developers.put(c, 1)
19:            bugTypes.replace(type, developers)
```

Figure 1: The Algorithm of Developer Group Creation

Next, the procedure gets the list of developers mapped against the identified bug *type* (line 7). If no developers are yet mapped against this *type*, a new instance of inner map named *developers* is initialized (line 8-9). All the *contributors* are then populated into the *developers* map which links each developer to their initial contribution frequency (line 10-11). This *developers* map is then put against the identified bug *type* (line 12). On the other hand, if a list of *developers* is already mapped against the identified *type*, another *for* loop is declared for updating the *developers* list (line 14). The loop then checks whether the *developers* list already contains the *contributors* and updates the contribution frequency of each contributor, *c* (line 15-18). Finally, the procedure updates the outer map *bugType* with the changed *developers* list (line 19).

2) Preference Elicitation: This step focuses to elicit the bug solving preference of new developers for ensuring their inclusion in the allocated team. When a new developer arrives, the list of most representative words of each bug type is offered to the developer. The chosen bug types are initially considered as the types of bugs the developer can contribute to. So, the developer is then grouped with the developers who have worked on similar bugs determined by the previous step.

B. New Bug Report Processing

On arrival of a new bug report *B*, the type of the report needs to be identified for extracting the developer group to which it can be assigned. The *summary, description* and *severity* properties of the report are extracted and processed. As these property values generally contain irrelevant and noisy terms, pre-processing is done. The processing step includes identifier decomposition based on CamelCase letter and separator character, number and special character removal, stop word removal and stemming. A score for each bug type is computed using (1) similar to [15], as follows-

$$typeScore(i) = \sum_{\forall w \in B} (Probability_i(w) * Distribution_i(w)) \quad (1)$$

where, *i* represents the *i-th* type in the LDA model, *w* represents each word in *B*, $Probability_i(w)$ is the probability of *w* in the *i-th* bug type, and the distribution of *w* in the new bug report is indicated by $Distribution_i(w)$. Finally, the bug type which gets the highest score having most similar vocabulary with the new bug report, is determined as the type of the new bug report. Thus, the developer's group associated with the determined bug type is selected. The top-*K* members of this group, who have higher contributions are considered as the developers from which a bug fixing team needs to be allocated.

C. Developer Collaboration Extraction

It is mentioned above that bug resolution is a collaborative task. To allocate a team, the collaboration among the developers needs to be considered. So, this step extracts the collaboration among the developers of the identified group. A heterogeneous directed network is constructed from the previous *fixed* bug reports [6]. The four types of nodes include - Bug (B), Developer (D), Component (C) and Comment (T). The eight types of possible relations among these nodes are listed in Table I. For example, Type 1 relationship connects a D node to a B node depicting the developer (D) has *worked on* the bug report (B). The term *work* refers assignment, report, reassignment, reopening, fixing, verifying or tossing event of a bug. Similarly, Type 4 and Type 5 relations denote that a comment (T) *is contained by* a bug (B), and a developer (D) *has written* the comment (T), respectively.

Developer collaboration can be identified by factors such as how frequently two developers contribute to the same bugs and components of the system. Keeping these factors in mind, six types of paths similar to [6] are extracted from the network each of which connects two developers using combinations of the above relation edges. The paths are listed in Table II. For example - 'D-B-T-D' represents that a developer (D) has worked on a bug (B), which has a comment (T) written by another developer (D). Similarly, 'D-B-C-B-D' depicts that a developer (D) has worked on a bug (B) of a component (C), having another bug (B), which was worked on by another developer (D).

TABLE I. EIGHT TYPES OF RELATIONSHIPS AMONG NODES

Type No.	Specification
1	D *works on* B
2	B *is worked on by* D
3	B *contains* T
4	T *is contained by* B
5	D *writes* T
6	T *is written by* D
7	B *contains in* C
8	C *is contained by* B

TABLE II. SIX TYPES OF DEVELOPER COLLABORATION

Path Type	Collaboration on	Path
1	Same Bug	D-B-D
2	Same Bug	D-B-T-D
3	Same Bug	D-T-B-T-D
4	Same Component	D-B-C-B-D
5	Same Component	D-B-C-B-T-D
6	Same Component	D-T-B-C-B-T-D

D. Expertise and Recency Combination

As mentioned before, ignorance of recent activities may result in inactive developer assignment. So, this step adds recency information with the extracted developer's collaboration. The more recent developers work or comment on a bug, the higher the priority of that developer. For combining the recent activities, the time when the developers collaborate on the bug, is considered. The algorithm in Figure 2 is proposed to compute a score called TAEN score for each developer, by combining the expertise and recency of collaboration.

The *CalculateScore* procedure of Figure 2 takes a complex data structure, named *devInfos* as input. This data structure maps the developers to their identified collaboration information of type *DeveloperCollaboration*.

```
procedure CALCULATESCORE(Map < String,
        DeveloperCollaboration > devInfos)
    Map < String, Double > devScores
    for each d ∈ devInfos do
        for each path ∈ d.sameBugs do
            ADDSCORE(path.firstEdge,
                        BugReport.date)
            ADDSCORE(path.lastEdge,
                        BugReport.date)
procedure ADDSCORE(Edge e, Date date)
    if e.srcNode = D then
        dev ← e.srcNode
    else
        dev ← e.destNode
    if !devScores.keys.contains(dev) then
        devScores ← 1/(date − e.Date)
    else
        devScores+ ← 1/(date − e.Date)
```

Figure 2: The Algorithm of Expertise and Recency Combination

Each instance of *DeveloperCollaboration* contains two properties - *sameBugs* and *sameComponents*. The former property contains a list of paths which depicts the associated developers collaboration on same bugs. Similarly, the later one represents developers collaboration on same components. The *CalculateScore* procedure represents the partial score calculation process based on the same bugs only. A similar approach is also used for calculating the collaboration score of same components. The procedure starts with defining a data structure called, *devScores* which connects the developers to their calculated TAEN score (line 2). An outer *for* loop is defined for iterating on each developer and an inner loop is defined for iterating on their collaborated paths (line 3-4). Each collaboration path generally connects two developers. Therefore, for each collaborated path the score of the two developers needs to be added or updated (line 5,6). To perform this task, another procedure, *AddScore* is declared (line 7).

This procedure takes an edge and a date as input. It is seen from Table I that developers directly collaborate by working or commenting on bugs. So, the collaboration edge is sent as parameter for the *AddScore* function. Besides, for adding the recency information of these activities, the collaboration date is also sent to this function. It first extracts the developer node from the inputted edge (line 8-11). It then checks whether the developer has a TAEN score already assigned (line 12). Based on this checking, it adds or updates the score (line 13-15). The score for each collaboration path is initially considered as 1. However, this score is divided by the date difference between the reporting date of the new bug report (*date*) and the collaboration date of the developer (*e.date*). The smaller the difference, the more recent the developer collaborated on the bug, thus the higher the score the developer gets. Lines 13-15 ensure the effect of recency information on the developer's TAEN score.

E. Team Allocation

Finally, for allocating a team consisting of N developers where $N<K$, the technique first checks the *severity* property of the newly arrived bug report. The *severity* property refers to how severe the bug is, or whether it is an enhancement request. If the *severity* value is any of *blocker*, *critical* and *major* [7], the reported bug is considered as one that needs to be handled by existing developers. So, TAEN considers only the top-K contributors and sorts the developers based on their TAEN score. The top scored N developers are allocated as the fixer team.

If the *severity* value contains *normal*, *minor*, *trivial* or *enhancement* [7], it can be handled by new developers. In this case, TAEN considers the new developers along with the top-K, and counts their current workload (assigned bugs). The N developers with least workload are included in the team. This step ensures bug assignment to new developers based on their bug solving preference. If two developers have the same workloads, the tie is resolved using the TAEN score. When a bug report is fixed by a developer, this contribution is updated in the groups of Subsection III-A. This update ensures incremental contribution enhancement of developers as well as their participation in bug resolution.

IV. Case Study

For initial assessment of compatibility, TAEN was applied on an open source project, Eclipse JDT [17]. This project was chosen because this has been used for evaluation in various related approaches [15]. Secondly, the bug repository of JDT is available in open source. A total of 2500 *fixed* bug reports between years 2009 and 2015, and 676 *open* bug reports between 2015 and 2016 have been collected for experimental analysis of TAEN.

As stated before, TAEN first takes system bug reports in XML format [7]. The *summary* and *description* properties are collected from the *<short_desc>* and *<thetext>* tags respectively. It then applies LDA on the properties to determine the most relevant type of each bug report. Various techniques are available in the literature for identifying the natural number of topics when applying LDA [15]. The case study divides the bug reports into n=17 distinct types, as 17 has already been used as number of topics in Eclipse [15]. The contributors, severity, reporting time, activity properties are also extracted from different XML tags in a similar manner. The contributors are then grouped against the corresponding bug types identified by LDA.

Now, on arrival of new developers, they are presented with the most representative words of each bug type. Table III shows a few top most representative words of bug Type-2 and 11. The table depicts that the representative keywords give an idea about the corresponding type. For example, the enlisted keywords against Type-2 indicates User Interface (UI) related terms as well as bugs. If a developer selects Type-2, the developer is added to the group of developers associated with Type-2 bugs.

TABLE III. Few top representative words of bug Type-2 and 11

Type 2	Click	Editor	Select	Display	Dialog	Event
Type 11	Mozilla	Agent	Gecko	Build	User	Windows

For comparative analysis, TAEN is compared with a team assignment approach, KSAP [5]. A randomly selected test dataset containing 250 *fixed* and 30 *open* bug reports have been used for checking the allocation validity. The experimental analysis allocates a team of N developers, where N is set to 10. The reason behind setting N to 10 is that it is reported that Eclipse bug reports include on average 10 developers contributions [6]. Besides, for ensuring validation consistency between KSAP and TAEN, K=50 top most contributors are taken from both techniques for processing of *Developer Collaboration Extraction* step.

The compatibility of TAEN is evaluated using the following metrics - recall, effectiveness and workload distribution. Recall@N refers to whether the top N allocated developers contain the actual developers who fixed the report. The higher number of actual developers included in the top N places, the more correct the allocation is. The recall is calculated using (2) similar to [6] -

$$Recall@N = \frac{|\{dev1, dev2, ..., devN\} \cap \{GroundTruth\}|}{|GroundTruth|} \quad (2)$$

Here, *{dev1,dev2,...,devN}* is the set of N allocated developers, and *{GroundTruth}* refers to the set of actual fixers containing the reporter, fixer and commenters. Table IV illustrates the average Recall@10 achieved by TAEN and KSAP. TAEN had a higher average recall (68.51) than KSAP. Consideration of both recent and previous activities enabled TAEN to improve the recall from 52.88 to 68.51.

TABLE IV. COMPARISON OF AVERAGE TEAM ALLOCATION RECALL@10

Approaches	Average Recall@10
KSAP	52.88
TAEN	68.51

Effectiveness refers to the position of the first *GroundTruth* developer in the allocated list. Not all the members of a team generally play similar roles in an assigned task. Therefore, the ranking in the suggested team plays a vital role in determining task division. Approaches that allocate relevant developers at the top of the list are considered more effective. A lower value of this metric indicates higher effectiveness of the allocated list. The values in Table V shows allocation effectiveness of TAEN and KSAP. They also show the percentage of suggesting the first relevant developer at Position 1 to 3. In 66.36% cases TAEN shows the first revelant developer at Position 1 whereas KSAP shows that in only 2.73% cases. The consideration of recent activities enables TAEN to prioritize active developers at top of the list. The percentage of Position 2 and 3 for TAEN is less than KSAP because, TAEN covers most of the cases at Position 1. The last column shows TAEN shows the relevant developers on average near position 1.98 which is lower than KSAP (3.1).

TABLE V. COMPARISON OF AVERAGE EFFECTIVENESS

Approaches	Average No. of Cases (%)			Average
	Position 1	Position 2	Position 3	Effectiveness
KSAP	66.36	7.27	10.91	1.98
TAEN	2.73	57.27	11.82	3.1

In order to validate the task assignment to new developers, current workload among the developers are counted from *open* bug reports of 2016. The developers who do not have any past history, i.e. they are not grouped under any of the bug types are considered as new developers in the experimentation. The bug solving preference of these new developers is determined by the type of bugs they are currently assigned to. Based on this preference, these developers are initially grouped with one of the bug types. The 30 above mentioned *open* bug reports are analyzed on both KSAP and TAEN. A partial view of workload distribution among developers preferring bug Type-15 is shown in Figure 3. The bars of Figure 3 clearly show that KSAP assigns no tasks to the 6 new developers plotted at the right end of the graph. However, TAEN successfully allocates the new developers based on their preference.

For better understanding the variability of task assignment, standard deviation of the workloads is calculated. Standard deviation of a dataset depicts the variability of the data from their mean point. A lower value of this metric represents less variability i.e. equal workload distribution among developers. The average standard deviation of workloads assigned by the two techniques are enlisted in Table VI. TAEN has a

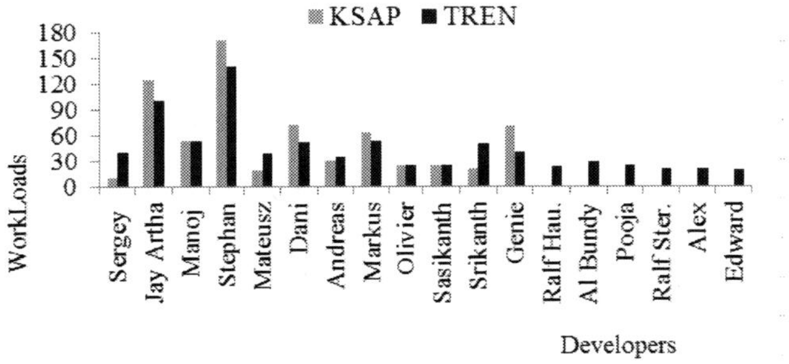

Figure 3: Workload Distribution of KSAP and TAEN

lower standard deviation of 30.05 than KSAP (46.33). The preference based inclusion of new developers in the assignment process, enabled TAEN to achieve lower standard deviation. This significant decrease in the value of standard deviation represents higher consistency of resource utilization by TAEN.

TABLE VI. COMPARISON OF VARIABILITY IN WORKLOAD DISTRIBUTION

Approaches	Average Standard Deviation
KSAP	46.33
TAEN	30.05

V. CONCLUSION

Team allocation is generally done from previous fixed reports. Due to ignoring recent activities, these approaches may allocate inactive fixers. Both previous reports and recent commits do not contain any information regarding the newly joined developers. Not considering new developers in the final allocation leads to improper workload distribution. To overcome these limitations, TAEN is proposed, which assigns bugs to both existing and new developers combining the expertise and recency information.

The *Bug Solving Preference Elicitation* step first determines new developer's choice of fixing certain types of bugs, and adds them to the group of developers of the chosen type. The *New Bug Report Processing* step identifies the type of the incoming reports to extract the corresponding grouped developers. Next, the *Developer Collaboration Extraction* step generates a heterogeneous network from the previous reports to find the collaboration of the extracted developers over the network. The *Expertise and Recency Combination* step then assigns a TAEN score to each developer based on their collaboration expertise and recency. After checking the severity of incoming reports, the *Team Allocation* step allocates a fixer team by using TAEN score and current workloads.

For performing a case study on Eclipse JDT, 2500 *fixed* and 676 *open* bug reports were collected. A test set of 250 *fixed* and 30 *open* bug reports were used for comparison with an existing technique, KSAP. The result shows that TAEN improves recall from 52.88 to 68.51, and achieves increased effectiveness by identifying the correct bug fixer near position 1.98. The results also depict a significant decrease of standard deviation from

46.33 to 30.05 which indicates equal workload distribution. In future, bug reports which are not previously handled by any developers should be observed to check TAEN's performance.

ACKNOWLEDGMENT

This work is supported by the fellowship from ICT Division, Bangladesh. No - 56.00.0000.028.33.065.16 (Part-1)-772 Date 21-06-2016.

REFERENCES

[1] S. Banitaan and M. Alenezi, "Tram: An approach for assigning bug reports using their metadata," in *Proceedings of the 3rd International Conference on Communications and Information Technology (ICCIT), June 19–21, 2013, Beirut, Lebanon.* IEEE, 2013, pp. 215–219, URL: http://info.psu.edu.sa/psu/cis/malenezi/pdfs/TRAM.pdf [accessed: 2016-10-30].

[2] V. Dedík and B. Rossi, "Automated bug triaging in an industrial context," in *Proceedings of the 42th Euromicro Conference on Software Engineering and Advanced Applications (SEAA), August 31–September 2, 2016, Limassol, Cyprus.* IEEE, 2016, pp. 363–367, URL: https://www.researchgate.net/profile/Bruno_Rossi2/publication/308417176_Automated_Bug_Triaging_in_an_Industrial_Context/links/57e3e3df08ae8d5908c1617b.pdf [accessed: 2016-12-01].

[3] H. Hu, H. Zhang, J. Xuan, and W. Sun, "Effective bug triage based on historical bug-fix information," in *Proceedings of the 25th International Symposium on Software Reliability Engineering (ISSRE), October 23–26, 2014, Toulouse, France.* IEEE, 2014, pp. 122–132, URL: https://hal.inria.fr/hal-01087444/document [accessed: 2016-05-20].

[4] O. Baysal, M. W. Godfrey, and R. Cohen, "A bug you like: A framework for automated assignment of bugs," in *Proceedings of the 17th International Conference on Program Comprehension (ICPC), May 17–19, 2009, British Columbia, Canada.* IEEE, 2009, pp. 297–298, URL: http://citeseerx.ist.psu.edu/viewdoc/download?doi=10.1.1.143.7283&rep=rep1&type=pdf [accessed: 2016-10-29].

[5] A. Khatun and K. Sakib, "A bug assignment technique based on bug fixing expertise and source commit recency of developers," in *Proceedings of the 19th International Conference on Computer and Information Technology (ICCIT), December 18–20, 2016, Dhaka, Bangladesh.* IEEE, 2016, pp. 592–597, URL: http://sci-hub.cc/10.1109/iccitechn.2016.7860265 [accessed: 2017-03-05].

[6] W. Zhang, S. Wang, and Q. Wang, "Ksap: An approach to bug report assignment using knn search and heterogeneous proximity," *Information and Software Technology*, vol. 70, pp. 68–84, 2016, ISSN: 0950-5849.

[7] "Afrina/TREN," Jan. 2017, URL: https://github.com/Afrina/TREN/blob/master/TeamAssignMSTestProject/Data/TeamData/bug_data_2009_2015.xml [accessed: 2017-01-10].

[8] V. B. Sawant and N. V. Alone, "A survey on various techniques for bug triage," *International Research Journal of Engineering and Technology*, vol. 2, pp. 917–920, 2015, ISSN: 2395-0056.

[9] R. V. Sangle and R. D. Gawali, "Auto bug triage a need of software industry," *International Journal of Engineering Science*, vol. 6, pp. 8668–8670, 2016, ISSN: 2321-3361.

[10] M. Linares-Vásquez, K. Hossen, H. Dang, H. Kagdi, M. Gethers, and D. Poshyvanyk, "Triaging incoming change requests: Bug or commit history, or code authorship?" in *Proceedings of the 28th International Conference on Software Maintenance (ICSM), September 23–30, 2012, Trento, Italy.* IEEE, 2012, pp. 451–460, URL: http://www.cs.wm.edu/~mlinarev/pubs/ICSM'12-DevRecAuthorship.pdf [accessed: 2016-10-20].

[11] D. Matter, A. Kuhn, and O. Nierstrasz, "Assigning bug reports using a vocabulary-based expertise model of developers," in *Proceedings of the 6th International Working Conference on Mining Software Repositories (MSR), May 16-17, 2009, Vancouver, Canada.* IEEE, 2009, pp. 131–140, URL: http://flosshub.org/system/files/131AssigningBugReports.pdf [accessed: 2016-02-26].

[12] P. Bhattacharya and I. Neamtiu, "Fine-grained incremental learning and multi-feature tossing graphs to improve bug triaging," in *Proceedings of the 26th International Conference on Software Maintenance (ICSM), September 12–18, 2010, Timisoara, Romania.* IEEE, 2010, pp. 1–10, URL: http://www.cs.ucr.edu/~pamelab/icsm10bhattacharya.pdf [accessed: 2016-02-26].

[13] G. Jeong, S. Kim, and T. Zimmermann, "Improving bug triage with bug tossing graphs," in *Proceedings of the 7th joint meeting of the European software engineering conference and the ACM SIGSOFT symposium on The foundations of software engineering (ESEC/FSE), August 24–28, 2009, Amsterdam, Netherlands.* ACM, 2009, pp. 111–120, URL: http://143.89.40.4/~hunkim/images/6/65/Papers_jeong2009fse.pdf [accessed: 2016-05-30].

[14] L. Chen, X. Wang, and C. Liu, "An approach to improving bug assignment with bug tossing graphs and bug similarities," *Journal of Software*, vol. 6, pp. 421–427, 2011, ISSN: 1796-217X.

[15] J.-W. Park, M.-W. Lee, J. Kim, S.-W. Hwang, and S. Kim, "Cost-aware triage ranking algorithms for bug reporting systems," *Knowledge and Information Systems*, vol. 48, pp. 679âĂŞ–705, 2015, ISSN: 0219-3116.

[16] R. Shokripour, J. Anvik, Z. M. Kasirun, and S. Zamani, "A time-based approach to automatic bug report assignment," *Journal of Systems and Software*, vol. 102, pp. 109–122, 2015, ISSN: 0164-1212.

[17] "JDT Core Component - Eclipse," Jan. 2017, URL: https://eclipse.org/jdt/core/ [accessed: 2017-01-10].

Self-Governance Developer Framework

Mira Kajko-Mattsson
School of ICT
KTH Royal Institute of Technology
Stockholm, Sweden
email: mekm2@kth.se

Gudrun Jeppesen
Department of Computer and Systems Sciences
Stockholm University
Stockholm, Sweden
email: gudrunjep@telia.com

Abstract—**Success of software developers should be attributed to developers' knowledge of what to do and their discipline and trust to their self-organization. To achieve this, the software community should provide appropriate process frameworks recommending developers what needs to be done, still however, allowing maximal freedom, flexibility and self-discipline. The Self-Governance Software Developer (SGD) Framework is the solution to this. In this paper, we suggest and motivate the SGD Framework. We also benchamark it against Personal Software Process (PSP). Our results show that SGD has a higher coverage of the developer activities. Still, however, it needs to be evaluated within the industrial context.**

Keywords-personal software process; self-discipline; self-organization; software development; software methods, process models, coding, unit testing.

I. INTRODUCTION

Discipline and know-how takes many forms and permeates almost every aspect of software development. Disciplined and knowledgeable developers and/or teams know what is expected from them in specific development contexts. They know best what activities to choose and how to organize their work for the success of their projects. Undisciplined and/or less experienced developers/teams, on the other hand, may not always know what to do and are not always able to deliver quality code on time and within budget.

Many sources tell software developers what to do. The most common ones are various software development methods [1]-[3][7]-[9][12][16], or guidance from managers [4], or organizational in-house methods [2]. Irrespective of whether they are waterfall, iterative or of any other nature, most methods impose sets of development activities that are not always applicable in all kinds of development contexts. Also, managers and/or organizations impose specific methods to developers which are not always explicitly stated and/or well motivated. This may limit the freedom of developers and make them into passive workers who conduct tasks to which they are not always convinced [5]-[7][13][18].

There is a big difference between developers deciding what to do and being told what to do. Making decisions on your own implies freedom. Developers become more self-driven, enthusiastic and motivated about their work [3][6][12][14]. By learning on their own mistakes, they become more experienced, and hopefully, more mature software developers. The modern methods have recognized this, and therefore, they have given more freedom to developers by eliminating the rigidity of development methods and by decreasing the authority of the managers. The modern methods give more trust and freedom to developers by allowing them to self-govern their own work, learn from their own experience and mistakes, and take their consequences [4][5][7][8][10][11].

Currently, the idea of self-governance is becoming more and more omnipresent within software development. Individual developers and/or teams are expected to exercise most of their necessary functions without intervention from others. This may work well, as long as developers and teams know what to do in order to achieve the best possible results. Unfortunately, there are not many process models providing them with this type of knowledge.

Today, there are no standard process models specifying complete lists of activities as required of software developers. Regarding the current software engineering literature, the lists of activities to be conducted by developers are scattered across various books or articles. The most relevant and all-inclusive sources are (1) Personal Software Process (PSP) as written by Watts Humphrey [7] and (2) our works on developer tests [8][9]. Usually, complete lists may be found only in the industry.

Most of the companies provide some kind of support telling developers what to do. This support is realized in form of process models or methods. The level of formality and rigidness of these models may vary from company to company. Some provide developers with strict sequences of activities which must be conducted step by step. Some others give free hands to developers in deciding what to do. Here, the choice of activities strongly depends on the developers, their knowledge of software development process, maturity, experience, and most importantly, their ability to self-govern themselves.

Even if it is highly desired, self-governance does not always function in many development contexts. There are many reasons to this. Some of them are that developers may not always be aware of what to do and when, or they may not be disciplined enough, or due to various external forces, they may be forced to choose the shortest, however, not always the most optimal way of organizing and conducting their own work.

Success of today's developers should be attributed to their knowledge, discipline and trust. To achieve it, the software community should provide process frameworks

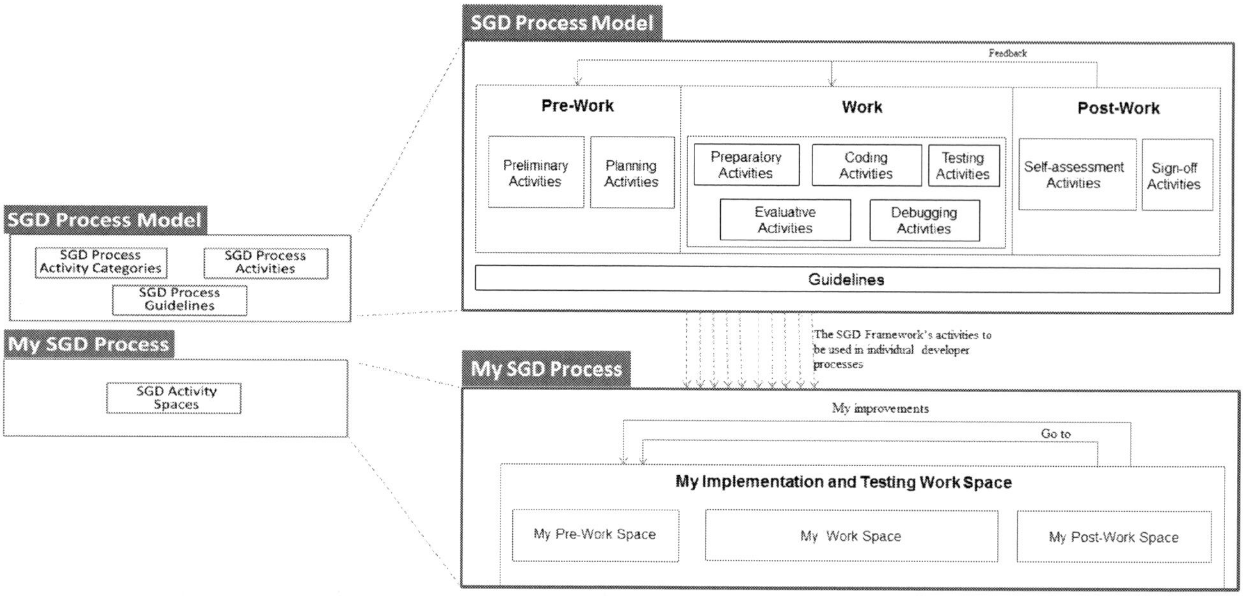

Figure 1. Structure of *the Self-Governance Developer Framework*

telling developers what needs to be done, still however, giving them maximal freedom to organize their own work [15][17][18]. The *SGD Framework* is the solution to this.

In this paper, we suggest and motivate the SGD Framework. SGD is an extension of PSP [7]. To illustrate the enhancements, we benchmark SGD against PSP [9]. The remainder of this paper is as follows. Section II presents the SGD Framework. Section III benchmarks the framework against PSP. Finally, Section IV makes concluding remarks.

II. THE SGD FRAMEWORK

The *SGD Framework* provides generic activities that can be selectively chosen by software developers or teams while implementing software code and unit (developer) testing it. The goal of SGD is to support developers in their daily work by assisting them in self-managing, monitoring and controlling their own assignments. The framework's target groups are software developers and teams whose main task is to code, compile, unit test and integrate their own code units before delivering them for integration and system testing. It is an extension of Watts Humphrey's PSP and of our former work [7]-[9].

The *SGD Framework* is structured into two parts. As shown in on the left-hand side of Fig. 1, these are (1) *SGD Process Model* and (2) *My SGD Process*. The *SGD Process Model* consists of (1) *SGD Process Activity Categories*, (2) *SGD Process Activities*, and (3) *SGD Process Guidelines*. This paper only focuses on (1) *SGD Process Categories* and (2) *SGD Process Activities*. It excludes *SGD Process Guidelines*.

A. SGD Process Model

The *SGD Process Model* consists of three main process parts. These are (1) *Pre-Work* (2) *Work*, and (3) *Post-Work*. The model's activities cover a wide and all-inclusive spectrum of activities that are relevant for conducting implementation and unit (developer) testing. In actual development endeavors, however, not all of the activities need be conducted. In some contexts and/or programming environments, only their subsets may be relevant. For this reason, the *SGD Process Model* includes the *SGD Process Guidelines* providing suggestions for what activities to conduct, when and why.

As illustrated on the right-hand side of Fig. 1, the SGD activities are grouped into nine categories that are distributed across the three above-listed *SGD* process parts. In the model, they are put in the part and category in which they are contextually relevant. They are also listed in the order that may correspond to a logical workflow. This may make the model be understood as traditional and heavyweight. However, the *SGD Framework* does not impose any specific order of activities. The activities may be conducted in any order and they may be included in any process phase that suits the developers and their environments. For simplicity reasons, however, they are mentioned in the *SGD Process Model* part only once. Developers are free to use them in the order that best suits their requirements, needs, formality levels, development approaches, contexts and specific working and/or technological environments as long as their choice contributes to product and process quality.

1) Pre-Work Activities: The SGD Process Model's first part, the *Pre-work* part, includes activities that need to be conducted before starting the implementation work. The *Pre-Work* activities are listed in Table I. They deal with

TABLE I. PRE-WORK ACTIVITIES (+ IMPLIES PRESENCE, – IMPLIES ABSENCE, P STANDS FOR PARTIALLLY)

SGD PRE-WORK ACTIVITIES	
SGD PRE-WORK: PRELIMINARY ACTIVITIES	**PSP**
PR-1: Review and agree on the overall or part of the project plan	+
PR-2: Revise and ensure that the technology to be used is tested and understood	–
PR-3: Revise and understand any appropriate internal (organizational) and external standards	I
PR-4: Learn/relearn the organization's implementation and unit (developer) testing way of work	–
PR-5: Review and revise your personal implementation and unit (developer's) testing way of working	I, P
PR-6: Sign your personal Service Level Agreement (Work Contract)	P, I
SGD PRE-WORK: PLANNING ACTIVITIES	**PSP**
PL-1: Review the requirement(s) for the unit(s) to be developed	–
PL-2: Prepare (make) and/or review the design specifications for the unit(s) to be developed	+
PL-3: Resolve unclear questions and uncertainties	P, I
PL-4: Determine your implementation and unit(developers) testing goals	+
PL-5: Determine your implementation and unit (developer's) testing strategy/ies	I
PL-6: Determine your implementation and testing practices	I
PL-7: Identify standards to be used for meeting your goals	P
PL-8: Set you own personal deadlines to be met during your implementation and unit (developer's) testing work	+
PL-9: Estimate effort and resources required for carrying out your work	+
PL-10: Schedule your work	+
PL-11: Review your implementation and unit (developer) testing plan to ensure that it is realistic and achievable	I
PL-12: Identify risks related to your plan	–
PL-13: Plan for managing any identified risks	I, P

identifying goals to be achieved, formulating strategies for achieving the goals, arranging or creating ways for reaching them, and with monitoring and controlling the implementation and unit (developer) testing steps. They aid developers in achieving an optimal balance between the development requirements and the available resources.

The *Pre-work* part consists of *Preliminary* and *Planning Activities*. They support developers in initiating their work and in creating their own implementation and unit testing personal plans. Although they are listed in the *Pre-Work* category, they may very well be conducted both before and during the actual implementation and testing work. This, of course, depends on the development context at hand and the needs that have arisen in that context.

a) Preliminary Activities: The *Preliminary Activities* are to be conducted before starting the implementation and unit (developer) testing work. They should be carried out before the actual implementation work begins. They prepare developers for performing high quality work. Here, the concerns are making sure that methodologies, technologies, standards, ways of working, commitments are understood and are in place. The SGD Framework strongly recommends that developers consider them before launching their individual development endeavors. Their non-performance may imply various risks that may jeopardize development work and results.

To carry out their work in the best possible way, developers should frequently learn or relearn the organizational ways of working, revise and ensure technologies and revise and understand standards that they are going to use (see Activities PR-2 – PR-4 in Table I). They must also pay attention to their past experiences in order to be able to improve and determine their ways of working (see Activity PR-5 in Table I). This is pivotal for sustaining quality and technologically up-to-date and standard-adhering work. If developers do not spend enough time on these activities, they may run the risk of repeating pitfalls of previous projects.

To find out about available resources and timescales for their work, developers should review and agree on the overall project plan in case of small projects or on parts of the project plan in case of large projects (see Activity PR-1 in Table I). This will enable them to plan their own work so that they can meet the stated requirements and customer expectations. Finally, the SGD Framework recommends that all developers sign their personal Service Level Agreements (SLAs) – contracts in which they commit themselves to conduct their work according to the agreed upon standards and expectations (see Activity PR-6 in Table I).

b) Planning Activities: The *Planning Activities* aid in formulating the initial and continuous development plans. They deal with (1) reviewing the necessary documents, (2) determining ways of conducting the work, and (3) planning the work.

Developers should review the documents that provide important input for understanding the scope of their work. This includes reviewing of requirements and preparing and/or reviewing of design specifications (see PL-1 – PL-2 in Table I). In many cases, requirements and design specifications may not be easy to understand. To free themselves from any misunderstanding and/or confusion, developers should resolve all kinds of unclear questions and uncertainties (see PL-3 in Table I). In this way, they make sure that they acquire a true picture of the user requirements, that the design correctly reflects the requirements, and that their plans are based on realistic premises. Having understood the requirements and design specifications aids developers in determining the limits and approaches while planning their individual work.

The SGD Framework recommends that developers determine implementation and unit (developer) testing goals and strategies and practices that will guide them in their planning (see PL-4 – PL-6 in Table I). Developers should

TABLE II. WORK ACTIVITIES (+ IMPLIES, – IMPLIES ABSENCE, I MEANS IMPLICITLY, P STANDS FOR PARTIALLY)

SGD WORK ACTIVITIES	
SGD WORK: PREPARATORY ACTIVITIES	PSP
P-1: Prepare (make) and/or review your low-level design(s) of the code to be written or changed	+
P-2: Prepare (make) an impact analysis of your low-level design(s)	–
P-3: Determine the types of unit (developer) test cases and their order	I
P-4: Create and/or revise your unit (developer) test case base	+
P-5: Revise the existing unit (developer) regression test base, if relevant	–
P-6: Create or modify stubs and drivers, if required	–
P-7: Prepare your unit (developer) testing environment and check whether it is appropriate for you work	–
SGD WORK: CODING ACTIVITIES	PSP
C-1: Write/rewrite your code	+
C-2: Compile/recompile your code	+
C-3: Make notes on your compilations errors, if necessary	+
C-4: Make notes your defects	I, P
SGD WORK: TESTING ACTIVITIES	PSP
T-1: Check whether the unit (developers) test case base meets the given requirements and design	–
T-2: Check whether the unit (developers) regression test case base meets the given requirements and design	–
T-3: Remedy requirement problems in your unit (developers) regression and/or test case base, if any	–
T-4: Perform dynamic testing by executing code	+
T-5: Perform static (human) testing by reviewing your code	+
T-6: Record/write down test results	+
SGD WORK: EVALUATIVE ACTIVITIES	PSP
E-1: Analyse your unit (developer) testing results	+
E-2: Depending on the unit (developers) testing results, determine your next step(s)	P
SGD WORK: DEBUGGING ACTIVITIES	PSP
D-1: Identify the source of error(s)	+
D-2: Determine solutions(s) for eliminating the sources of error(s)	+

then identify all kinds of standards that need be considered during implementation, set deadlines that need be met, estimate effort and resources and make their personal work schedules (see PL-7 – P-10 in Table I).

After having created their individual plans, developers evaluate them (see PL-11 in Table I), identify risks related to the plans (see PL-12 in Table I) and plan for managing the identified risks (see PL-13 in Table I). In this way, their plans will achieve the right balance of scope, approaches, resources and risks allowing developers to achieve their goals in the best possible way.

2) The Work Activities: The SGD Process Model's second part, the *Work Activities*, includes activities required for producing code and for assuring its quality. It consists of five categories of activities: (1) *Preparatory Activities*, (2) *Coding Activities*, (3) *Testing Activities*, (4) *Evaluative Activities*, and (5) *Debugging Activities*. They are all listed in Table II.

a) Preparatory Activities: The *Preparatory Activities* include the activities needed for preparing the implementation work. They help developers to become ready for writing and unit (developer) testing code. The activities deal with low-level designs, unit (developer) test case designs, stubs and drivers, and unit (developer) testing environment.

Before coding, developers should make the low-level designs of the code they are going to write or, in cases when someone else is responsible for making low-level designs, they should review them. They should also make impact analysis of the designs. The SGD Framework recommends that developers prepare and/or review several design solutions, analyze the impact of the solutions and select the most appropriate solution for the work at hand (see P-1 and P-2 in Table II). This will aid them in creating the best possible solutions for the user requirements and the given premises.

Developers should determine the types of unit (developer) test cases and the order in which they should be run. They should create or revise their own unit test case bases and regression unit test case bases (see P-3 – P-5 in Table II) and create or modify stubs and drivers, if necessary (see P-6 in Table II). Finally, developers should prepare or check their testing environments to enable continuous and smooth testing without any technical interruptions (see P-7 in Table II).

b) Coding Activities: The *Coding Activities* deal with code production including writing or rewriting code and compiling it. The SGD Framework recommends that code be produced using the chosen low-level design. If code is not based on any low-level design, then the risk is that it may not meet the stated requirements. The coding activities even include making personal notes on the compilation errors and on the detected defects (see C-1 – C-4 in Table II). This will help developers monitor their work, evaluate the quality of their work and help them learn from their own coding mistakes.

c) Unit Testing Activities: The *Unit Testing Activities* aid in assuring that the code meets the stated quality goals. They include (1) unit testing activities and (2) control of unit test cases. The unit testing activities encompass dynamic and static testing and the recording of the test results (see T-4 – T-6 in Table II). The control of the unit test cases, on the other hand, encompasses the review of the unit test case bases with the purpose of checking whether they still meet the given requirements and/or designs. Even if developers have created or revised the unit test case bases before starting coding, they should check them anew after

TABLE III. POST-WORK ACTIVITIES (+ IMPLIES PRESENCE, – IMPLIES ABSENCE, I MEANS IMPLICITLY, P STANDS FOR PARTIALLY)

SGD POST-WORK ACTIVITIES	
SGD POST-WORK: SELF-ASSESSMENT ACTIVITIES	PSP
A-1: Assess your own development work	+
A-2: Identify sources of your mistakes	+
A-3: Identify improvement areas in your own way of working	+
SGD POST-WORK: DELIVERY AND SIGN OFF ACTIVITIES	PSP
S-1: Check that your code fulfills the commitment(s) stated in the Service Level Agreement	P
S-2: Deliver your code	+
S-3: Sign-off your personal Service Level Agreement	–

having implemented the code. If they find any problems in them, then they should remedy them. It is only after coding that developers may clearly see what changes need to be done to the unit test case bases (see T-1 – T-3 in Table II).

d) Evaluative Activities: The *Evaluative Activities* deal with the evaluation of unit (developer) testing results and determination of the next step (see E-1 and E-2 in Table II). They should be conducted right after the unit (developer) testing activities and before starting the next series of implementation and unit (developer) testing steps. In this way, developers will make sure that they have chosen the workflow that is appropriate for their work context at hand.

e) Debugging Activities: The *Debugging Activities* aid developers in identifying the sources of the errors that have been discovered during compilation and unit testing and in suggesting solutions for eliminating them (see D-1 and D-2 in Table II). The errors are only symptoms of defects and they may not always be visible. Therefore, it is important that developers (1) debug code for the errors that are not easy to interpret and (2) confirm their underlying defects before deciding on how to attend to them. Otherwise, the defects may reappear either in the same or some other disguise.

3) The Post-Work Activities: The Process Model's third part, the *Post-Work* part, includes activities required for finalizing the implementation and unit testing. They are listed in Table III. Here, the SGD Framework suggests that developers make a self-assessment of their own development work before they deliver their code to integration and system testing and that they sign-off their personal SLAs. When assessing their development work, developers should identify causes of their mistakes and identify improvements that should help them avoid future mistakes (see A-1 – A-3 in Table III). This will help developers become more effective and efficient.

When signing off their personal SLAs, developers should first check that their code fulfills the commitments that they have agreed to before starting their work (see S-1 in Table III). They should then deliver their code (see S-2 Table III) and, finally, sign-off their assignments (see S-3 in Table III). In this way, developers will make sure that they have performed all the work stipulated in their personal SLAs.

B. My Process Part

My *SGD Process* corresponds to the actual developer process as planned and conducted by individual developers and/or teams. As shown in Fig. 1, it consists of three essential activity spaces. Activity spaces are empty spaces that are to be filled in by developers themselves with the activities from the *SGD Process Model.*

Not all of the SDG process model activities may be necessary to conduct in all development contexts. In some contexts, only their subsets may be relevant. For this reason, the *SGD Framework* only provides empty activity spaces that are to be filled in by the developers with the activities which they have selected by themselves. The selected activities are the reflection of developer's workflows that have been conducted or are going to be conducted. Their choice depends on the chosen strategies, methodologies and individual developer or team preferences.

As shown in Fig. 1, the SGD Framework suggests three main activity spaces. These are (1) *My Pre-Work Space* to be filled in with the start-up activities, (2) *My Work Space* to be filled in with the actual development and testing activities, and (3) *My Post-Work Space* to be filled in with concluding activities.

The *My Pre-work* activity space is to be filled in with the activities that developers need for initiating and planning their work. The activities to be used in this space are mainly the activities from the *SGD Pre-Work* part including *Preliminary* and *Planning Activities* (see Fig. 1).

The *My Work* activity space is to be filled in with the activities that developers perform when implementing and testing their code. The activities to be used in this space are mainly the activities from the *SGD Work* part including *Preparatory Activities, Coding, Unit Testing, Evaluation* and *Debugging* (see Fig. 1). In addition to this, the *My Work* space may include sets of activities from the *SGD Pre-work* part that developers need for conducting their continuous preparation and planning.

Finally, the *My Post-Work* activity space is to be filled in with the activities that conclude the implementation and unit testing work. The activities to be used in this space mainly come from the *SGD Post-Work* part including *Self-Assessment* and *Delivery* and *Sign-Off Activities* (see Fig. 1). However, this space may also include the activities from the *Pre-Work* and *Work* parts in cases when developers have not fulfilled their SLA commitments and, thereby, have to finalize their work before submitting their code for system integration.

III. BENCHMARKING THE SGD FRAMEWORK

The SGD Framework was benchmarked against PSP [7]. While benchmarking, we simply checked whether PSP included the SGD activities. The presence of the activities is marked with a plus (+), the absence is marked with a minus

(–). Unclear cases, such as implicit or partial presence of the activities, are marked with I standing for implicit and P standing for partial implementation.

The benchmarking results are presented in Tables I-III. As can be seen there, PSP does not fully cover any of the SGD Framework categories. Below, we briefly comment on the benchmarking results for each of the categories.

Regarding the *Pre-Work* activities, PSP has performed poorly. It does not encourage developers to revise and ensure that the technology to be used is tested and understood (Activity PR-2 in Table I). Neither does it suggest that developers learn or relearn the organizations' implementation way of working (PR-4 in Table I). We believe that these activities are pivotal for succeeding with the implementation work. Both technology and ways of working continuously evolve. Lack of knowledge about them may lead to substantial productivity loss. Finally, PSP is not clear about whether developers should review and revise their own implementation ways of working (Activity PR-6 in Table I). In our opinion, this is a severe omission considering the fact that this activity is driving the whole personal software process.

Regarding the *Planning* activities, PSP fails to suggest that developers review the requirements for the units to be developed (Activity PL-1 in Table I). This may lead to the fact that developers may misunderstand the requirements and develop things that have not been expected from them. PSP also fails to suggest that developers identify risks related to their own personal plans (Activity PL-12). Again, this activity is one of the driving wheels of a disciplined personal developer process.

PSP is not explicit enough about activities related to determining implementation and testing strategies and practices (Activity PL-5 and PL-6 in Table I) and in reviewing the developer plan for assuring that the work is realistic and achievable (PL-11 in Table I). We believe that this activity is very important. Not considering it may lead to failure of delivering code in time or it may result in never delivering it due to the unrealistic personal plans.

Considering the *Preparatory* activities in the *Work* part, PSP does not consider the fact that developers should make an impact analysis of their low-level designs (Activity P-2 in Table II). Neither does it consider the fact that developers should revise the existing regression test base (P-5 in Table II) and that they should prepare and check whether the testing environment is appropriate (P-7 in Table II).

PSP covers all the SGD coding activities with one exception. It does not encourage developers to make notes on their defects (Activity C-4 in Table II). We believe that this activity is important from the perspective of individual professional development. By remembering defects and analysing their root causes, that is, mainly mistakes, developers will improve their professional skills and become better at developing software.

In addition to traditional testing activities, SGD includes checks whether unit test bases and regression test bases meet the given requirements and designs (T-1 – T-2 in Table II). PSP does not consider these activities at all. Neither does it assume that there may be requirement problems in the regression test bases (T-3 in Table II). Requirements may change with time and this should be reflected in the regression test base. Lack of the activities T-1 – T-3 may lead to the omission of testing important requirements and late discovery of defects, either during integration and system testing or even during operation.

Regarding the remaining *Work* activities, such as *Evaluative* and *Debugging* activities, PSP has implemented them all. PSP also implements all but one *Post-Work* activity. The activity that it does not implement concerns signing off SLAs (see Activity S-3 in Table III).

IV. Final Remarks

Self-governance should bring value in form of improved developer productivity and job satisfaction. Developers should be able to decide upon what activities to choose based on the value the activities bring. This has been recognized in PSP as suggested by Watts Humphrey [7].

In this paper, we have suggested Self-Governance Developer Framework outlining the activities aiding developers and/or teams in designing their own personal processes. SGD only provides a basic conceptual structure of the activities and provides guidelines for performing them. It does not provide any suggestion for any order among the activities. Neither does it define inputs and outputs of the activities. As a framework, it constitutes a platform for creating developer process models, which in turn, are free to define their own order, inputs and outputs, and provide guidance in decision making.

The SGD Framework is a continuation and extension of PSP [7] and of our earlier work on developer testing process [8][9]. So far, it has only been evaluated against PSP. It has not yet been evaluated against other standards and industrial or academic models. Evaluation, however, is on its way. Right now, we are conducting active research by studying activities as conducted by software engineering students at KTH Royal Institute of Technology [19][20]. We are also in the process of evaluating the SGD with the industrial software engineering professionals.

References

[1] P. Abrahamssom and K. Kautz, "The Personal Software Process: Experiences from Denmark," Proc. Euromicro Conference, IEEE, Sept. 2002, pp. 367-374, doi: 10.1109/EURMIC.2002.1046223.

[2] F. Abdolazimian and S. Mansouri, "Business Process Reengineering by Rational Unified Process (RUP) Methodology,". *World Applied Sciencies Journal 4, (Supple 2)*, IDOSI Publications, pp. 33-42, 2008.

[3] K. Beck, M. Beedle, A. van Bennekum, A. Cockburn, W. Cunningham, F. Fowler, J. Grenning, J. Highsmith, A. Hunt, R. Jeffries, J. Kern, B. Marick, R. C. Martin, S. Mellor, and K. Schwaber, "*Manifesto for Agile Software Development*,". [Online]. Available from: http://agilemanifesto.org/, 2017.03.15.

[4] K. Culver-Lozo, "The Software Process from the Developer's Perspective: A Case Study on Improving Process Usability," Proc. Ninth International Software Process Workshop, IEEE, Oct. 1995, pp. 67-69, doi: 10.1109/ISPW.1994.512766.

[5] W. Hayes, "Using a Personal Software Process[SM] to improve performance," Proc. Fifth International Software Metrics Symposium. Metrics, IEEE, pp. 61-71, 1998.

[6] A. Heravi, V. Coffey, and B. Trigunarsyah, "Evaluating the level of stakeholder involvement during the project planning processesss of building projects," International Journal of Project Management, ELSEVIER, vol. 33, pp. 985-997, 2015.

[7] W. S. Humphrey, Introduction to the Personal Software Process, Addison-Wesley, 1997.

[8] G. Jeppesen, M. Kajko-Mattsson and J. Murphy, "Peeking into Developers' Testing Process," Proc. International Conference on Computational Intelligence and Software Engineering, IEEE, pp. 1-8, 2009. doi: 10.1109/CISE.2009.5366347.

[9] M. Kajko-Mattsson and T. Bjornsson, "Outlining Developers' Testing ProcessModel," Proc. 33rd EUROMICRO Conference on Software Engineering and Advanced Applications, IEEE, pp. 263-270, 2007, doi: 10.1109/EUROMICRO.2007.45.

[10] Z. Lasio, "Project portfolio management: An integrated method for resource planning and scheduling to minimize planning/scheduling-dependent expenses," International Journal of Project Management, ELSEVIER, vol. *28*, pp. 609-618, 2010.

[11] M. Lavallé and P. N. Robillard, "The Impacts of Software Process Improvement on Developers: A Systematic Review," Proc. 34th International Conference on Software Engineering, pp. 113-122, 2012, doi: 10.1109/ICSE.2012.6227201.

[12] M. Maccoby, "Self-developers: why the new engineers work," IEEE Spectrum, IEEE, vol. 25, no. 2, pp. 50-53, 1996, doi: 10.1109/6.4511.

[13] N. H. Madhavji, X. Zhong, and E.E. Emam, "Critical Factors Affecting Personal Software Processes," IEEE Software, IEEE, vol. 17, no. 6, pp. 76-83, 2000, doi: 10.1109/52.895172.

[14] C. d. O. Melo, C. Santana, and F. Kon, "Developers Motivation in Agile Teams," Proc. 38th Euromicro Conference on Software Engineering and Advanced Applications, IEEE, pp. 376-383, 2012, doi: 10.1109/SEAA.2012.45.

[15] S. Priestley, *Scientific Management in the 21th Century*. [Online]. Available from: http://www.articlecity.com/articles/business_and_finance/article_4161.shtml, 2017.03.15.

[16] K. Schwaber and J. Sutherland, *The Scrum Guide TM*. [Online]. Available from: ttp://www.scrumguides.org/docs/scrumguide/v2016/2016-Scrum-Guide-US.pdf#zoom=100, 2017.03.15.

[17] C. M. Thomas, "An Overview of the Current State of the Test-First vs.Test-Last Debate," Scholarly Horizons: University of MinnesotaMorris Undergraduate Jounal, vol. 1, iss. 2. [Online]. Available from: http://digitalcommons.morris.umn.edu/cgi/viewcontent.cgi?article=1015&context=horizons, 2017.03.15.

[18] S. Wambler, *Choose the Right Software Method for the Job*. [Online]. Available from: http://www.agiledata.org/essays/differentStrategies.html, 2017.03.15.

[19] University Degree Programme in Information and Communication Technology (CINTE), KTH Royal Institute of Technology in Sweden. [Online]. Available from: https://www.kth.se/student/kurser/program/CINTE/HT13/kurslista?l=en, 2017.03.15.

[20] University Degree Program in Information and Communication Technology (TCOMK), KTH Royal Institute of Technology in Sweden. [Online]. Available from: https://www.kth.se/student/kurser/program/TCOMK/HT14/genomforande?l=en, 2017.03.15.

Security and Software Engineering: Analyzing Effort and Cost

Callum Brill, Aspen Olmsted
Department of Computer Science
College of Charleston, Charleston, SC 29401
Email: brillch@g.cofc.edu, olmsteda@cofc.edu

Abstract— There are many systems developed to model and estimate the software development lifecycle of a product, such as Constructive Cost Model (CoCoMo) II and SEER for Software (SEER-SEM). As the demand for security in software engineering rises, engineers are proposing changes to the development lifecycle to better integrate security. These changes in the Software Development Lifecycle (SDLC) come with the need for changes in how we model the associated costs. Specifically, this paper analyzes the costs of a Web Content Management System with regards to security and proposes adjustments, based on lifecycle changes, to the CoCoMo II cost model that would allow for security to be better factored into project management.

Keywords- Software Engineering; Cyber Security.

I. INTRODUCTION

The cost of software development projects can be quite difficult. The Software Development Lifecycle (SDLC), the lifecycle software engineering project undergoes, consists of the following stages [1]:

- Analysis–Developing the goals to be achieved by the software and defining the scope of the software with regards to those problems to ensure that the project does not fall victim to scope creep.
- Requirements–Translating project goals into concrete operations of the software.
- Design–Formulating detailed descriptions of the previously defined operations, including but not limited to the design of user interfaces, internal logic decisions and modeling system interactions.
- Implementation–Encoding the agreed upon design choices into a working software application.
- Testing–Evaluating the correctness of the implementation to remove potential defects.
- Deployment–Deploying the tested implementation into a production environment so that the software may be consumed by end users.
- Maintenance–Resolving issues that arise during use by consumers, ensuring that the software can continue to be used and keeping the software from becoming obsolete. This is typically the longest stage and is an ongoing effort.

However, this lifecycle is becoming less appropriate for representing software development, as security is becoming more important. Many of the existing models to estimate cost are based on this lifecycle, which means the need to update those cost models rises along with the need to replace the SDLC with a more secure process.

Another cost that models do not account for is Information Technology (IT) and technical debt. IT debt is the idea that systems can accrue liability over time, usually by having maintenance operations postponed or added to an ever-growing backlog; and if that liability is not recognized and dealt with, it can grow exponentially [2]. Similarly, technical debt is the liability that one assumes when producing software products and deciding to produce code that may not necessarily be the most optimal solution in the hopes that it will ease schedule pressure [3]. In both cases, this liability may be reduced by devoting man-hours to either, in the case of IT debt, performing maintenance tasks from a back log or, in the case of technical debt, refactoring, i.e. changing code without changing the external functionality. With the potential to become wildly expensive, it is important to incorporate the potential of these debts into cost models.

Our paper examines the position of IT and technical debt in the current software development lifecycle and cost models, as well as changes to the SDLC, and proposes factors to better estimate the amount of effort necessary to resolve these issues.

The organization of this paper is as follows. Section 2 describes related work and the limitations of current methods. In Section 3, we give a motivating example from which we draw our information. Section 4 describes our proposed changes to current models and methodologies. Section 5 contains the conclusion and possible future work using our models and the field of secure software engineering.

II. RELATED WORK

A. Constructive Cost Model

There are multiple models used to estimate the cost of developing software: The Constructive Cost Model (CoCoMo) [4] and its offshoots, such as SEER for Software [5] (SEER-SEM) and the numerous in-house models used by software development firms. CoCoMo II, the model proposed by Boehm et al. [4], is designed to consider a shift in development paradigms away from waterfall development and towards iterative patterns, such as agile and extreme programming. CoCoMo II has various factors that determine cost, including a reliability factor, however it has no factor indicative of security development costs. Prior versions of CoCoMo had a factor related to security; however, it was an effort modifier that dealt with the development of classified software. The shift to cover software built on off the shelf platforms [4] has resulted in the removal of such security factors. The driving motivation in the shift is the belief that the platform will be secure; therefore, any software built upon it will be secure. Our paper suggests factors to estimate the cost of developing software using a secure process. Madachy has developed a Web application to using CoCoMo II to be used to estimate costs [6].

B. Effort Cost And Reduction

Using the platform as a service (PaaS) model is a common method of saving on costs as it removes the need for end-users to develop from scratch. Olmsted et al. estimate the total cost of an platform to be approximately 13 million dollars by using a metric consisting of a measure of source lines of code (SLOC) and a trace of code execution *[7]*. We use methodologies from this analysis to estimate cost factors related to the security of these platforms and the hypothetical cost to have been developed using an alternate lifecycle.

C. Secure Sofware Development Lifecycle

There are many proposed enhancements for the Software Development Lifecycle from many different sources. Microsoft advocates a secure development lifecycle to complement the security of their operating system. Microsoft's proposed Development lifecycle add several stages to the development lifecycle, including [8]:

- Security Education and Awareness – Ensuring that developers are educated on the ideals surrounding security.
- Determining Project Security Needs – Analyzing if the project has a crucial need to follow the Secure Development Lifecycle
- Designing Best Practices – Fitting common best practices to your project and determining new best practices as necessary.
- Product Risk Assessment – Estimating the appropriate amount of effort to create an appropriate level of security.
- Risk Analysis – Analyzing possible threat vectors.
- Security and Best Practice Documentation and Tooling – Creating tools and best practices which can be easily followed by an end user to help ensure the security of their environment.
- Secure Coding Policies – Following prescribed methodologies in order to prevent poor implementations of design e.g. avoiding certain functions, leveraging compiler features, and using the latest version of tools.
- Secure Testing Policies – Applying secure testing policies in order to verify the security of you application. This does not make the product secure, only verifies that it is.
- Security Push – Pushing to ensure that any legacy code that is used is secure.
- Security Audit – Determining if the product is appropriately secure to ship to consumers.
- Security Response and Execution – The creation, and execution if necessary, of plans with which to respond to security breaches.

Some of these steps are relegated to technical debt and often not handled at the appropriate points in development and cut due to cost, especially in agile development and commercial off the shelf products. With these steps in mind, our paper our paper provides a factor to add to CoCoMo to estimate the cost of integrating these procedures into a development lifecycle.

III. MOTIVATING EXAMPLE

WordPress [9], Drupal [10], and Joomla! [11] are three of the most widely used COTS Web platforms. These platforms allow end-users to create Websites with significantly less effort than creating their own Website; however, Websites running these platforms are among some of the most exploited on the internet due to the low barrier of entry. Our paper examines one of these platforms, Drupal, in order to determine factors that should be added to CoCoMo II in order to adequately cover the costs of secure development.

According to work by Meike, Sametinger and Wiesaur, Joomla and Drupal both have serious design flaws that place the platforms at definite risk. Currently identified flaws include the allowance of file uploads with unchecked contents, the existence of HTTP headers that contained data capable of being manipulated and escalations of privilege. These flaws in the code exist because of flaws in the design process [12].

IV. CONTRIBUTION

We determined the factors to add to CoCoMo II through an analysis of an unsecure, obsolete version of Drupal. This analysis is an examination of the number of lines of source code involved in flaws in the platform. We determine that that is the cost of the flaw, valued in source lines of code (SLoC). We then run a similar analysis on the latest version of Drupal. We then compare those costs with the cost of the newest version and compare vulnerabilities to determine if the design flaws still exist. Here all costs are equivalent to the number of lines of source code, so our calculation can give us a comparable measure.

In Table 1, we have an explanation of several pain points and security vulnerabilities in two common Web content management systems Drupal and Joomla! in versions 5.2 and 1.0.13, respectively. In this table ✓indicates and issue that is not present in the software, × indicates an issue that is present in the software and an ! indicates that the issue has been partially resolved in the software. Using these unresolved and partial resolved issues, we measured the number of lines of code per function call, using a PHP module called xDebug.

Table 2 contains a list of flaws, the status of that flaw in Drupal 5.2, the number of lines of source code necessary to achieve the functionality present in Drupal 5.2, the status of the flaw in Drupal 8.2.3, the number of lines necessary to achieve the functionality in Drupal 8.2.3, and the technical debt balance. In this table the technical debt balance is a value based on whether or not the flaw had been resolved. Should the flaw have been resolved, the SLoC from the obsolete version of Drupal is subtracted from the SLoC of the later version of Drupal. Should the flaw not have been resolved, the amount of technical debt is represented by the SLoC of the current version of Drupal.

Examining the measurements, based on a measurement of flaws present in Drupal version 5.2 and 8.2.3, in Table 2 we can see that some of the more serious flaws that were present in 5.2

TABLE I WCMS VULNERABILITIES [8]

	Joomla!	Drupal
Community		
Security patches	✓	✓
Reporting of vulnerabilities	✓	✓
Hints to countermeasures	✓	✓
Installation		
Security hints	✓	×
Security settings	×	×
Parameter Manipulation		
HTTP header data	×	×
Super global arrays	✓	✓
Cookies	✓	✓
Remote Command Execution	✓	✓
Forms	!	×
Cross-Site Scripting		
APIs against XSS	✓	✓
XSS via URL parameter	✓	✓
XSS via search fields	✓	✓
XSS in other forms	✓	✓
XSS in back-end	✓	✓
SQL-Injection		
Any countermeasures	✓	✓
User Administration		
Login: XSS or SQL-Injection	✓	✓
Secure Passwords	×	!
Sessions at the Server	×	!
Sessions at the Client	✓	✓
Session Hijacking	!	×
Access to Functions	!	✓
Spam		
Contact forms like CAPTCHA	✓	!
Spam Relays	✓	✓
E-mail addresses	✓	×
Malicious File Upload		
Checking File Endings	✓	✓
Checking File Contents	×	×
Elevation of Privilege		
Privileged users	×	!
Administrators	×	×
Optional Modules		
Warnings	✓	✓
Security measures in core	×	×

were resolved. These flaws allow authors or users who had escalated their privileges to that of an administrator to post code directly into Webpages. In our Drupal 5.2 test environment, we executed code that showed the server information, but it would be fully possible for a malicious user to deploy a Web shell through these vulnerabilities. There is also a clear difference in the overhead code between the two versions. For example, during the installation the obsolete code required 638 lines of code, while the modern version required 4616 to execute that same function. It is clear, however, that even though some issues are resolved there are several issues that remain and would need to be resolved through the effort of the end user.

TABLE II ANALYSIS OF COST PER FLAW

Security Feature	Drupal 5.2 Status	Drupal 5.2 SLoC	Drupal 8.2.3 Status	Drupal 8.2.3 SLoC	Technical Debt Balance
Security Hints during Installation	None	638	Hints present	4616	3978
Installation Security Settings	None	638	None	4616	4616
Secure Passwords	Not Enforced	860	Not Enforced	4694	4694
File Content Scan	Does not scan file contents.	798	Incorrect file types are detected	1566	768
Administrators	Can Execute PHP at will	907	PHP not Executed	1953	1046

Using the data gathered from our Drupal test environment, we have developed two factors which increase the accuracy of the CoCoMo cost Models to reflect the true costs of developing secure software. The first factor, a multiplier of 3.47, is applied to greenfield engineering projects to estimate the effort of designing a project using a Secure Software Development Lifecycle (SSDLC) rather than using the standard SDLC. This value was calculated by comparing the SLoC of flaws which had been resolved between versions of Drupal (8135 lines / 2343 lines).

The second factor, a multiplier of 1.607, should be used to calculate the effort that will be needed to handle technical debt when a software product has already been developed and the development team did not use a SSDLC. This multiplier was determined by comparing the technical debt balances of the unresolved flaws with the technical debt balances of the resolved flaws (9310 lines / 5792 lines).

V. CONCLUSIONS AND FUTURE WORKS

In this paper, we have proposed an additional factor to CoCoMo II. This was done by calculating and comparing the cost of code in flawed portions of a Web platform and a less secure, obsolete version of the same platform. We believe that the use of these factors would accurately describe the amount of additional effort necessary to integrate a SDLC as well as the possible pitfalls that arise as technical debt.

Future works may include the analysis of several other off the shelf Web content management systems, using the same analytical method, to increase the size of the data set and consequently the accuracy of the secure development factor or the development of such a factor for other costing models.

REFERENCES

[1] I. Sommerville, Software Engineering, Harlow: Addison-Wesley, 2001.

[2] D. Britton, "Why IT Debt is Mounting," Micro Focus, 22 09 2014. [Online]. Available: http://www.networkworld.com/article/2686761/it-skills-training/why-it-debt-is-mounting.html. [Accessed 27 9 2016].

[3] P. Kruchten, R. L. Nord and O. Ipek, "Technical Debt: From Metaphor to Theory and Practice.," *IEEE Software,* vol. 29, no. 6, pp. 18-21, 2012.

[4] B. Boehm, B. Clark, E. Horowitz, C. Westland, R. Madachy and R. Selby, "Cost Models for Future Software Life Cycle Processes: COCOMO 2.0," *Annals of Software Engineering,* vol. 1, no. 1, pp. 57-94, 1995.

[5] D. Galorath, Galorath, [Online]. Available: http://galorath.com/products/software/SEER-Software-Cost-Estimation. [Accessed 15 April 2017].

[6] R. Madachy, "CoCoMo II - Constructive Cost Model," [Online]. Available: http://csse.usc.edu/tools/COCOMOII.php. [Accessed 27 9 2016].

[7] A. Olmsted and K. Fulford, "Platform As A Service Effort Reduction," in *Proceedings of The Eighth International Conference on Cloud Computing, GRIDs, and Virtualization (Cloud Computing 2017),* Athens, 2017.

[8] M. Howard and S. Lipner, The security development lifecycle, Redmond: Microsoft Press, 2006.

[9] Wordpress.org, [Online]. Available: https://wordpress.org/. [Accessed 16 April 2017].

[10] Drupal, [Online]. Available: https://www.drupal.org/. [Accessed 2017 16 April].

[11] "Joomla!," Open Source Matters, Inc., [Online]. Available: https://www.joomla.org/. [Accessed 2017 16 April].

[12] M. Meike, J. Sametinger and A. Wiesaur, "Security in Open Source Web Content Management Systems," *IEEE Security and Privacy,* vol. 7, no. 4, pp. 44-51, 2009.

[13] A. Olmsted and K. Fulford, "Platform As A Service Effort Reduction".

Improving a Travel Management Procedure: an Italian Experience

Antonello Calabró*, Eda Marchetti*, Giorgio Oronzo Spagnolo*
Pierangela Cempini†, Luca Mancini†, Serena Paoletti†

*Software Engineering Area
†Administrative Staff
Institute of Information Science and Technologies"A. Faedo"
Italian National Research Council (CNR)
via G. Moruzzi, 1 - Pisa, Italy
Email: firstnames.lastname@isti.cnr.it

Abstract—**Recently, a lot of attention has been dedicated by the Public Administrations to reduce/optimize the costs of travel management. Indeed, automatic support may increase the quality of the proposed services, drastically decreasing the time required for document production and validation, and promoting the integration with different PA (Public Administration) systems and services. However, due to the critical nature of the exchanged data, the interaction with the customers (personnel and citizens), the complexity of the considered procedures, the quality aspect becomes a crucial point to be considered during the development of automatic supports. In this paper, we focus on the quality aspects of the PA travel management automation, and we present the evaluation of a prototype implementation of a framework for automating the travel management process adopted inside an Italian PA. The experience highlighted important challenges in the application of automatic facilities for the travel management and nd allowed the detection of inconsistencies and improvements of the process itself.**

***Keywords*–usiness process; Monitoring; Adequacy Criteria; Learning assessmentusiness process; Monitoring; Adequacy Criteria; Learning assessmentB**

I. Introduction

Automatic support is currently consolidated practices for increasing the quality of services provided by administrations and drastically decreasing the time required for documents production and validation. In line with this policy, the Italian Public Administrations (PAs) are currently moving towards the "digital maturity", i.e., massive adoption of Information and Communication Technologies) facilities to increase the quality and efficiency of their internal procedures, integrating the different PA services and speeding up the overall PA management [1]. However, due to the critical nature of the exchanged data, the interaction with the customers (personnel and citizens), the complexity of the considered procedures, the quality aspect becomes a crucial point to be considered during the development of automatic supports. In this paper we focus on the PA travel management automation, which has been recognized as one of the PA hot topics for cost reduction, according to a recent research of the School of Management in collaboration with AirPlus [2]. In particular, this analysis evidenced that only one third of the considered PAs has an accurate, organized, quality satisfactory travel management system. Most of the times, only a partial automation is provided and the single employees are forced to organize their travels with the help of on-line travel services.

The main issues of the existing facilities have been identified into the persistency of: an hard copy collection of travel documentations; an inaccurate, incomplete or erroneous collection of travel data; a manual checking and validation of the produced travel documentation by the administrative personnel. A more satisfactory travel management system could, on one hand drastically reduce the time and effort necessary for the procedure completion, and from the hand, provide optimized travel schedule, conventions with public transports accommodations and digitalization of travel documentation. A preliminary analysis of the impact of the adoption of proper automatic support for the travel management on the PAs overall costs can be summarized as:

- n evident increase of the quality of the filled modules due to the reduction in the number of errors and inconsistencies inside them;
- an accurate collection and cataloguing of data, avoiding loss of documentations;
- a reduction of the time required for checking and validating the different costs and expenses;
- automatic and periodic statistical travel reports useful for the stipulation of conventions with travel or accommodation companies;
- an accurate and more organized annual budget analysis useful for a faithful schedule and planning of PA costs;
- an integration with the different PA systems and services, with an important decrease in the cost and effort necessary by the administrative staff to process the documentation, record travel data information and complete the overall travel refund.

On the basis of the above considerations, and continuing a preliminary work presented in [3], this paper presents the procedural steps followed from requirements elicitation to the definition of a specific quality model and the relative customized software measurement plans for its internal travel management system of an Italian PA: the Institute of Information Science and Technologies "A. Faedo" (ISTI) of the Italian National Research Council (CNR) in Pisa [1]. In collaboration with the administrative staff of such institute, we analyzed the possible quality improvements starting from three points

[1] http://www.isti.cnr.it/

of view: the technical position, related to the quality of the systems itself; the view of the user, which is more related to the usability experienced and the quality level obtained in the fulfilment of his/her tasks; and finally, the view of the PA personnel, which is interested in the maximization of the revenues in management.

Thanks to our previous experience in different context domains, [3], [4], [5], [6], [7], we followed a storytelling approach [8] [9] to collect through interviews the most important requirements, quality attributes, interesting behaviors and critical activities of the travel management process. Then, using the basic guidelines of the Business Process Management [10], we developed a Business Process Model (BPM) representing the steps that have to be performed by the different participants (people, teams distributed organizations or systems) during the execution of the travel management process. This approach allowed us to focus on important quality aspects and an easy model for the travel refund process. Concise definitions have been used both during discussions with the ISTI administration and for the preliminary validation of the executable framework, called COSO (COmpilazione miSsiOni) [11], implementing the process itself. n particular, to simplify the quality attributes measurement, track activities evolution and the information exchange, monitoring capabilities have also been included in the developed framework.

Recently BPM modeling has been adopted in many sectors, such as financial services, business services and construction, manufacturing, public sector and healthcare, retail and wholesale, and telecommunications. Especially in the public administration, many governments are taking advantage of the multiple benefit that BPM software solutions offer [12]. There are various examples of successful BPM adoption in public administrations like for instance those experienced in Germany, Switzerland, Austria [13] and Sweden [14]. In particular, the authors in [15] describe the BPM System for benchmarking, monitoring, simulation and redesigning processes, that will be deployed into the Greek government agencies. However, despite the importance of the topic, there is very little attention paid on the definition of precise quality aspects useful both for guiding the development and subsequent assessment of such system.

The experience of this paper highlighted that the identification of the proper quality attributes, as well as the BPM elements can be a key factor for the final results. It also revealed important challenges in the application of automatic facilities for the travel management in a specific PA context and and revealed the detection of inconsistencies and improvements of the process itself.

Summarizing, the contribution of this paper is: the BPM modeling of the natural language rules of the CNR manual for travel management process, the definition of a quality model focused on productivity, efficient time management, usability and performance aspects, and the feedbacks and results of the preliminary assessment of the COSO framework.

In the rest of the paper, some background concepts are presented in Section II, while in Section III, the procedure followed for deriving BPM is presented. The set of quality attributes used for the COSO assessment is schematized in Section IV, while the main COSO components are introduced in Section V. Preliminary assessment results are collected in Section VI and discussion and conclusions follow in Section VII.

II. BACKGROUND

In this section, we briefly provide some details about the CNR travel management procedure. The formalism chosen to represent this procedure is the Business Process Model and Notation (BPMN) [16], which is the de facto standard for process modeling. It is indeed a rich and expressive but also complex language to be used for the tasks associated with process modeling [17]. Usually, the BPMN refers to any structured collection of related activities or tasks that are carried out to accomplish the intended objectives of an organization. Tasks within a business process may represent steps that can be performed manually by a human or automatically by an IT system [18].

As any other PA, ISTI and more in general the CNR, has a well-defined collection of travel policies and procedures. According to CNR rules, the travel expenses have to be previously authorized using a specific authorization module. Once travel has been completed, the expenses have to be reported into a specific refund module, supported by appropriate documentation and legitimated by the administrative staff. Variations from the established policies represent exceptional cases and have to be approved by the authorized department approver (Director). One of the main traveler's responsibility is to be familiar with, and strictly follow, the policies and procedures specified in the manual. It is out of the scope of this paper to provide a detailed rules list; in the following we only mention the most important ones. Additional information regarding travel authorization, reimbursement process as well as accounting practices and procedures is available in [19].

Authorization: The travel should be authorized by the Director, and an authorization module should be produced at least five working days before departure. Travelers should provide their personal details, the motivation of the travel, the location, and an estimated amount of the total travel cost.

Transportation: Class depends on the category of travelers and varies from national to international transportation.

Accommodation: Type of allowed accommodation depends on the category of travelers.

Reimbursing Travel Related Expenses: Rules vary in case of national or international travels an reported through specific module.

Meal expenses: Only two meals are allowed and the total meal expenses for day are limited by specific boundaries.

Documentation: Original receipts for all expenses must be submitted to administrative staff and PDF copy provided.

Mileage Reimbursement Rate: Reimbursements for mileage are made following specific mileage reimbursement rate in effect at the time of the trip.

Reimbursable Expenses: Reimbursable travel expenses also include: airline baggage fees, automobile rentals and meeting/-conference fees.

However, the Italian legislation about PA travel management is continuously modifying and due to its natural language specification, it often rises misunderstandings and misinterpretations. Being informed and knowledgeable about the travelers management evolution is one of the most difficult points for the travelers. Therefore, the documentation provided both for travel authorization and travel refund are often full of errors and inconsistencies.

III. Model Creation

In this section, we briefly present the method used requirement elicitation. The requirements have been then translated into the Business Process Models of the ISTI travel management process, called ISTI Travel Model (ITM). In order to develop the ITM, we followed a storytelling methodology [8], [9]. Therefore, through interviews with ISTI personnel and domain experts, we collected the most interesting behaviors and critical activities of the travel management process.

The method is summarized in Figure 1, where three main stakeholders are: the *Tellers*, who are asked to describe their activities explicitly through stories; the *Facilitators*, who provide support to story tellers for producing coherent stories and to modelers for the definition of the first abstraction of the models; *Modelers*, who are the process analysts defining the graphical models on the bases of information collected from the tellers and facilitators. Following the storytelling methodology three specific phases, each one involving all the roles, have been executed as briefly described in the rest of this section.

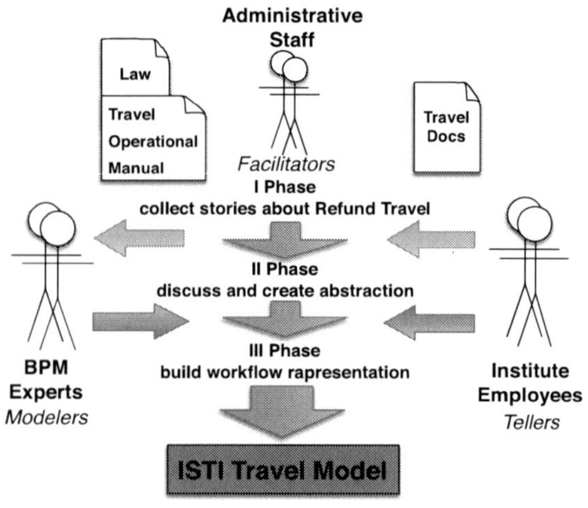

Figure 1. Methodology to create the model

At the end of the three phases of the storytelling methodology, we have produced one high-level model that describes the main process of the ITM and sixteen lower level models that describe in details the sub-processes. For simplicity, we report in Figure 2 just the high-level model of the ITM concerning reimbursement of travel related expense.

As in the Figure 2, the actors interact with the COSO framework according to the following procedure: (1) The employee authenticates himself/hersef though COSO and starts a request of travel refund expenses; (2) Using an Identity Provider (IdP is responsible for providing identifiers for users looking to interact with a system) COSO identifies the users; (3) GEKO [20], the ISTI internal Internet service managing administrative projects funding, sends to COSO the data related to the selected travel; (4) the employee fills/uploads and accepts travel data and documents. The COSO framework aids the employee in the module completion implementing the rules and policies of the CNR travel management procedure concerning the accomodations, transportation, meal expenses; (5) Finally, the refund request is printed and sent to the SIGLA framework [21], which is the official CNR system for the management of the accounting and financial reporting.

IV. Quality aspects

Nowadays, modern societies and administrations take more and more in consideration quality aspects of their business process and try to improve them by the adoption of automatic support. The International Organization for Standardization (ISO) in its definition for quality, namely "(the) degree to which an inherent characteristic (a distinguishing feature) fulfils requirements (a need or expectation that is stated, generally implied or obligatory)" [22]. Thus, an important aspect becomes the possibility of evaluating both the user satisfaction and the quality of the proposed service in terms of parameters that can be obtained by directly measuring the business process. Considering in particular the PAs business processes, they involve several collaborative activities shared among different, possibly many, offices, personnel, companies. Moreover, the introduction of laws/regulations concerning the improvement of automatic documentations management as well as the necessity of costs reduction provide new challenges for the enactment and automation of PA business process such as productivity, timeless, and usability and performance.

In this section, considering the specificity of the ISTI travel business management, the information collected in the phase 2 of the storytelling methodology (see Section III), and the set of attributes expressed in the ISO/IEC 25010 standard [23], a customized set of quality attributes has been selected and adapted for assessing the COSO framework.

In the following subsections, the quality model is briefly presented considering the attributes divided into five target perspectives: business, security, performance, configuration and enhancement.

1) Business Perspective: The attributes considered according to the business perspective are:

Suitability: Degree to which the system provides a set of functions that meet the ISTI personnel requirements (both from administrative and user perspective). It is measured in the number of requirements implemented into the specifications.

Accessibility: Degree to which the system can be used by people with the widest range of characteristics and capabilities to achieve a specified goal in a specified context of use. Two measures are associated to this attribute: the number of functions a user with a physical handicap can access; the number of different categories of ISTI personnel mapped into the system.

Learnability: Degree to which the system can be used by the ISTI personnel to learn the rules of the CNR travel management procedure. It is measured in terms of the completeness of user documentation and /or help facilities.

User error protection: Degree to which the system protects users against making errors. It is measured in terms of the number of rules of the CNR travel management procedure implemented in the system.

Adaptability: Degree to which the system can effectively and efficiently be adapted to different or evolving rules of

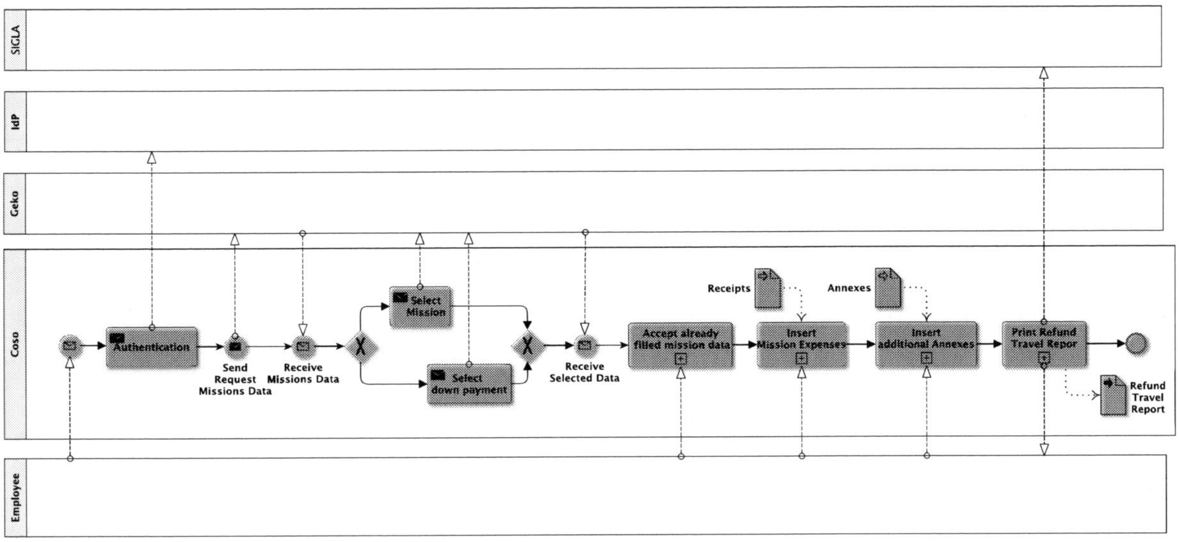

Figure 2. COSO high-level Model

CNR travel management procedure. It is measured in terms of number of implemented rules per functionality in the system.

Modularity: Degree to which new features or customization can be added to the system. It is measured in terms of the average number of dependencies between system components.

2) Security Perspective: The attributes considered according to the security perspective are related to the degree to which the system protects travel information. Therefore, the ISTI personnel or other interacting systems should have the degree of data access appropriate to their types and levels of authorization. It is evaluated in terms of:

Confidentiality: The system ensures that data are accessible only by the ISTI authorized personnel. It is evaluated in terms of the possibility to control system accesses.

Integrity: The system prevents unauthorized access or modifications. It is measured in terms of the possibility to avoid data corruption.

Non-repudiation: Degree to which actions or events can be proven to have taken place. It is measured in terms of the possibility to use digital signature.

Accountability: Degree to which the actions of an entity can be traced. It is measured in terms of the possibility to use audit trail.

Authenticity: The system can prove the identity of a subject or resource. It is measured in terms of the use of the possibility to authenticate the identity of a subject or resource.

3) Performance Perspective: The attributes considered according to the performance perspective are related to the resources and the behaviour of the system. In particular, the considered attributes are:

Time behaviour: Time necessary to compile the modules for the travel authorization or refund. It is measured in terms of the mean time necessary for a module completion.

Capacity: Maximum amount of simultaneous accesses to the system. It is measured in terms of how many online requests can be processed per unit of time.

4) Configuration Perspective: The attributes considered according to the configuration perspective are related to the structure of the system. In particular, the considered attributes are:

Compatibility: Degree to which the system can exchange its results with other available systems or components. It is evaluated in terms of how flexible is the system in data sharing.

Interoperability: Degree to which the system can use (or produce) information from (for) other systems. It is evaluated in terms of supported data exchanged format.

5) Enhancement Perspective: Additional quality attributes, not included in the considered standard, have been defined for the framework assessment. In particular:

Traceability: Degree to which the system can keep track of a given set or type of information to a given degree. Specifically the system should log and trace activities execution according to user defined specific rules. It is measured in terms of number of tracking and storage facilities included into the system.

Customizable data collection: Degree to which the system can provide statistical analysis on the basis of travel data collection. It is measured in terms of the number of user defined statistical analysis the system can produce.

V. FRAMEWORK

For completeness, in this section we provide a short description of the automation of the CNR travel management procedure, thought the COSO framework, is provided. More details can be found in [3]. As described shown in Figure 3, the framework collaborates with the three main software products of ISTI that are SIGLA [21], for the management of the accounting and financial reporting, GEKO [20] for the management of funding and Identity Provider to manage authentication. However, during the development and validation stages, the prototype has been forced to work as a stand-alone framework. In Figure 4, additional architecture details of the COSO component are shown. To improve the

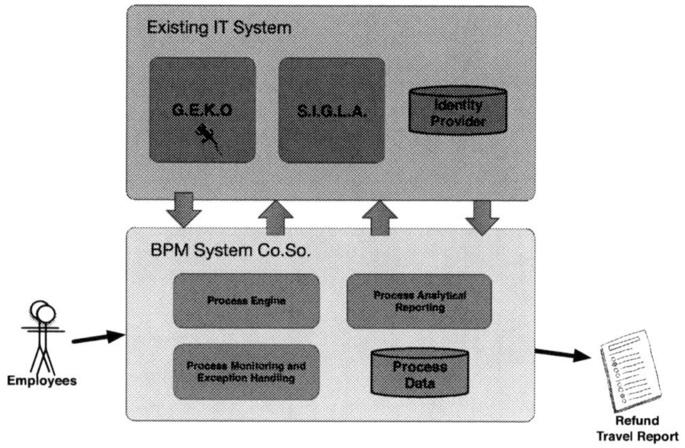

Figure 3. Overview of the high level architecture

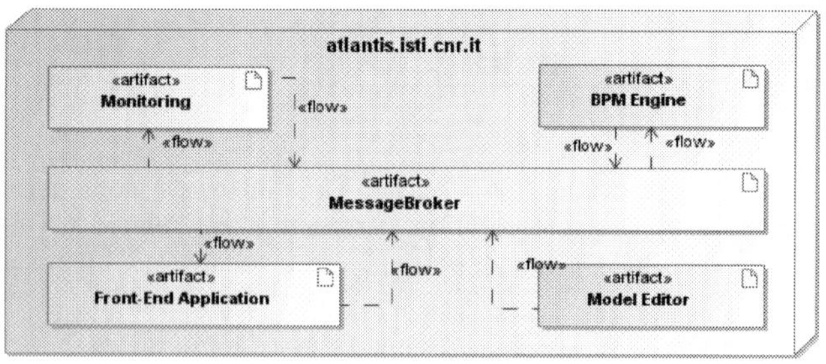

Figure 4. Overview of the architecture

adaptability, modularity and learnability of the proposal, five main components have been identified:

- the **editor**: it provides facilities both for creating and modifying the models representing the business process.
- the **front-end**: it is composed of several web-forms and help facilities. It provides both documentations and suggestions to the user and contributes to decrease the number of errors in module fulfilling.
- the **monitoring**: it keeps track of models execution and collects specific travel data useful for statistical analysis.
- the **message broker**: it deals with the communication between different components.
- the **BPM engine**: it executes the BP model relative the CNR travel management process.

VI. Assessment

According to the quality attributes defined in Section IV, the following sections recap how and where these attributes have been addressed. For the assessment, the specification described in section III and its current prototype implementation into the COSO framework [11] have been considered.

A. Business Perspective Assessment

Suitability: During the three phases of the storytelling methodology a set of functional and non functional requirements has been collected. In the model creation, these requirements have been mapped and realized into one or more activities or tasks of the BP model. Consequently, all the identified requirements have been implemented into the specifications.

Accessibility: The current implementation of COSO prototype provided a set of facilities specifically designed for administrative and research staff. Additional categories of ISTI personnel, such as external or associated staff, have still to be included in the implementation. The percentage of different categories of ISTI personnel mapped into the system is currently around 70%. Specific facilities for users with physical handicaps are currently under development and, therefore, this measure was not evaluated.

Learnability: A set of user documentation and help facilities has been defined in collaboration with Administrative Staff to make easier the learning of the rules of the CNR travel management procedure. In particular, for each of the activities and tasks of the derived BP model the front end of COSO framework provides a help menu reporting meaningful example, rules description and specific constraints.

User error protection: The BP model implements all the rules and policies defined in CNR travel management procedure [19]. Moreover, the front-end application of COSO framework has been developed to prevent rules violation or common users mistake.

Adaptability: During the BP model derivation, the process has been stiletted into more sub-processes, each one associated to a (or a restricted group of) requirement(s) so to simplify the maintenance or upgrading of the the framework. Moreover, the editor associated to the COSO framework allows to update the models in case of new requirements or rules.

Modularity: The development of the COSO framework followed the Model-View-Controller paradigm. The stand alone components as well as the use of messages paradigm and REST invocations guarantee the independency between system components.

B. Security Perspective Assessment

The attributes related to the security perspective, i.e confidentiality, integrity, non-repudiation, authenticity, are covered by the ISTI authentication system, and ISTI intranet in general, on which the users must authenticate themselves before. In particular, ISTI implements the authentication procedures, policies and the architecture required by the GARR consortium (Rete italiana dell'istruzione e della ricerca - Italian network for the research and instruction) [24], which is the top Italian Guarantor for the research networks, in order to protect data from any intruders. Moreover, to better focus on these quality aspects, as depicted in Figure 2, in the BP model a specific task has been entirely dedicated to the security aspects.

C. Performance Perspective Assessment

Time behaviour: We are currently collecting data for the complete evaluation of this attribute. However, the introduction of an automatic framework provided a drastic reduction in the time required for checking and validating the different costs and expenses. Before the introduction of the COSO framework the process was manually completed. Preliminary results evidenced that the time behaviour can be reduced to one third of the mean time required for a completion of a travel authorization and refund (currently estimated into 3 and 1.5 hours respectively). Moreover, the possibility of simultaneous accesses of from different users reduced the interactions and communications between the ISTI personnel and the Administrative staff.

Capacity: We do not have a statistical significant number or data to estimate this attribute. However, considering that inside ISTI the average number of travel authorizations and refunds per years is around 1500 this can represent a considerable budget and effort reduction for the overall institute.

D. Configuration Perspective Assessment

From the configuration perspective, the automatic framework provides the integration with GEKO, the ISTI internal internet service managing administrative projects funding, and SIGLA, the official CNR system for the management of the accounting and financial reporting. This decreases considerably the cost and effort necessary by the administrative staff to process the documentation, exchange personnel information and modules, record travel data, and complete the overall travel refund.

Finally, considering the enhancement perspective the monitoring component included in the framework, allows to log, trace and store activities execution according to specific rules defined in collaboration with ISTI administrative staff. The purpose is to improve costs management and predictions; establish a better distribution of ISTI budget and possibly establish specific (accommodation/transportation) conventions. In addition, monitoring component includes the possibility to defined customizable rules and store the relative data so to improve user defined statistical analysis. This guarantees a satisfied level of the enhancement quality attribute implementation.

VII. Discussion and Conclusion

This paper presented the procedure adopted for the BPM modeling of the natural language rules of the ISTI-CNR travel management manual and the definition of a quality model useful for the development and assessment of its automatic implementation. Preliminary feedbacks and results have been collected during the evaluation of the COSO framework. The lessons learned by this experience are: the model must be flexible enough to accommodate modifications and situations that are not explicitly described by the regulations; the model must be simple and intuitive to make easier its understanding; quality aspects are difficult to be defined and formalized by not software engineering expert and many times a mediator is necessary. As a future work, we will continue the COSO implementation and the collection of assessment results.

Acknowledgments

The authors would like to thank Claudio Montani, Director of the ISTI-CNR in Pisa, for his hints, incitements and useful discussions.

References

[1] Italian Parlament, "Codice dell'amministrazione digitale," http://www.parlamento.it/parlam/leggi/deleghe/05082dl.htm, [retrieved: Feb-2017].

[2] AirPlus, "Il Travel Management nella Pubblica Amministrazione," https://www.airplus.com/it/it/news_153185_172508/, [retrieved: Feb-2017].

[3] G. O. Spagnolo, E. Marchetti, A. Coco, P. Scarpellini, A. Querci, F. Fabbrini, and S. Gnesi, "An experience on applying process mining techniques to the tuscan port community system," in Software Quality Day 2016, 2016, pp. 49 – 60.

[4] A. Calabró, F. Lonetti, and E. Marchetti, "Monitoring of business process execution based on performance indicators," in The Euromicro Conference series on Software Engineering and Advanced Applications (SEAA), 2015, pp. 255–258.

[5] A. Calabrò, F. Lonetti, and E. Marchetti, "KPI Evaluation of the Business Process Execution through Event Monitoring Activity," in ES, 2015, pp. 169–176.

[6] S. Zribi, A. Calabrò, F. Lonetti, E. Marchetti, T. Jorquera, and J.-P. Lorré, "Design of a simulation framework for model-based learning," in Proceedings of International Conference on Model-Driven Engineering and Software Development, 2016, pp. 631–639.

[7] G. O. Spagnolo, E. Marchetti, A. Coco, and S. Gnesi, "Modelling and validating an import/export shipping process," ERCIM News, vol. 2016, no. 105, 2016, [retrieved: Feb-2017]. [Online]. Available: http://ercim-news.ercim.eu/en105/special/modelling-and-validating-an-import-export-shipping-process

[8] F. M. Santoro, M. R. S. Borges, and J. A. Pino, "Acquiring knowledge on business processes from stakeholders' stories," Advanced Engineering Informatics, vol. 24, no. 2, 2010.

[9] J. C. de A. R. Gonçalves, F. M. Santoro, and F. A. Baião, "Business process mining from group stories," in CSCWD, 2009, pp. 161–166.

[10] J. Jeston and J. Nelis, Business process management. Routledge, 2014.

[11] A. Calabró, E. Marchetti, G. O. Spagnolo, P. Cempini, L. Mancini, and S. Paoletti, Towards the Automation of the Travel Management Procedure of an Italian Public Administration. Springer International Publishing, LNBIP 269, 2016, pp. 175–187.

[12] N. Zhang and X. Hou, "Government Process Management under electronic government and its application," in E-Business and E-Government (ICEE), 2011 International Conference on, 2011, pp. 1–4.

[13] N. Ahrend, K. Walser, and H. Leopold, "Case Study of the Implementation of Business Process Management in Public Administration in Germany, Switzerland and Austria," in ECEG2013-13th European Conference on eGovernment: ECEG 2013. Academic Conferences Limited, 2013, p. 11.

[14] P. Wohed, D. Truffet, and G. Juell-Skielse, Business Process Management for Open E-Services in Local Government Experience Report. Springer Berlin Heidelberg, 2011, pp. 1–15.

[15] S. Gayialis, G. Papadopoulos, S. Ponis, P. Vassilakopoulou, and I. Tatsiopoulos, "Integrating process modeling and simulation with benchmarking using a business process management system for local government," International Journal of Computer Theory and Engineering, vol. 8, no. 6, 2016, p. 482.

[16] OMG, "Business Process Model and Notation (BPMN)," 2011, 20th ed.: Object Management Group.

[17] J. Recker, "Opportunities and constraints: the current struggle with BPMN," Business Proc. Manag. Journal, vol. 16-1, 2010, pp. 181–201.

[18] C. Gerth, Business Process Models. Change Management, ser. Lecture Notes in Computer Science. Springer, 2013, vol. 7849. [Online]. Available: http://dx.doi.org/10.1007/978-3-642-38604-6

[19] Roberto Tatarelli and Fabiana Carinici, "Le spese di trasferta - criteri e modalitá di corresponsione del trattamenti di missione e dei rimborsi spese," http://www.urp.cnr.it/documenti/c14-015-a.pdf, [retrieved: Feb-2017].

[20] Institute of Information Science and Technologies (ISTI), "Gestione Commesse," http://geko.isti.cnr.it:8180/CNR/, [retrieved: Feb-2017].

[21] Italian National Research Council (CNR), "Sistema Informativo Gestione Linee di Attivita," http://contab.cnr.it/portale/, [retrieved: Feb-2017].

[22] International Organization for Standardization, "Quality management principles," http://www.iso.org/iso/pub100080.pdf, [retrieved: Feb-2017].

[23] International Organization for Standardization, "Systems and software Quality Requirements and Evaluation (SQuaRE)," http://www.iso.org/iso/catalogue_detail.htm?csnumber=35733, [Online; accessed 19-Feb-2017].

[24] Gruppo per l'Armonizzazione delle Reti della Ricerca (GARR), "Acceptable Use Policy," http://www.garr.it/it/documenti/2133-acceptable-use-policy-eng-version, 2016, [retrieved: Feb-2017].

AUTHOR INDEX